NEW STUDIES IN BIBLICAL THEOLOGY 30

The God who became human

Titles in this series:

An index of Scripture references for all the volumes may be found at
http://www.thegospelcoalition.org/resources/nsbt

NEW STUDIES IN BIBLICAL THEOLOGY 30

Series editor: D. A. Carson

The God who became human

A BIBLICAL THEOLOGY OF INCARNATION

Graham A. Cole

APOLLOS

INTERVARSITY PRESS
DOWNERS GROVE, ILLINOIS 60515

APOLLOS
An imprint of Inter-Varsity Press, England
Norton Street
Nottingham NG7 3HR, England
Website: www.ivpbooks.com
Email: ivp@ivpbooks.com

InterVarsity Press, USA
P.O. Box 1400
Downers Grove, IL 60515-1426, USA
Website: www.ivpress.com
Email: email@ivpress.com

InterVarsity Press®, USA, is the book-publishing division of InterVarsity Christian Fellowship/ USA® <www.intervarsity.org> and a member movement of the International Fellowship of Evangelical Students.

Inter-Varsity Press, England, is closely linked with the Universities and Colleges Christian Fellowship, a student movement connecting Christian Unions throughout Great Britain, and a member movement of the International Fellowship of Evangelical Students. Website: www.uccf.org.uk

Unless stated otherwise, Scripture quotations are from the Holy Bible, NEW INTERNATIONAL VERSION® NIV®. Copyright © 1973, 1978, 1984, 2011 by Biblica, Inc.™ All rights reserved worldwide. Used by permission.

Scripture quotations marked ESV are from The Holy Bible, English Standard Version, published by HarperCollins Publishers © 2001 by Crossway Bibles, a division of Good News Publishers. Used by permission. All rights reserved.

Scripture quotations marked NRSV are taken from the New Revised Standard Version of the Bible, Anglicized edition, copyright © 1989, 1995 by the Division of Christian Education of the National Council of the Churches of Christ in the USA. Used by permission. All rights reserved.

First published 2013.

Set in Monotype Times New Roman
Typeset in Great Britain by CRB Associates, Potterhanworth, Lincolnshire
Printed and bound in Great Britain by Ashford Colour Press Ltd.

USA ISBN 978-0-8308-2631-5
UK ISBN 978-1-84474-800-6

 InterVarsity Press is committed to protecting the environment and to the responsible use of natural resources. As a member of Green Press Initiative we use recycled paper whenever possible. To learn more about the Green Press Initiative, visit <www.greenpressinitiative.org>.

British Library Cataloguing in Publication Data
A catalogue record for this book is available from the British Library.

Library of Congress Cataloging-in-Publication Data
A catalog record for this book is available from the Library of Congress.

P	18	17	16	15	14	13	12	11	10	9	8	7	6	5	4	3	2	1
Y	28	27	26	25	24	23	22	21	20	19	18	17	16	15	14	13

To Isaiah and Louka, who
bring me such joy

Contents

Series preface

New Studies in Biblical Theology is a series of monographs that address key issues in the discipline of biblical theology. Contributions to the series focus on one or more of three areas: (1) the nature and status of biblical theology, including its relations with other disciplines (e.g. historical theology, exegesis, systematic theology, historical criticism, narrative theology); (2) the articulation and exposition of the structure of thought of a particular biblical writer or corpus; and (3) the delineation of a biblical theme across all or part of the biblical corpora.

Above all, these monographs are creative attempts to help thinking Christians understand their Bibles better. The series aims simultaneously to instruct and to edify, to interact with the current literature, and to point the way ahead. In God's universe, mind and heart should not be divorced: in this series we will try not to separate what God has joined together. While the notes interact with the best of scholarly literature, the text is uncluttered with untransliterated Greek and Hebrew, and tries to avoid too much technical jargon. The volumes are written within the framework of confessional evangelicalism, but there is always an attempt at thoughtful engagement with the sweep of the relevant literature.

Books on the incarnation tend to deploy, early on in the discussion, the categories of systematic theology. The biblical proof texts that are adduced are mostly from the New Testament; much less effort has been poured onto tracing incarnation theology right through the canon. Although considerable effort in biblical theology has been devoted to such messianic themes as the Davidic monarch, the priesthood and the temple, relatively little has been devoted to the incarnation. This book by Dr Graham Cole takes steps to fill the need. Undoubtedly more can be said, but it is immensely satisfying to find an able systematician wrestling with the biblical texts – as it is to find biblical scholars tracing the lines from exegesis towards biblical and systematic theology – not least on a topic as central to Christian faith as this one. As I write these words, the world approaches the Christmas season, and around the globe, in their own languages, Christians will sing,

> Veiled in flesh, the Godhead see;
> Hail th' incarnate Deity!
> Pleased as man with men to dwell –
> Jesus our Emmanuel.

D. A. Carson
Trinity Evangelical Divinity School

Author's preface

This study has surprised me. In contributing to a series of biblical theology studies rather than to a systematic theology one, I expected to trace a biblical theme from Genesis to Revelation in biblical theology style with careful attention to the unfolding biblical plotline, and then to tease out some larger theological implications of the text.

What I found was that the incarnation per se was not explicitly part of the Old Testament hope, but if certain Old Testament texts are read with a subtle typological method, then arguably the idea is there in a hidden way. Augustine's argument that what was latent in the Old Testament becomes patent in the New comes readily to mind. This should not surprise, as Paul teaches us the incarnation is a mystery – something hidden in the plan of God that now stands revealed once Jesus has come.

Even so, there is a background in the Old Testament without which the incarnation would be unintelligible. Here is yet another instance where Christology needs to be done from behind in the light of God's dealings with Israel. The incarnation is a stupendous divine deed. To think that God incarnate wept human tears at the tomb of his friend Lazarus is astounding. There is continued debate as to whether suffering may be ascribed to the God of the Bible, but there is no debate that in classical Christianity Christ suffered in his human nature.

I am grateful to my graduate assistant at Beeson Divinity, David Matlak, who did so much fetching of material for me. I am also in the debt of Dr John Momson for alerting me to some important Jewish literature pertinent to this study. Dr Peter Adam and I spent more than one breakfast in Melbourne, Australia, talking on this theme. And I am thankful to him for his insights. The astute series editing and criticisms of D. A. Carson are always appreciated, as is the patient publishing editing of Philip Duce of Inter-Varsity Press. Eldo Barkhuizen did a superb job of copy-editing and I am grateful to him. My wonderful wife, Jules, has been as supportive as ever. This study has made me appreciate even more the wonder that we live on a visited planet and that the Father sent no surrogate to share our human lot but sent his Son, who, as the ancient Nicene Creed says, 'For us and for our salvation . . . came down from heaven, was incarnate of the Virgin Mary and became truly human.'

Graham A. Cole

Abbreviations

1QS	*Rule of the Community* (Dead Sea Scrolls)
4QFlor	*Florilegium* (Dead Sea Scrolls)
ACC	*Ancient Christian Commentary on Scripture: Old Testament 1*, ed. Thomas C. Oden, Downers Grove: InterVarsity Press, 2001
BBCNT	*IVP Bible Background Commentary: New Testament* (EIRC)
BBCOT	*IVP Bible Background Commentary: Old Testament* (EIRC)
CD	*Damascus Document* (Dead Sea Scrolls)
CD	K. Barth, *Church Dogmatics*, ed. G. W. Bromiley and T. F. Torrance, 4 vols., Edinburgh: T. & T. Clark, 1936–77
Chm	*Churchman*
CJCC	*The Comprehensive John Calvin Collection*, Rio, Wisc.: Ages Software, 2002, CD-ROM version
CNTUOT	*Commentary on the New Testament Use of the Old Testament*, ed. G. K. Beale and D. A. Carson, Grand Rapids: Baker Academic; Nottingham: Apollos, 2007
DBI	*Dictionary of Biblical Imagery*, ed. L. Ryken, J. C. Wilhoit and J. C. Longman III, Downers Grove: IVP Academic
DFTIB	*Dictionary of the Theological Interpretation of Scripture*, ed. K. J. Vanhoozer, London: SPCK; Grand Rapids: Baker Academic, 2005
DPHL	*Dictionary of Paul and His Letters* (EIRC)
EBC	*The Expositor's Bible Commentary*, ed. F. E. Gaebelein, Grand Rapids: Zondervan, CD-ROM version, 1976–
EIRC	*The Essential IVP Reference Collection*, Leicester: Inter-Varsity Press, 2001, CD-ROM version
ERT	*Evangelical Review of Theology*
ESV	English Standard Version

ExpTim	*Expository Times*
fl.	flourished
Gen. Rab.	*Genesis Rabbah*
Hebr.	Hebrew
HSOB	*Hard Sayings of the Bible* (EIRC)
Int	*Interpretation*
JANT	*The Jewish Annotated New Testament*, ed. A. Levine and M. Z. Brettler, New York: Oxford University Press, 2011
JETS	*Journal of the Evangelical Theological Society*
JSB	*Jewish Study Bible*, ed. A. Berlin and M. Z. Brettler, New York: Oxford University Press, 2004
Lat.	Latin
lit.	literally
LXX	Septuagint
NA	*New Advent: Featuring the Catholic Encyclopedia*, Pennsauken, N.J.: Disc Makers, 2007, 2nd ed., CD-ROM version
NBC	New Bible Commentary
n.d.	no date of publication given
NDBT	*New Dictionary of Biblical Theology* (EIRC)
NIB	*New Interpreter's Bible*: Complete Twelve Volume Commentary CD-ROM, New Interpreter's Bible Commentaries, by L. E. Keck, 2002
NIBD	*The New Interpreter's Dictionary of the Bible*, ed. K. D. Sakenfeld, 5 vols., Nashville: Abingdon, 2009
NIDOTTE	*The New International Dictionary of Old Testament Theology and Exegesis*, ed. W. A. VanGemeren, 5 vols., Grand Rapids: Zondervan, 1996, CD-ROM version
NIV	New International Version
NIVACNT	NIV Application Commentary, New Testament
NJB	New Jerusalem Bible
NRSV	New Revised Standard Version
OBC	Oxford Bible Commentary
OGB	*The Oxford Guide to the Bible*, ed. B. M. Metzger and M. D. Coogan, Oxford: Oxford University Press, 1993
P	Papyrus
pl.	plural
Q.	Question (*Summa Theologica*)
sg.	singular

ABBREVIATIONS

RTR	*Reformed Theological Review*
SBJT	*The Southern Baptist Journal of Theology*
TNTC	Tyndale New Testament Commentaries
TOTC	Tyndale Old Testament Commentaries
tr.	translated, translation
VTSup	Supplements to Vetus Testamentum
WBC	Word Biblical Commentary
WTJ	*Westminster Theological Journal*

Introduction

Why this book?

The discipline of biblical theology reads Scripture with attention both to its unfolding plotline from Genesis to Revelation and its accent on Christ as the fulfilment of the antecedent hope of Israel. The study of themes therefore is a major part of the undertaking. For example, take the theme of the leadership of God's people as in prophet, priest and king. Each category finds its apogee in Jesus Christ, as Calvin among others has seen. Any number of biblical theologies, as their tables of contents and indexes often show, trace the story of prophethood or priesthood or kingship as it canonically unfolds. But what of the incarnation? Here the treatment, if any, is sparse. Other great pivotal events in Christology, such as atonement or roles Christ assumed (e.g. servant of the Lord), can be successfully placed in a promise–fulfilment framework. Is incarnation an anomaly? Put another way, was incarnation part of the hope of Israel? This study attempts to address this question among others.

For years I have been intrigued by a quotation in one of Terence E. Fretheim's books. In his book on the suffering of God, Fretheim quotes Old Testament scholar E. Jacob. In the quotation Jacob connected the anthropomorphic language of the Old Testament and the incarnation of Christ. Eventually I was able to secure Jacob's book for myself and found that his point was made even more richly than Fretheim's brief quotation suggested. Jacob wrote:

> The God of the Old Testament is a God who seeks to manifest his presence in order to be recognized as the sovereign Lord; that is why the fear of God is at the basis of all piety and all wisdom. But God also and especially seeks to manifest his presence in order to save man. A line not always straight, but nonetheless continuous, leads from the anthropomorphisms of

the earliest pages of the Bible, to the incarnation of God in Jesus Christ.[1]

Could it be that Old Testament language about God's eyes, ears, arms, hands, fingers and so forth prepare the way somehow for the incarnation of God the Word become flesh?[2]

Kierkegaard famously said, 'Life lived forwards but understood backwards.'[3] Perhaps something similar may be said of God's providence: 'Life is lived forwards but providence is understood backwards.' Once the canon of Scripture was completed, God's people could read it in such a way as to see how rich it is in intra-textual allusion and reference, and with it see the exhibition to divine providence that led to an incarnation. Thomas F. Torrance puts the point this way:

> The background for Christ the Son of God can only be the background which the fact of the incarnation creates for itself out of the world. . . . [T]here is a long prehistory to Jesus, but theologically we must say that when the Son of God breaks into that historical development, he throws it all into critical reorientation. The prehistory is critically and creatively re-interpreted by the incarnate Word, and it is only in that light that we must look at the prehistory of the incarnation in Israel.[4]

To use Hendrikus Berkhof's helpful phrase, God's people can now do 'Christology from behind'.[5] (Torrance is one example.) That is to say that with reference to Jesus 'we see him in the line of redemptive history, how he arises out of the Old Testament problematic, and gives and is the answer to it'.[6] Again, Berkhof rightly contends, 'the appearance of Jesus Christ is no isolated epiphany'.[7] A surprising voice adds to the chorus. Rabbi Jacob Neusner writes:

---

[1] Jacob 1958: 32. See also the briefer quotation of Jacob in Fretheim 1984: 6.

[2] Berkhof (1979: 20) seems to think so: 'The very personal coming of God to man in the Old Testament, to the point of being anthropomorphic, is here immeasurably intensified [the Christ event], and thereby given a completion as well: he comes to men in a man, in one who as "the Son" stands in a unique relationship to him as "the Father".' This is an insightful statement, but not as helpful if read in the context of Berkhof's lack of a robust doctrine of the essential Trinity (cf. 1979: 20, 330–337).

[3] Kierkegaard 1941b.

[4] Torrance 1992: 38.

[5] Berkhof 1979: 267.

[6] Ibid.

[7] Ibid. 221.

On the basis of a large number of stories along these lines [with anthropomorphic descriptions of God], we might well contemplate composing the story of God on earth – a kind of gospel of God incarnate, walking among human beings, talking with them, teaching them, acting among them, just as, for the evangelists as the church received and venerated their writings, Jesus Christ, God incarnate, walked on earth, taught, and provided the example for humanity of the union of humanity and divinity. That is hardly to suggest that the Judaism of the dual Torah [the Hebrew Bible and those rabbinic works that reduced the oral Torah to writing] and the Christianity of Jesus Christ as God incarnate are to be matched. But they assuredly sustain comparison.[8]

Neusner recognizes that very often the God presented in the Old Testament is presented as though incarnate.

In this present work my aim is to explore this idea of how the incarnation was prepared for. However, every exploration is shaped by certain assumptions. To these assumptions we next turn.

Assumptions

Assumptions play a role in every claim to knowledge. For example, if I claim to know X, I express that claim in some language. In so doing I am assuming that language can convey thought from one mind to another. That is to say, I am assuming that language is a vehicle for communicative action. Part of my job is not only to read books and articles but to help students to do so intelligently. More often than not, writers do not make their assumptions visible. Consequently students need some help in detecting a given writer's assumptions. For example, if I read Scripture with materialist assumptions, then I need to explain – explain away? – any references to the supernatural.[9] In this view Saul of Tarsus did not meet the risen Christ

---

[8] Neusner 1992: 17–18.

[9] According to Halverson (1981: 414–415), the divide between naturalistic and non-naturalistic world views is the fundamental one. He contends, 'It may be helpful to bear in mind from the beginning, however, that one theme that underlies nearly all philosophical discussion is the perpetual conflict between *naturalistic* and *nonnaturalistic* world views. A *naturalistic* world view is one in which it is affirmed that (a) there is only one order of reality, (b) this one order of reality consists entirely of objects and events occurring in space and time, and (c) this one order of reality is completely self-dependent and self-operating. . . . Any world view that denies any of the above-stated tenets of naturalism, then, may be termed *nonnaturalistic*' (original emphases).

on the road to Damascus. Rather he had an epileptic fit or some other aberrant neurological episode.[10] The Christ he met was the Christ of a fevered imagination. So what assumptions underlie this work?

A key assumption is that there is a living God who is a personal agent. Walter Brueggemann captures the essence of the biblical testimony to this living God in a fine way. He is writing of the God revealed in the Old Testament, but what he writes is true of both testaments: '"God" as rendered in the Old Testament is a fully articulated personal agent, with all the particularities of personhood and with a full repertoire of traits and actions that belong to a fully formed and actualized person.'[11] It is this God who providentially orders human affairs. Nature and history are thus open to divine action.

According to Huston Smith, both moderns and postmoderns would have problems with such openness. He offers this analogy by way of explanation:

> If we think of traditional peoples as looking out upon a world through the window of revelation (their received myths and texts), the window that they turned to look through in the modern period (science) turned out to be stunted. It cuts off at the level of the human nose, which (metaphysically speaking) means that when we look through it our gaze slants downward and we see only things that are inferior to us. As for the post modern window, it is boarded over and allows no inclusive view whatsoever.[12]

In contradistinction to the above, this work assumes that God has provided Holy Scripture so that his people are not left in an epistemological black hole from which no epistemic light can escape. In other words this work assumes that there is a revelation of the character, will and ways of God to be found in the church's inspired Book. Holy Scripture – God's words in human words – exhibits an amazing unity of storyline in its diversity of genres. There is a metanarrative.[13] Or put another way, in the words of Augustine Scripture presents 'one discourse' (*unus sermo*) and from many mouths emanates 'one word'

---

[10] The classic attempt of such explaining away in relation to the apostle Paul is Sargant 1957.

[11] Brueggemann 2009: 2.

[12] Huston Smith in Anderson 1995: 206.

[13] That Scripture presents a metanarrative is ably brought out by both Carson 2010 and Webber 2008.

(*unum verbum*).[14] That one discourse found in Scripture tells of the triune living God who speaks and acts, creates and recreates, saves and judges in a narrative that moves through creation, Fall, redemption and consummation as the story unfolds from Genesis 1 to Revelation 22.

Praeparatio evangelica

The phrase *praeparatio evangelica* means 'preparation for the gospel'.[15] This concept featured early in Christian thought to explain how pagans got so much right about God. For example, Augustine wrote in his celebrated *Confessions* of the philosophers he had read:

> And therein I read, not indeed in the same words, but to the selfsame effect, enforced by many and various reasons, that, 'In the beginning was the Word, and the Word was with God, and the Word was God. The same was in the beginning with God. All things were made by Him; and without Him was not any thing made that was made.' That which was made by Him is 'life; and the life was the light of men. And the light shines in darkness; and the darkness comprehends it not.' And that the soul of man, though it 'bears witness of the light,' yet itself 'is not that light; but the Word of God, being God, is that true light that lights every man that comes into the world.' And that 'He was in the world, and the world was made by Him, and the world knew Him not.' But that 'He came unto His own, and His own received Him not. But as many as received Him, to them gave He power to become the sons of God even to them that believe in His name.' This I did not read there.[16]

Clearly Augustine thought that he found Johannine-like ideas in the writings of the philosophers (Platonists). Significantly, though, he also said he did not find the idea that the Word became flesh and dwelt among us in the pagan thought he knew. For early Christians *ex hypothesi* this preparatory work among the pagans was done by the Logos. This work paralleled that of the work of the *logos asarkos* ('Word without flesh' or *logos incarnandus*) with Israel in Old

---

[14] Wilkens 2003: 326, n. 9. Wilkens cites Augustine's *Exposition of Psalm 103.4.1*.
[15] This was the title of the fifteen-book work by Eusebius of Caesarea (AD 263–339), the first important early church historian.
[16] Augustine 2007b: 7.9.

Testament times in preparation for the incarnation, when *logos asarkos* became *logos ensarkos* ('Word enfleshed', or *logos carnatus*).[17]

This work is in the tradition of *praeparatio evangelica* with its focus on how the revelatory work of providence in Old Testament times 'represents a foreshadowing of incarnation'.[18] In pursuit of this aim, as discussed above, typology plays its part as does analogical correspondence. Both are important conceptual tools. Another tool employed in this study is 'descriptor fittingness', for want of a better phrase. This phrase refers to how Old Testament language provides apt descriptors for understanding incarnation as the quintessential expression of divine presence in the midst of God's people. T. F. Torrance in his work *The Mediation of Christ* offers a helpful insight regarding such descriptors when he writes, 'They constitute the essential furniture of our knowledge of God even in and through Christ. If the Word of God had become incarnate among us apart from all that, it could not have been grasped – Jesus himself would have remained a bewildering enigma.'[19] In another work, *Incarnation: The Person and Life of Christ*, Torrance points out that if you need to make something, you need tools. Likewise if you are to understand something, you need conceptual tools. God provided those conceptual tools in his revelatory and redemptive dealings with ancient Israel.[20] There is a famous Bill Cosby skit in which the comedian plays Noah. God commands him to build an ark. Cosby ask what an ark is. Next God tells him to get wood to build the ark so many cubits in length, height and width. To which Cosby asks what a cubit is. The relevant point is that revelation is unintelligible without the requisite categories already being in place. So too the Christ event.

The plan of the book

Chapter 1 explores the purpose of creation in terms of God's creating and fashioning a palace-temple as his habitation for dwelling with the creature made in the divine image. In particular how God prepared the way for his ultimate incarnate concomitance by revealing himself in anthropomorphic, anthropopathic and anthropopraxic ways is canvassed. In this chapter these latter three crucial terms are defined.

[17] Muller 1986: 152, 238.
[18] Ibid. 152.
[19] Torrance 1992: 18.
[20] Torrance 2008: 41.

Also in this chapter I argue that a third category is needed in discussing God's relation to the world. The idea of concomitance (the God-with-us motif) needs to be added to the traditional categories of transcendence and immanence. In so doing I hope that the reader of Scripture may take away a more sophisticated set of categories by means of which to understand the portrayal of God in Scripture than the general categories of anthropomorphism *simpliciter* and transcendence or immanence to understand how God relates to creation with its culmination in the incarnation. An excursus is attached to the chapter that addresses a long-standing question that still attracts debate today: Would the incarnation have taken place if there had been no Fall?

In the second chapter the biblical portrait of God is amplified as he acts in Israel's history to redeem a people of his own among whom he can dwell. Once more God's anthropomorphic, anthropopathic and anthropopraxic ways are reviewed as we follow the biblical plotline. In particular the theophanic language of the patriarchal, Mosaic, former and latter prophetic periods is examined. God is rendered as a person who speaks, acts and feels as though embodied. In two places at least the Lord is rendered in human terms as someone who eats and wrestles, and does so in history (e.g. Gen. 18 and 32 respectively). In other places the experience is visionary, more fragmentary and heavenly (e.g. Isa. 6). We follow James Barr in describing such phenomena as anthropomorphic theophanies. However, there is no incarnation of deity as such in view.

The third chapter explores Israel's hope and the promise of the divine presence with his people in the midst of the created order. For B. B. Warfield – as we shall see – the keeping of the promise meant that the Messiah to come would be divine. R. C. Ortlund, Jr., argues similarly. This contention is examined. In chapter 3 particular attention is given to some key Old Testament texts (Pss 45:6; 110; Isa. 9:6; Dan. 7:13) that both Warfield and Ortlund, Jr., employ to argue for the deity of the Messiah. The question is whether these texts demand such a reading. Certainly the Old Testament expected human agents or even divine agents of the divine purpose to come to Israel's aid at some juncture in its future: a prophet like Moses, a Davidic king, the heavenly Son of Man, the child born bearing the names 'Immanuel' and 'mighty God'. Moreover the Old Testament writers also expected God himself to come. But an incarnate, divine-human deliverer? That's the key question. The section on typology goes some of the way in addressing that question.

In chapter 4 the preparatory gives way to the actual. The testimony of the New Testament now comes into full view as we continue to follow the biblical plotline. God stooped and entered the arena of human affairs in the most personal of ways. Concomitance is now enfleshed. Matthew's testimony to Jesus as both the truly human Davidic king of promise (Matt. 1) and as Emmanuel ('God with us', Matt. 1:23), Mark's presentation of Jesus as the one in whom God comes to Zion (Mark 1 – 2) and the writer to the Hebrews' account of Jesus as both deity and humanity (Heb. 1 – 2) are considered along with the Johannine witness that Jesus is the Word become flesh who dwelt among us (John 1:14). The implicit incarnation theology of Matthew and Mark becomes more explicit in Hebrews and patent in John. What could be seen in retrospect after the coming of Christ and what could be seen in prospect are not to be confused, however. In Pauline terms the incarnation is a mystery that in Old Testament times was a hidden part of the divine plan. Also in this chapter, philosopher Nicholas Wolterstorff's theory of theories is drawn upon to provide an important conceptual tool to analyse how the anthropomorphisms, anthropopathisms and anthropopraxisms of the Old Testament together with other Old Testament testimonies might point to incarnation and contribute to the intelligibility of the idea. An excursus is attached that treats the question of whether the Christ per se was known by Old Testament saints to be active in their history.

Chapter 5 addresses the question raised by Anselm of Canterbury in the Middle Ages: Why did God become human? Unlike Anselm, however, we seek New Testament answers to the question, rather than speculative ones. The appeal is to Scripture, not to reason with the Bible shut. Happily there is an abundance of New Testament testimonies that address the question. Christ's revelatory, representative, substitutionary, defeating the devil and moral modelling roles are predicated on his assuming a truly human nature. An excursus is attached that treats the question of whether the divine Son assumed fallen or unfallen human nature in the incarnation.

Chapter 6 considers the significance of the incarnation in two aspects: theological and existential. It explores the value of the incarnation for theological method, for the doctrine of God and change, for the affirmation of the created order, for the valuing of human life, for our understanding of mission, for the encounter between Christianity and other religions with special reference to Islam, for the question of theodicy and defence, given evils, and for matters of dogmatic rank. This chapter also explores the value of the incarnation at the personal or existential level. The incarnation matters with regard to our appreciation of the depths of the divine love and our cultivating a sense of wonder.

The last chapter draws the threads of the argument together in summary form and is followed by an appendix that addresses the question of how biblical theology interfaces with systematic theology in the theological interpretation of Scripture.

My hope is that by the time the reader closes this study he or she will have a deeper sense of the astonishing providence of God that subtly prepared the way for the mystery of the incarnation, a greater appreciation of the magnitude of the divine stooping that in the incarnation saw God weep human tears, and a profounder joy at the depth of the love of God that sent no surrogate as the final revelation but the beloved Son who became flesh.

Chapter One

God prepares the way from the beginning

Origins are fascinating. At present I am doing some research on my Jewish grandfather on my mother's side of the family. He was known to the press as a flamboyant character who had emigrated from the Crimea after the First World War. He called himself a professor and ran a dance studio in Sydney, Australia, in the first half of the twentieth century. Some of the dances he invented and put into print are in the National Library of Australia and are also listed in a Stanford University catalogue that begins with Domenico da Piacenza in 1425 and concludes with Elizabeth Gibbons in 2007. I learned that one of the dancing teachers he employed, Nellie Cameron, was a notorious character in the underworld of Sydney. He died when I was two so I have no memory of him, only a photo or two.

Origins matter to individuals and indeed to an entire people. They mattered to Israel. Genesis as the name implies is about origins. The most basic of questions are addressed in the text: Where does humanity in general come from and where does Israel in particular come from? Why is the world so broken and we with it? Do we have a future?

In this chapter we consider how from the beginning the Creator prepared a way to be present among his creatures. As Thomas F. Torrance rightly says, 'The incarnation of the Son of God has a pre-history, a background or hinterland of preparation and significance which we must not overlook.'[1] In addition an excursus will address a venerable question: Would the incarnation have occurred irrespective of the Fall? But first, who is this God who prepares the way and who not only has his own glory but has humanity's best interests at heart?

God and God's image

The God who comes into majestic relief in Genesis 1:1 – 2:3 is the creator of all things who acts with purpose and not caprice. The

[1] Torrance 1992: 37.

language is simple, the thought profound.[2] God is pictured in terms any Israelite would understand. He is the great worker who does six days on the job and then comes rest. The first three days see the creation of environments: day one, the heavens (Gen. 1:3–5); day two, the waters (Gen. 1:6–8); and day three, the earth (Gen. 1:9–13). Each day is pronounced as good and the presentation of each day's creative work has an evening-and-morning formula attached to it. If the first three days represent the forming of three different environments, the next three days articulate their filling with different kinds of creatures suitable for them. And so on the fourth day the heavens are populated with sun, moon and stars (Gen. 1:14–18). The fourth day is pronounced good and God applies the evening-and-morning formula. The fifth day sees the waters populated with all sorts of sea creatures and the air with winged creatures. Both the populating of the sea and earth are thematized. It too is good and once again the evening-and-morning phrase is in evidence (Gen. 1:20–23). On the sixth day God focuses on the earth and the creatures suitable for inhabiting it. It is on this day that a unique creature appears, humankind (more anon). The creation of various earth creatures is good, according to the text, but there is a qualitative leap in relation to the creature uniquely in the image of God. Now we read that the creation is very good (Gen. 1:24–31). And once more the evening-and-morning formula is in view. The seventh day moves the reader onto a different plane. Here is the climax of all the events that have gone before. The language of holiness is used in the Bible for the first time, as this time 'frame' itself is hallowed. Significantly the evening-and-morning phrase drops from view. There is something very different about this end point. Chaos has thus given way to cosmos. The process has been an orderly one.

The nature of those days is controversial still. Richard Dawkins is not the first person to raise questions. Aquinas (1225–74) in his era

---

[2] For a brief discussion of various Christian approaches to reading the Genesis creation account see Carson 2010: 14–15. Carson's own view (15) is that 'the Genesis account is a mixed genre that feels like history and really does give some historical particulars. At the same time, however, it is full of demonstrable symbolism.' Thus for Carson (30) the serpent of Gen. 3 'may be the embodiment of Satan, or he may be the symbol for Satan, and the Bible doesn't really care to explain which'. My own view is similar. Real events are narrated, albeit in a highly stylized and symbolic way. It is no accident in my view that both protology ('first things', as in Gen. 1 – 3) and eschatology in the narrow sense ('last things', as in Rev. 20 – 22) are both presented in Scripture with a great deal of symbolism. Both paradise lost and paradise regained lie beyond our experience, so this should not surprise the sensitive reader.

was faced with multiple ways of understanding those days, as can be seen in Paul J. Glenn's paraphrase of part of the *Summa Theologica*:

> There are different interpretations of the term day as used in the scriptural account of creation. Some say the six days of active creation are not periods of time but a listing of the order in which creatures were made. Others think these days have time significance, but hardly in the sense of our twenty-four hour day, for that is measured by the sun, and the sun was not created until the fourth day. In any case the six days of creation and the seventh day of rest give an adequate account of the works of creation and their sanctification. St. Augustine makes the days of creation into one period in which God manifests worldly creatures to the angels in seven ways. It must be acknowledged that Scripture uses suitable words to express the works of creation, and to suggest or imply the operation of the three persons of the divine Trinity in these works.[3]

So what we have seen is how Aquinas explores the options: six days of revelation to the angels (Augustine), an orderly listing (others) and special days (still others). He concludes that, whichever it was, God created in an appropriate manner. Wise words.

On the way to the Sabbath God created creatures to image his ways (Gen. 1:27):

> So God created mankind in his own image,
> in the image of God he created them;
> male and female he created them.

The divine intent is stated in the previous verse (Gen. 1:26): 'Then God said, "Let us make mankind in our image, in our likeness, so that they may rule over the fish in the sea and the birds in the sky, over the livestock and all the wild animals, and over all the creatures that move along the ground."' God exercises dominion. They exercise dominion. He subdues. They subdue. The notion of humankind in the image of God (*imago Dei*) is also an essentially contested concept to this day. Are human beings images of God like the image of President Lincoln stamped on an American coin? Is the image ontological or substantival? Or are human beings images of God like the image we

---

[3] Aquinas, *Summa Theologica* I.a, Q. 74, in Glenn 1963: 59–60.

see of ourselves in a mirror? What we do, so the image does. So is the image functional?[4] Or is it neither but rather a relational idea? Just as male and female are the image of God, so there is something relational about God on the inside (*ad intra*). Ultimately the doctrine of the Trinity lies behind our being the images of God in this view. C. John Collins wisely suggests, 'Scholars will advocate one of these three over the others, but we will note that they need not be mutually exclusive. Perhaps none is right, or some combination is right, or maybe we simply cannot come to a firm conclusion.'[5] Following Aquinas here one could say whatever 'image' means, it is an appropriate way to describe who we are as creatures, vis-à-vis God. What is clear is that on this sixth day the creature is to act in Godlike ways in the created order. Furthermore Genesis 2 and 3 make plain that this creature can be God's speech partner. These three foundational chapters merit closer attention from this angle of vision. What portrayal of God is found in them? How is God rendered?

The portrayal of God in the beginning

The word to sum up the God of Genesis 1 is 'transcendent'. This God has no rivals. He stands on the other side of the ontological ledger to creatures. He is beyond creatures. Creation is spoken into being by God. God's repeated speech acts are causative. As we observed previously, over the first three days various environments are formed: sky, next the waters and finally earth (Gen. 1:2–13). Over the remaining three they are filled: sun, moon and stars, next come the sea creatures and lastly the animals and humankind (Gen. 1:14–31). God is like a great emperor. His word works and is enough. Divine action is speech action. His words do things. And with that speech the Spirit also is at work. Indeed spirit or breath is the vehicle for the spoken word with us and with God.

In Genesis 2 God not only speaks but he fashions. Like a potter with clay Adam is formed from the earth: 'Then the LORD God formed

---

[4] Dearman (2002: 39) favours the functional view in the light of 'the discovery in 1979 of a statue of an Aramean king with a bilingual inscription (Assyrian, Aramaic), where the statue is referred to as the "image" and "likeness" of the king. According to the inscription, King Hada-Yithi placed the statue of himself in a city to remind his subjects of him and his rule when he is physically absent from them.' Dearman does not tease this out at any length. But in this view Adam and Eve arguably are living 'statutes' representing the living God and marking the rest of the created order as belonging to God.

[5] Collins 2006: 63.

a man from the dust of the ground and breathed into his nostrils the breath of life, and the man became a living being' (Gen. 2:7).[6] God commands Adam regarding the task to control and care for the garden sanctuary: 'The LORD God took the man and put him in the Garden of Eden to work it and take care of it' (Gen. 2:15). If Genesis 1 presents humankind in royal terms as rulers, Genesis 2 renders Adam as a priest who is to relate to the garden zone like the later Levites are to relate to the tabernacle and temple. Gordon J. Wenham comments:

> Similarly, [*šmr*] 'to guard, to keep', has the simple profane sense of 'guard' (4:9; 30:31), but it is even more commonly used in legal texts of observing religious commands and duties (17:9; Lev 18:5) and particularly of the Levitical responsibility for guarding the tabernacle from intruders (Num 1:53; 3:7–8). It is striking that here and in the priestly law these two terms are juxtaposed (Num 3:7–8; 8:26; 18:5–6), another pointer to the interplay of tabernacle and Eden symbolism already noted (cf. *Ber. Rab.* 16:5).[7]

Significantly the garden sanctuary does not appear to constitute the geographical limits for the Adamic task. Following the logic of the narrative that begins in the previous chapter, humankind is to exercise dominion over the fish of the sea. This is hardly satisfied by a horticultural existence. In other words, the garden sanctuary is best seen as a staging post for the task of Edenizing the entire world. William J. Dumbrell makes the point well: 'As a paradigm of the end, Genesis 2 thus displays the harmony that humankind's dominion was to secure the world at large. Adam's role in Eden was to extend the contours of the garden to the whole world.'[8]

Clearly in Genesis 2 God is portrayed as transcendent once more. What the human experience of being so commanded by God sounded or felt like is not explored. The text has little interest in human psychology per se. Moreover this chapter presents God as a farmer who planted the garden that became the Adamic responsibility: 'Now the

---

[6] Dunn (2008: 32) fancifully argues that 'In a not improper sense the account of the man's creation in Gen. 2:7 is an incarnation – God breathing the breath of life into the human shape formed from the clay of the ground so that man comes to be as a living being.' Dunn admits (31) that he has difficulty in distinguishing 'a person inspired to the nth degree by the spirit of the deity and one who incarnates the word of that deity'.

[7] Wenham 2004, comment on Gen. 2:15.

[8] Dumbrell in Hafemann 2002: 62.

LORD God had planted a garden in the east, in Eden; and there he put the man he had formed' (Gen. 2:8).

As literary scholar Leland Ryken suggests, the scriptural story is a comedy in literary terms. He writes regarding comedy that it is 'a work of literature in which the plot structure is U-shaped, with the action beginning in prosperity, descending into potentially tragic events, and ending happily'.[9] The *Dictionary of Biblical Imagery* amplifies his point in relation to the Bible per se:

> The overall plot of the Bible is a U-shaped comic plot. The action begins with a perfect world inhabited by perfect people. It descends into the misery of fallen history and ends with a new world of total happiness and the conquest of evil. The book of Revelation is the story of the happy ending par excellence, as a conquering hero defeats evil, marries a bride and lives happily ever after in a palace glittering with jewels. From Genesis to Revelation we see the U-shaped structure working itself out: from the harmony of Genesis 1 – 2 through the disharmony of Genesis 3 – Revelation 20 to harmony again and albeit of a higher kind in Revelation 21 – 22.[10]

This is a refreshing way to view the biblical accounts. Clearly Scripture seen in these terms is no scientific monograph.[11] Its interests lie elsewhere.

In Genesis 3 the comedy takes its dark turn in what Augustine famously termed 'the Fall' and more recently Jacques Ellul 'the Rupture'. Importantly for our purposes in this section the transcendent God of Genesis 1 and 2 is also now to be understood as concomitant as well. God comes alongside his creature made in his image, as Genesis 3:8 shows. This God walks in the garden: 'Then the man and his wife heard the sound of the LORD God as he was walking in the garden in the cool of the day, and they hid from the LORD God among the trees of the garden.'

---

[9] Ryken 1998.

[10] Ibid. Interestingly the comedic curve is seen in the story of Christ's incarnation and exaltation, as in Phil. 2:5–11. The state of glory gives way to the state of humiliation, which in turn gives way to the state of glory regained.

[11] That Scripture is not a scientific text has not always been appreciated. The so-called Mosaic Science of the seventeenth century comes to mind and those on the continent and England who wanted to found cosmology, astronomy, physics and chemistry on the exegesis of Scripture in conscious opposition to the 'heathenish' philosophy of Aristotle. See the discussion in Cole 1990: 22–23.

The idea of divine concomitance adds an important nuance in understanding the divine relation to creatures. The traditional categories are transcendence and immanence. Transcendence has been thematized earlier in the discussion. Immanence refers to God's indwelling creation and working within it. Concomitance adds to these categories the notion of alongsideness or God with us. The notion of the divine alongsideness is important in both Old Testament and New. For example, Moses pleaded for the divine accompaniment in Exodus 33:15–16: 'Then Moses said to him, "If your Presence does not go with us, do not send us up from here. How will anyone know that you are pleased with me and with your people unless you go with us? What else will distinguish me and your people from all the other people on the face of the earth?"' And Jesus promised it to the eleven disciples in Matthew 28:18–20 in the famous Great Commission passage:

> Then Jesus came to them and said, 'All authority in heaven and on earth has been given to me. Therefore go and make disciples of all nations, baptizing them in the name of the Father and of the Son and of the Holy Spirit, and teaching them to obey everything I have commanded you. And surely I am with you always, to the very end of the age.'

Indeed Jesus arguably is entrusting to the disciples the Adamic task that Adam and Israel failed in, namely to be fruitful and multiply.[12]

Process theologian Norman Pittenger articulates these categories clearly when he writes:

> This God, who is the one and only God, is above and transcendent to the creation – inexhaustible and beyond our human grasping. This God is active within the creation, enabling its response to the divine intention – here is the divine immanence. This God is also alongside the creation too, disclosed by act in the affairs of the world; here is what I like to name the divine concomitance.[13]

The supreme instantiation of divine concomitance is the incarnation of the divine Son of God (John 1:14), as I shall argue in a later chapter.

---

[12] Beale 2004: 198.

[13] Pittenger n.d. One does not need to buy into Pittenger's process metaphysic to appreciate his insight on this particular point.

Importantly divine transcendence allows no room for pantheism. The Creator–creature distinction is the most basic metaphysical one in Scripture. The divine immanence and concomitance leave no room for deism as though the Creator has lost interest in creation.

Another significant question arises from reviewing the early chapters of Genesis. How are we to understand the language of speaking and seeing of Genesis 1, of resting, planting and commanding in Genesis 2 and walking in Genesis 3? The traditional way of addressing the question is to view this language as anthropomorphic.[14] An anthropomorphism (*anthrōpos*, 'human'; *morphē*, 'shape') is a description of God in human terms.[15] R. T. France makes an important observation in relation to biblical anthropomorphisms when he writes:

> It is one of the marks our departure from the biblical way of thinking about God, as the living God, that we are inclined to be ashamed of anthropomorphism. . . . We pass it off as a rather regrettable primitive phase in the evolution of thinking about God, just a step higher than sheer idolatry, a crude and unsophisticated language which our more advanced and respectable theology has translated into abstract concepts.[16]

Herman Bavinck, for one, felt no such embarrassment. As he put it, 'If it is improper to speak about God in anthropomorphic language, the only logical alternative is not to speak about God at all.'[17] For him biblical anthropomorphisms as a category covers the application to God of language about 'human organs, members, sensations, affections . . . human actions, a certain office, profession, or relation. . . . [and even] language derived from the organic and inorganic

---

[14] The theological defence of such a term is to argue that it is predicated on an even more profound proposition, namely that humankind – according to Gen. 1 – is theomorphic (God shaped).

[15] Ironically what has become a technical term in theological discussion was first propounded by an eighteenth-century atheist, Paul Henri Thierry, Baron d'Holbach (1723–89). Baron d'Holbach (2007: 124) argued, 'Thus, in truth, the moral qualities with which he has clothed the divinity, supposes him material, and the most abstract theological notions, are, after all, founded upon a direct, undeniable *Anthropomorphism*' (original emphasis). According to d'Holbach, theologians could not do otherwise because they themselves are material beings who project on the deity human qualities carried to perfection by a process of abstraction. For a handy discussion of d'Holbach's views see Banks 2011: 56–58.

[16] France 1970: 17.

[17] Bavinck 1977: 90.

creation'.[18] Useful though this conventional approach is, I believe that more precision would be clarifying. But what would more precision look like? Terence E. Fretheim offers some clarifying distinctions regarding categories of anthropomorphic speech: '(a) form, with its function (mouth, speaking, Num. 12:8); (b) emotional, volitional and mental states (rejoicing, Zeph. 3:17); (c) roles and activities, within the family (parent, Hos. 11:1) or the larger society (shepherd, Ps. 23.1)'.[19] With debts to Fretheim, I propose that when Scripture speaks of divine action in a way that is analogous to human action and roles such as 'speaking', 'seeing' and 'walking', the descriptor to employ is 'anthropopraxism'. However, when Scripture uses terms of God that have their analogues in human emotion, then 'anthropopathism' is the more precise descriptor.[20] Lastly, when Scripture ascribes human organs to God or facial features or limbs, then 'anthropomorphism' is the appropriate term.[21] In fact this last category admits of further refinement. When the text speaks of an appearance of God in human form per se, then we are dealing with an anthropomorphic theophany.[22] (In scholarly discourse, a theophany is an appearance of a god.[23]) Genesis 6 is a case in point: 'The LORD saw how great the wickedness of the human race had

[18] Ibid. 86–88. His is the most expansive view of biblical anthropomorphism that I have encountered. To include 'language derived from the organic and inorganic creation' I find puzzling.

[19] Fretheim 1984: 6.

[20] For a more sophisticated taxonomy see Hamori 2008: 26–34. Her categories include, in order of discussion, concrete anthropomorphism, envisioned anthropomorphism, immanent anthropomorphism, transcendent anthropomorphism and figurative anthropomorphism. It is worth noting that some scholars reject the attempt to refine the category of anthropomorphism. For example, Caird (1980: 173) does not accept the distinction between anthropomorphism and anthropopathism. His main argument is that these two categories do not cover the range of biblical materials. What is needed is coverage of 'metaphors of activity and relationship'. My category of anthropopraxism addresses precisely that desideratum.

[21] Fretheim 1984: 6.

[22] 'Anthropomorphic theophany' is borrowed from Barr 1960: 34. I prefer Barr's 'anthropomorphic theophany' to Terrien's (1978: 68) 'epiphanic visitation'. Terrien argues that theophany involves natural phenomena (e.g. light, darkness, whirlwinds, lightning, thunder, smoke, *inter alia*). However, I believe that the qualifier 'anthropomorphic' is precise enough to aid, not hinder, discussion of certain biblical accounts (e.g. Jacob and the wrestler in Gen. 32:22–32).

[23] Niehaus (1997: 1247) points out that the Greek term *theophaneia* lies behind our word 'theophany' (*theos*, 'god', and *phainō*, 'I appear'), and 'was used to describe a festival at Delphi at which images of the gods were shown to the people'. The whole article is an excellent treatment of theophany in brief compass. For a more sustained treatment of theophany and one that Niehaus heavily draws upon see Kuntz 1967, esp. ch. 1.

become on the earth, and that every inclination of the thoughts of the human heart was only evil all the time. The LORD regretted that he had made human beings on the earth, and his heart was deeply troubled' (Gen. 6:5–6). The Lord sees human wickedness (anthropopraxism). He is grieved and has pain (anthropopathism). This pain fills God's heart (anthropomorphism).

Some early Christian commentary

Early Christian commentators and preachers had to face the challenge of anthropomorphisms, anthropopathisms and anthropopraxisms. The depiction of God's walking in the garden in Genesis 3:8 provides a case in point. Ephrem the Syrian (born c. 306; fl. 363–373) comments:

> It was not only by the patience he exhibited that God wished to help them [Adam and Eve]; He also wished to benefit them by the sound of his feet. God endowed his silent footsteps with sound so that Adam and Eve might be prepared, at that sound, to make supplication before him who made the sound.[24]

This early church poet seems to be working with some notion of divine accommodation to human need to account for the language.

John Chrysostom (344/354–407; fl. 386–407), the famous early church leader and preacher, wrestles with the question 'Does God have feet?' There were some in his context who appeared to take Genesis 3:8 with a naive literalism. Chrysostom asks:

> What are you saying – God strolls? Are we assigning feet to him? Have we no exalted conception of him? No, God does not stroll – perish the thought. How could he, present as he is everywhere and filling everything with his presence? Can he for whom heaven is his throne and earth a footstool be confined to the garden? What right minded person could say this?[25]

Having dismissed literalism, what positively can be said according to Chrysostom?

---

[24] Ephrem the Syrian, *Commentary on Genesis 2.24.1*, quoted in Louth 2001: 82.
[25] John Chrysostom, *Homilies on Genesis 17:3–4*, quoted in Louth 2001: 82.

So what is the meaning of this statement, 'They heard the sound of the Lord as he strolled in the garden in the evening?' He wanted to provide them with such an experience as would induce in them a state of anguish, which in fact happened: they had so striking an experience that they tried to hide from the presence of God.[26]

Significantly Chrysostom's doctrine of God trumps a literalist hermeneutic: 'Have we no exalted conception of him?' He seeks to protect the idea of the divine transcendence with his question. This insight will prove important, for, as we shall see in subsequent chapters, the biblical writers were very much aware that God belongs to a different order of being to ourselves.

God prepares the way to what end?

More than once in this chapter thus far the notion that God has prepared the way from the beginning has been thematized. The question now must be put as to the end in view. Hints have been given. The Adamic task is royal and priestly. Recent scholarship throws great light on the question, and for the purposes of this chapter I shall follow John H. Walton's discussion.[27] In a nutshell God from the start has created with the end in view of living with the creature in his image. Put another way, the purpose of creation is divine habitation in a cosmic palace-temple. This is such a crucial point that elaboration is needed.

According to Walton, Genesis 1 is a temple text. The accent in the chapter is not on the material origins of the universe but on how God prepares a habitation for himself. In the ancient Near East such a habitation is a temple. He sums up his argument in the following way: 'In summary, we have suggested that the seven days are not given as the period of time over which the material cosmos came into existence, but the period of time devoted to the inauguration of the functions of the cosmic temple and . . . the entrance of the presence of God to take up his rest that creates the temple.'[28]

---

[26] Ibid.

[27] Beale (2004: 81–121) also provides an excellent discussion of this idea. He acknowledges his debts to Walton.

[28] Walton 2009: 92. Fascinatingly the making of the creation, the tabernacle and the temple is structured around seven successive divine acts or a time period involving seven. See the fine discussion in Beale 2004: 60–61.

Walton's thesis needs amplification in that the early chapters of Genesis not only present the making of a temple but a palace-temple.[29] Rikki E. Watts asks a crucial question:

> But is there any evidence of this notion in the Bible? The data is overwhelming. . . . In fact, the Hebrew Bible is awash with architectural imagery when describing creation. It speaks of the foundations of the earth (Ps 18:15; 82:5; 102:25; 104:5; Prov 8:29; Isa 51:13, 16; 2 Sam 22:8, 16; Zech 12:1; cf. 2 Sam 22:8), the pillars of the earth and of the heavens (1 Sam 2:8; Job 9:6; Ps 75:3; Job 26:11), the heavens' windows (Gen 7:11; 8:2; Isa 24:18; Mal 3:10; 2 Kgs 7:2; Ps 104:2), the stretching out of the heavens like a canopy/tent (Isa 40:12, 22; 42:5; 44:24; 45:12; 48:13; 51:13; Jer 10:12; 31:37; 32:17; 51:15; Amos 9:6; Zech 12:1; Job 9:8; Ps 102:25), and storehouses (Deut 28:12; Jer 10:13; 50:25; 51:16; cf. Ps 33:7; 135:7; Job 38:22).[30]

He asks a further question:

> But what kind of building is this? As Isaiah 66:1 makes clear, 'Heaven is my throne, and the earth is my footstool. Where is the house you will build for me? Where will my resting place be?' Where does one find a throne and a footstool if not in a palace, and what is the palace of Yahweh if not a temple? And note too the image of resting in his house (= Temple) in the light of Yahweh's resting in his completed abode on the seventh day of Genesis 1. In this sense, the whole of creation is seen as Yahweh's palace-temple, and hence the reason for his Jerusalem temple itself being a microcosm, a mini universe: it serves to remind Israel that the whole world is Yahweh's. Granted, Genesis 1 does not explicitly describe Yahweh as actually rolling up his sleeves and 'building' why should it when a truly Lordly Yahweh would merely have to give the word? But given the rather widespread Ancient Near Eastern notion linking creation, defeat-of-chaos, and temple-building, and the thorough-going architectural imagery which characterizes the biblical conceptualizing of creation, it would be very odd if Genesis 1 were not

---

[29] Walton (2009: 75) touches on the palace idea but does not develop it. He writes, 'In the same way, temple is built in the ancient world so that deity can have a center for his rule. The temple is the residence and palace of the gods.'

[30] R. E. Watts 2002.

to be understood along the lines of cosmic palace-temple building. As the Great King, Elohim, naturally creates realms for the lesser rulers (cf. Gen 1:16) as he forms his palace-temple out of the deep and gives order to and fills it. And as the Great King, having ordered his realm, he now rules over all in 'Sabbath' rest (see Exod 20), sitting in the great pavilion of his cosmos-palace-temple (cf. Ps 93).[31]

The idea of Emmanuel, 'God with us', is there in the biblical account from the very beginning.

God prepares the way by promise

As mentioned previously, in the divine comedy the harmonies of Genesis 1 – 2 with God and humankind at peace, humankind and the rest of creation at peace, humankind and the environment at peace give way in Genesis 3 to discord and fracture. As Thomas F. Torrance argues, 'It belongs to the nature of sin to divide, to create disorder, to disrupt, to destroy fellowship.'[32] In Genesis 3:1–5 we learn that the catalyst comes from outside the garden sanctuary in the guise of the serpent armed with dark innuendo:

> Now the snake was more crafty than any of the wild animals the LORD God had made. He said to the woman, 'Did God really say, "You must not eat from any tree in the garden"?'
>
> The woman said to the snake, 'We may eat fruit from the trees in the garden, but God did say, "You must not eat fruit from the tree that is in the middle of the garden, and you must not touch it, or you will die."'
>
> 'You will not certainly die,' the snake said to the woman. 'For God knows that when you eat from it your eyes will be opened, and you will be like God, knowing good and evil.'

---

[31] Ibid. Dumbrell (in Hafemann 2002: 58) adds a further insight: 'The placement of humankind in the garden as God's image furthers the analogy to the temple, with its image of the deity, drawing together the motifs of kingship and the temple at the beginning of the Bible.' Watts (2002) points out that the last act in temple construction was the placement of the image of the deity in the sacred space. In the light of the temple idea, theological reflection suggests that only a living image is able to be the image of a living God. This may be another reason why idolatry is such folly in biblical perspective.

[32] Torrance 2008: 38.

The character of God cannot be trusted. His word is not to be believed.[33] Something good is being held back from the man and the woman. The tree of the knowledge of good and evil is not to be resisted but embraced. After all it is so alluring, a sensual delight (Gen. 3:6): 'When the woman saw that the fruit of the tree was good for food and pleasing to the eye, and also desirable for gaining wisdom, she took some and ate it. She also gave some to her husband, who was with her, and he ate it.'[34] The results of the disobedience are catastrophic. No longer is there the fellowship between God and his image. Fellowship gives way to fear and flight from the presence (Gen. 3:8): 'Then the man and his wife heard the sound of the LORD God as he was walking in the garden in the cool of the day, and they hid from the LORD God among the trees of the garden.' Meredith G. Kline offers an intriguing interpretation of this episode:

> We may then translate Genesis 3:8a: 'They heard the sound of Yahweh God traversing the garden as the Spirit of the day.' The frightening noise of the approaching Glory theophany told them that God was coming to enter into judgment with them. The sound of judgment day preceded the awesome sight of the parousia of their Judge. It was evidently heard from afar before the searching, exposing beams of the theophanic light pierced through the trees in the midst of the garden. Momentarily, then, it seemed to them possible to hide from the eyes of Glory among the shadows of the foliage. Thus, inadvertently, they positioned themselves at the place of judgment in the midst of the trees of the garden, at the site of the tree of judicial discernment between good and evil.[35]

---

[33] For a brief but very useful treatment of Gen. 3 and how to understand the account as well as the catastrophic entailments it delineates see Carson 2010: 29–34. Beale (2004: 396) comments, 'Adam and Eve did not remember God's word, and they "fell", and they failed to extend the boundaries of God's Edenic temple.' The first part of the comment is hardly strong enough. The second part is extremely insightful.

[34] Some argue that Adam and Eve stand for every man and every woman. Thus Gen. 3 is the story of each one of us told in a highly symbolic way. In this view Adam and Eve were not historical individuals. Guinan (2008) argues, 'The man and woman of Genesis 2–3, as well as other characters of the primal stories, are intended to represent an Everyman and Everywoman.' But as I have written elsewhere (Cole 2009b: 57), 'logically speaking, if the Genesis stories are about all of us *ex hypothesi*, then they are about the first of us, and consequently belief in real personages and a real space-time fall is unavoidable even on the parabolic or mythic view'.

[35] Kline 1977–8.

In brief Adam and Eve meet with God's Spirit in judicial mode. Hence they hide. There is merit in his argument. The questioning is indeed confrontational in Genesis 3:9, 11 and 13. Furthermore in verse 24 the man and the woman are sent out of the garden and not simply led out. Even so, there is grace in the provision of a better and more permanent covering in Genesis 3:21 to address their nakedness.[36]

The cascading consequences of the primordial disobedience are manifold. The rupture is not simply an external one between God and humankind, but an internal one. There is shame at one's nakedness. Adam answers God, 'I heard you in the garden, and I was afraid because I was naked; so I hid' (Gen. 3:10). Consciousness of the other has become self-consciousness. The first pair has entered the dungeon of self-preoccupation. Furthermore there is not only the vertical relational rupture with God but a horizontal one between the sexes. The will to relate, exemplified in the one-flesh union of Genesis 2:24, becomes the will to blame ('the woman you put here with me') and the will to dominate ('he will rule over you'). Lastly, the downward relation to the rest of creation is disrupted such that ultimately the environment triumphs over us and back to dust we go. The world of Genesis 1 – 2 is no longer accessible. The cherubim with the flaming swords exclude the possibility of a simple return to paradise (Gen. 3:23–24): 'So the LORD God banished him from the Garden of Eden to work the ground from which he had been taken. After he drove the man out, he placed on the east side of the Garden of Eden cherubim and a flaming sword flashing back and forth to guard the way to the tree of life' – paradise lost, as Milton wrote. And yet there is evidence of mercy in the midst of judgment. The man and woman attempted to cover their nakedness with fig leaves (Gen. 3:7). The text does not elaborate but clearly they were no Versaces. And so God provides (Gen. 3:21): 'The LORD God made garments of skin for Adam and his wife and clothed them.' Indeed as I have written elsewhere, 'Even the banishment from the garden zone may have been a mercy, given

---

[36] Ibid. Some of his interpretation is more eisegesis than exegesis though: 'It was evidently heard from afar before the searching, *exposing beams of the theophanic light pierced through the trees in the midst of the garden*' (my emphasis). Matthews, Chavalas and Walton (2000) in their comment on Gen. 3:8 lend some independent support to Kline's view: 'Akkadian terminology has demonstrated that the word translated "day" also has the meaning "storm." This meaning can be seen also for the Hebrew word in Zephaniah 2:2. It is often connected to the deity coming in a storm of judgment. If this is the correct rendering of the word in this passage, they heard the thunder (the word translated "sound" is often connected to thunder) of the Lord moving about in the garden in the wind of the storm. In this case it is quite understandable why they are hiding.'

THE GOD WHO BECAME HUMAN

the narrative logic of the account. Man and woman are prevented from eating of the tree of life and thus kept mercifully from being locked into their alienated state.'[37]

By the end of Genesis 1 – 3 we see that the creation purpose to provide a dwelling place for God with humanity is challenged by both human and angelic sin. But there is light in this darkness: in the midst of judgment the text of the *protoevangelium* comes into view. God will remove the challenge but at a cost. He addresses the serpent as follows:

So the LORD God said to the snake,

> 'Because you have done this,
> "Cursed are you above all livestock
>   and all wild animals!
> You will crawl on your belly
>   and you will eat dust
>   all the days of your life.
> *And I will put enmity*
>   *between you and the woman,*
>   *and between your offspring and hers;*
> *he will crush your head,*
>   *and you will strike his heel."* '
>   (Gen. 3:14–15, my emphasis)

The blessing language of the creation account in Genesis 1 is now counterbalanced by the words of cursing in the Fall narrative of Genesis 3 (cf. Gen. 1:22, 28; 2:3, 14, 17). According to Gordon J. Wenham the reference to the serpent's eating dust is full of significance: '"Eat dust." The serpent will experience abject humiliation. Metaphorically eating dust is what happens to one's enemies (cf. Ps 72:9; Isa 49:23; Mic 7:17).'[38] Furthermore, the 'enmity' in view suggests a long period of conflict rather than a short one (cf. Num. 35:21–22; Ezek. 25:15; 35:5).[39]

C. John Collins, in a careful discussion of Genesis 3:15, captures the programmatic nature of the Genesis text:

> Hence, this is in fact a promise that God will act for the benefit of mankind by defeating the serpent (really the Dark Power that used

---

[37] Cole 2009b: 57.
[38] Wenham 2004, comment on Gen. 3:14.
[39] Ibid., comment on Gen. 3:15.

the serpent as its mouthpiece) in combat and defeat him, thus bringing benefits to mankind. That is, he is a champion. We are further entitled to say that he will be a human (an offspring of the woman), but one with power extraordinary enough to win. . . . The rest of Genesis will unfold the idea of this offspring and lay the foundation for the developed messianic teaching of the prophets. We must remember that an author put this text here, and we suppose that he did so with his plan for this unfolding in mind; hence for us to ask whether this is messianic may mislead us: instead, we may say that Genesis fosters a messianic expectation, of which this verse is the headwaters.[40]

There is admirable caution here in not overstating the case. It is in the retrospective light of the canonical unfolding of the biblical story that the programmatic nature of the *protoevangelium* comes into view. Hence the coining of a term meaning 'first gospel', which presupposes the gospel that came much later.

Genesis 3 does not make clear in any deep way just how the serpent's fate will be sealed. What is clear is that a male descendant of the woman will be involved. Triumph will come through suffering and that suffering will involve both the male offspring and the serpent:

> he will crush your head,
> and you will strike his heel.
>
> (Gen. 3:15)

The serpent will lose definitively, a crushed head, while the seed of the woman will sustain a struck heel. A subsequent book in the Torah underlines the nature of the challenge posed by the divine to human life in the new normal or abnormal (the post-Fall world). Leviticus reads strangely to modern Western ears: priests, sacrifices, blood and ritual. However, once the issue comes into view, namely of how a holy

---

[40] Collins 2006: 157. According to Dumbrell (2001b: 27–28), 'Such [interpretation], in fact, is found in the Septuagint, a very early witness to a traditional interpretation, where the neuter noun seed of verse 15 is treated syntactically as masculine to refer to the messiah. In the Palestinian Targums, Aramaic translations of the Hebrew noun *'āqēb* (heel, end) leads to a messianic understanding. The verse is taken to mean that the serpent and his descendants will bite the woman's descendants on the "heel" but also that there will be a remedy at the "end," in the day of the messiah. (Interestingly there is no evidence in later rabbinic sources of a messianic interpretation.) According to Irenaeus and the early church fathers, the woman's seed refers to humankind generally and then to Christ specifically.'

God can be present in the midst of an unholy people, then the logic of Leviticus becomes much less opaque. Ultimately atonement is needed, and at a cost.

Conclusion

In this chapter we have explored the idea of preparation from the beginning. That preparation is for the dwelling of God with humankind in a sacred space that is a palace-temple. The six-day process is best seen in architectural terms. God is building a habitation for himself. The divine largesse is shown in the way God creates a creature as his image with whom he can dwell. This is sheer grace in that there is no hint in the Genesis text that there was divine necessity to so create. Creation is an expression of divine freedom and generosity. However, discord entered the scene with devastating consequences for the habitation of God with humankind. Even so, the divine project is not abandoned. There is not only judgment but also the promise (the *protoevangelium*) of the world set right. The divine comedy will reach its harmony once more, the serpent will be defeated and a male descendant of the woman will be the key to the resolution of the conflict. The depiction of God in these early chapters is filled with anthropomorphism, anthropopathism and anthropopraxism. This depiction we shall continue to explore as we follow the biblical plotline.

Excursus: Would the incarnation have taken place irrespective of the Fall?

The question is whether the incarnation would have taken place irrespective of the Fall of Genesis 3. In other words was an incarnation of deity always the divine intention? It is not a new question.

The major figure in the early church period who turned his mind to the question was Maximus the Confessor (c. 580–662). Maximus argued that the incarnation would have taken place irrespective of the Fall. The incarnation of the Logos was always the divine intention and the grand eschatological goal of creation.[41] The question received more attention in the medieval period in the Western church.[42] (According to Meyendorff it was never a major question of interest in the Byzantine church.) In the West, Honorius of Acun (fl. c. 1106–35) believed that

[41] Meyendorff 1975: 160–161.
[42] For a useful discussion of how the medieval Christians addressed the question see Sheppard 2005: 61–76.

the incarnation was always the divine intention, as did Rupert of Deutz
(c. 1075–1129). Aquinas (c. 1225–74) was more cautious than Honorius
and Rupert. Aquinas was well aware of differences of theological
opinion on the question, but on balance thought that the incarnation
was God's remedy for sin and presupposed the Fall. Aquinas argued:

> Some say that the Son of God would have become incarnate, even
> if humanity had not sinned. Others assert the opposite, and it
> would seem that our assent ought to be given to this opinion. For
> those things that originate from God's will, lying beyond what is
> due to the creature, can only be known to us through being
> revealed in Holy Scripture, in which the divine will is made known
> to us. Therefore since the sin of the first human being is described
> as the cause of the incarnation throughout Holy Scripture, it is
> more in accordance with this to say that the work of the incar-
> nation was ordained as a remedy for sin, so that, if sin had not
> existed, the incarnation would never have taken place.[43]

Even so, Aquinas had a healthy respect for the freedom of God: 'Yet
the power of God is not limited in this way. Even if sin had not existed,
God could still have become incarnate.'[44]

Among those who believed that the incarnation would have taken
place irrespective of the Fall, two main rationales for the divine
purpose were suggested. Both Maximus the Confessor and Honorius
of Acun saw deification as the key. The divine purpose was to make
humanity divine through union with the divine-human Son.[45] Rupert
of Deutz suggested another reason: 'he [Christ] had no necessary
cause for becoming man, other than that his love's "delights were to
be with the children of men"'.[46] For Rupert the incarnation was the
climax of concomitance.

The medieval debate may seem particularly esoteric to those whose
high view of Scripture makes them cautious about going beyond what
is written. However, it does raise the importance of having some
concept of dogmatic rank. Dogmatic rank is the idea that not all
doctrinal claims stand on the same level. As we saw above, Aquinas
was sensitive to the fact that 'those things that originate from God's

---

[43] Quoted in McGrath 2011: 282. McGrath offers no opinion of his own on the
question.
[44] Ibid.
[45] Sheppard 2005: cf. 288–299 and 354.
[46] Ibid. 361.

will, lying beyond what is due to the creature, can only be known to us through being revealed in Holy Scripture, in which the divine will is made known to us'.[47] The Christian past is indeed helpful here. In the Reformation era the early Lutherans and later Reformed divines posited three levels of theological claim. Fundamental articles are those doctrines 'without which Christianity cannot exist and the integrity of which is necessary to the preservation of the Faith' (e.g. the resurrection of Christ).[48] Secondary fundamental articles are derived from the primary ones (e.g. how Christ is present in the Lord's Supper). The Lutherans argued that Calvinists were Christians because they held the primary fundamental articles but were clearly not Lutherans because of their view of the Lord's Supper. The Calvinists denied the Lutheran doctrine of consubstantiation.[49] Non-fundamental articles were those theological claims that did not affect one's salvation and the maintenance of the faith (e.g. the exact identity of the Antichrist).

In the light of the above I would assign the answer to the question of whether there would have been an incarnation irrespective of the Fall to the non-fundamental article category. The ever-present danger to the evangelical movement is to confuse these categories. The main thing is to make the main thing the main thing. This wisdom also applies to doctrine. Even so, if John H. Walton is correct, then Old Testament scholarship and ancient Near Eastern analogies throw fresh light on this old question. If Genesis 1:1 – 2:3 is a temple text, then the divine design was always to establish the divine presence on earth among God's creatures in a cosmic temple, which the Garden of Eden anticipates. This thesis, in my view, tips the speculative balance in favour of Maximus the Confessor, Honorius of Acun and Rupert of Deutz. The incarnation is no afterthought.

In terms of dogmatic rank, both the question and my answer are speculative and to some presumptuous.[50] Even so, Colin E. Gunton wisely argues, 'Would Christ have come even had there been no fall? Hypothetical questions are dangerous in theology, because it [theology]

---

[47] Quoted in McGrath 2011: 282.

[48] Muller 1986: 45. For the substance of this paragraph I am indebted to Muller's work, 45–46.

[49] McGrath (2011: 467) sums up the Lutheran doctrine in these terms: 'The theory of the real presence especially associated with Martin Luther, which holds that the substance of the Eucharistic bread and wine are given together with the substance of the body and blood of Christ.'

[50] For example, Calvin (2002b: 2.12.4) argues, 'But since all Scripture proclaims that to become our Redeemer he was clothed with flesh, it is too presumptuous to imagine another reason or another end.'

is concerned with what God has done, not what he might have done instead. But in this case the question enables us to bring out the point of what has happened.'[51] He maintains – following Edward Irving – that sin and evil may have dictated the form of Christ's coming but not the fact that he would come.

[51] Gunton 2002: 67–68.

Chapter Two

God prepares the way in his dealings with Abraham and Abraham's Old Testament children

In this chapter we continue to follow the biblical plotline as we consider first God's dealings with the patriarchs and then Israel itself. The angle of vision remains the same. With special attention to anthropomorphisms, anthropopathisms and anthropopraxisms we are asking how God is portrayed in the relevant texts. Of particular interest will be those texts that present an encounter with Yahweh in human form on the one hand, and those texts on the other hand that suggest that in the divine revelatory encounters there is both a veiling and unveiling of the nature of God. We shall also see if there is merit in W. Eichrodt's view that in the Old Testament, God 'can temporarily incarnate himself', and in the even more provocative suggestion from Terence E. Fretheim that 'There is no such thing for Israel as a nonincarnate God.'[1]

The patriarchal story and the 'embodied' God

There is much continuity in the way God is rendered in the patriarchal texts with the ones we have already explored in Genesis 1 – 6. Abram/Abraham serves as our example. Abram becomes God's speech partner (Gen. 12:1) just as Adam and Noah had been in pre-patriarchal times. And for the first time in the canonical story God is said to appear to, and not simply speak to, an individual (Gen. 12:7).[2] A second new feature is that divine speaking now also takes place in vision (Gen. 15:1) and dream (Gen. 15:12–13). Esther J. Hamori usefully describes

---

[1] Fretheim 1984: 106. Eichrodt is quoted in ibid. 102. Niehaus (1997) points out that temporariness is a defining characteristic of theophany.

[2] 'Appear' is in the passive (niphal from the root r'h). The Lord 'was seen'. The revelatory initiative lies with the Lord.

such textual evidence that presents a vision or a dream as 'envisioned anthropomorphism'.[3] Other anthropopraxisms, besides speech, include the Lord's taking Abram outside the tent (Gen. 15:5). This spatial idea is not elaborated in this text. Nor is the language of divine appearance filled out in Genesis 17:1: 'When Abram was ninety-nine years old, the LORD appeared to him and said, "I am God Almighty; walk before me faithfully and be blameless."' Here an empirical dimension is suggested implicitly ('appearance') as well as divine speaking explicitly ('He said').

Two patriarchal stories are of particular interest, because for the first time in canonical unfolding we meet what Hamori describes as ''îš' theophanies.[4] She writes, 'There are two biblical texts in which God appears to a patriarch in person and is referred to by the narrator as a "man," both times by the Hebrew word 'îš. Both of these identifications of God as an 'îš [man] are accompanied by graphic human depiction.'[5]

Abraham and the three visitors

The first of these stories involves Abraham and is found in Genesis 18. It has been said that Judaism is a four-thousand-year argument with God. In this view, Genesis 18 would describe the fountainhead. For in this chapter, Abraham famously argues with God about the

---

[3] Hamori 2008: 29. Jacob likewise experienced God in an anthropopraxic way in the dream at Bethel: 'He had a dream in which he saw a stairway resting on the earth, with its top reaching to heaven, and the angels of God were ascending and descending on it. There above it stood the LORD, and he said: "I am the LORD, the God of your father Abraham and the God of Isaac. I will give you and your descendants the land on which you are lying"' (Gen. 28:12–13).

[4] Fretheim (1984: 80–81) usefully distinguishes two types of theophany in Scripture: 'Theophanies of God as Warrior' and 'Theophanies of God as Bearer of the Word'. The two patriarchal narratives that concern us at present fall into the latter category. A subset of Bearer of the Word theophanies is that of anthropomorphic theophanies as opposed to non-anthropomorphic theophanies. The wrestler at the Jabbok is an example of the former and the burning bush of Exod. 3 is an example of the latter.

[5] Hamori 2008: 1. To be more precise, both patriarchal accounts contain andromorphisms. That is to say God is presented as having a male form rather than a female form (gynemorphism). For a useful discussion of the differences between anthropomorphism, andromorphism and gynemorphism see Scobie 2003: 118. These 'îš texts make Rabbi Meir Y. Soloveichik's (2010: 45) comments puzzling: 'God's presence dwells in the Temple and amidst the people of Israel, and the "glory of God" descends onto Sinai and leads Israel through the desert. In that sense, God may be considered to be present in the flesh of the Jewish people. . . . But Hebrew Scripture never depicts the divine appearing before the Jewish people in human form.'

fate of his nephew Lot in the face of the news that the Lord is about
to overthrow the cities of Sodom and Gomorrah (Gen. 18:23–32).[6]
That disturbing news is prefaced by the good news that the aged Sarah
will indeed have a son in a year's time (Gen. 18:10). This then is no
minor encounter. God is keeping covenant. The account itself opens
in a surprising way in Genesis 18:1–2: 'The LORD appeared to
Abraham near the great trees of Mamre while he was sitting at the
entrance to his tent in the heat of the day. Abraham looked up and
saw three men ['ănāšîm] standing nearby.'[7]

Interpreting the text is challenging because by the time one has read
both Genesis 18 and 19 the visitors are described variously as 'the
LORD' (Gen. 18:1, 13, 17, 20, 22, 26, 33), 'three men' (Gen. 18:2),
'my Lord' ('ădōnāy, Gen. 18:3), 'the men' (Gen. 18:16, 22; 19:10), 'two
angels' (Gen. 19:1) and finally, 'two men' (Gen. 19:12). The following
catena displays the diversity:

Genesis 18:1	The LORD appeared to Abraham near the great trees of Mamre while he was sitting at the entrance to his tent in the heat of the day.
Genesis 18:2	Abraham looked up and saw *three men* standing nearby.
Genesis 18:3	He said, 'If I have found favour in your eyes, *my lord*, do not pass your servant by.'[8]
Genesis 18:13	Then *the LORD* said to Abraham, 'Why did Sarah laugh and say, "Will I really have a child, now that I am old?"'
Genesis 18:16	When *the men* got up to leave, they looked down towards Sodom, and Abraham walked along with them to see them on their way.
Genesis 18:17	Then *the LORD* said, 'Shall I hide from Abraham what I am about to do?'

---

[6] That the Lord discloses to Abraham what he is about to do is significant. This is
knowledge that friends might share. It is no accident that Abraham is described as
God's friend (cf. Gen. 18:17; Isa. 41:8; John 15:15). Friends can also argue with each
other and not break the relationship.

[7] According to Niehaus (1997), in theophany God takes the initiative always. There
are no biblical examples of the creature's engineering the divine appearance. In other
words the God of the Bible is not subject to magical manipulation.

[8] Friedman (1995: 10) observes that 'my Lord' ('ădōnāy, Gen. 18:3) 'elsewhere
in the Bible refers only to God'. Friedman is a Jewish scholar and so when he refers to
the Bible it is the Hebrew Bible that is in view.

Genesis 18:20	Then *the* Lᴏʀᴅ said, 'The outcry against Sodom and Gomorrah is so great and their sin so grievous . . . '.
Genesis 18:22	*The men* turned away and went towards Sodom, but Abraham remained standing before *the* Lᴏʀᴅ.
Genesis 18:26	*The* Lᴏʀᴅ said, 'If I find fifty righteous people in the city of Sodom, I will spare the whole place for their sake.'
Genesis 18:33	When *the* Lᴏʀᴅ had finished speaking with Abraham, he left, and Abraham returned home.
Genesis 19:1	The *two angels* arrived at Sodom in the evening, and Lot was sitting in the gateway of the city. When he saw them, he got up to meet them and bowed down with his face to the ground. . . .
Genesis 19:10	But *the men* inside reached out and pulled Lot back into the house and shut the door.
Genesis 19:12	The *two men* said to Lot, 'Do you have anyone else here – sons-in-law, sons or daughters, or anyone else in the city who belongs to you? Get them out . . . '.[9]

At first Abraham does not recognize that he has encountered the Lord. True, he addresses one of them as 'Lord' when he offers hospitality (Gen. 18:3). But this seems simply to mean, as Gordon J. Wenham suggests, that he recognized one of them as the leader of the three, even though all three replied to him (Gen. 18:5).[10] It is not until Genesis 18:13–14 that the proverbial penny drops. Abraham is speaking with Yahweh: 'Then the Lᴏʀᴅ said to Abraham, "Why did Sarah laugh and say, 'Will I really have a child, now that I am old?' Is anything too hard for the Lᴏʀᴅ? I will return to you at the appointed time next year, and Sarah will have a son."' Sarah now knows in whose presence she stands. She is afraid (Gen. 18:15). It is intriguing that recognizing the presence of Yahweh himself took time, as Gordon J. Wenham notes.[11] Was it the supernatural knowledge of Sarah's laughing to herself that betrayed the divine visitation? Or was it that Abraham finally recognized a voice he had heard in the past (Gen. 12:1; 15:1; 17:1)? Hamori is in no doubt: 'In the *'iš* theophany, Yahweh appears as man,

---

[9] The emphases in italics are mine.
[10] Wenham 2004, comment on Gen. 18:5.
[11] Ibid., comment on Gen. 18:1.

with such anthropomorphic realism that Abraham does not recognize him until Yahweh's verbal self-revelation.'[12]

In this account we are dealing with anthropopraxisms. The Lord stands (Gen. 18:2), eats (Gen. 18:8), speaks (Gen.18:13) and walks (Gen. 18:16). However, there is also anthropomorphism here in a startling way. We are dealing not with figurative references to the divine heart or arm or ears but with the form of a male human being. Early church fathers had no doubts as to who was in view in the story. Irenaeus is representative and his comments apply to the patriarchal story regarding Abraham we have been considering and the one to come involving Jacob: 'The Son of God is implanted everywhere throughout Moses' writings. At one time, indeed, He spoke with Abraham, when about to eat with him [Gen. 18]. . . . At another time, He brought down judgment upon the Sodomites. And again, He became visible and directed Jacob on his journey [Gen. 32, more anon].'[13] As David W. Bercot suggests, 'The early church taught that in all of the Old Testament theophanies, it was the pre-incarnate Son of God who appeared.'[14]

Interestingly Calvin largely follows early church interpretation but also allows the following:

> The reason why Moses introduces, at one time, three speakers, while, at another, he ascribes speech to one only, is, that the three together represent the person of one God. We must also remember what I have lately adduced, that the principal place is given to one; because Christ, who is the living image of the Father, often appeared to the fathers under the form of an angel, while, at the same time, he yet had angels, of whom he was the Head, for his attendants.[15]

According to Calvin the three speakers are angels clothed in human form, one of whom is the pre-incarnate Christ, who is 'the chief of the embassy'.[16]

Unlike the early church fathers considered above, some modern interpreters have struggled to explain the portrayal of God in the story. John H. Sailhamer for instance:

---

[12] Hamori 2008: 13.
[13] Quoted in Bercot 2002: 643.
[14] Ibid.
[15] Calvin 2002a, comment on Gen. 18:9.
[16] Ibid., comment on Gen. 18:2.

The explanation seems to be that the three men, as such, are to be understood as the physical 'appearance' of the Lord to Abraham. In other words, though God himself did not appear to Abraham in physical form, the three men are to be seen as representative of his presence. In much the same way the Burning Bush of Exodus 3:2–3 was a physical representation of God's presence but yet was not actually the physical presence of God. In such a way the actual presence of God among his covenant people was assured but without leaving the impression that God may have a physical form.[17]

For Sailhamer the three men represent the one God. Others, however, for example R. W. L. Moberly, see in the account that Yahweh appears 'in the form (apparently) of a normal human being' in one of the individuals.[18] But is it a metaphor only? Moberly thinks yes. Hamori argues no and convincingly so in the light of thorough treatment of comparative ancient Near Eastern materials: 'The human form is no more metaphorical in the *'îš* theophany of Genesis 18 than in the fire in the theophany of Exodus 3.'[19]

Jacob and the wrestler

The second *'îš* theophany is found in another famous patriarchal narrative. Jacob, Abraham's grandson, is on his way to meet his estranged brother Esau and is aware that danger may well lie ahead. On the way Jacob meets a strange figure at the ford of the Jabbok. Martin Luther says of the story that 'Every man holds that this text is one of the most obscure in the Old Testament.'[20] The account in Genesis 32:22–32 is so striking and so mysterious it needs quoting in full:

> That night Jacob got up and took his two wives, his two female servants and his eleven sons and crossed the ford of the Jabbok. After he had sent them across the stream, he sent over all his possessions. So Jacob was left alone, and a man wrestled with him

---

[17] Sailhamer 1997, comment on Gen. 18:1.
[18] Quoted in Hamori 2008: 10.
[19] Ibid. 11.
[20] Quoted in Kaiser, Jr., et al. 2001. Recent commentators concur. Jewish scholar Levenson (2003: 67), for example, maintains, 'The fateful encounter at the Jabbok is one of the best-known episodes in the life of Jacob, but also surely the most enigmatic.'

till daybreak. When the man saw that he could not overpower him, he touched the socket of Jacob's hip so that his hip was wrenched as he wrestled with the man. Then the man said, 'Let me go, for it is daybreak.'

But Jacob replied, 'I will not let you go unless you bless me.'

The man asked him, 'What is your name?'

'Jacob,' he answered.

Then the man said, 'Your name will no longer be Jacob, but Israel, because you have struggled with God and with humans and have overcome.'

Jacob said, 'Please tell me your name.'

But he replied, 'Why do you ask my name?' Then he blessed him there.

So Jacob called the place Peniel, saying, 'It is because I saw God face to face, and yet my life was spared.'

The sun rose above him as he passed Peniel, and he was limping because of his hip. Therefore to this day the Israelites do not eat the tendon attached to the socket of the hip, because the socket of Jacob's hip was touched near the tendon.

As with the earlier *'iš* theophany, this second one is no minor episode. After it Jacob will bear a name that remains with Abraham's progeny to this very day: 'Israel'.

According to Hamori this narrative needs to be taken at face value as depicting an appearance of the divine in a human form. She argues:

As in Genesis 18, God appears here in anthropomorphically realistic form. There is no indication that there is anything unusual about his physical form as a man. He is scarcely a match for Jacob, who is himself not drawn as a terrifically intimidating character. The man is thus implicitly not larger than human size nor beyond human strength. He is not stronger than Jacob even when the latter has a dislocated hip. He engages in very human activity, as in Genesis 18, and never acts outside the bounds of his human form.[21]

Bringing Genesis 32 and 18 into conversation she concludes, 'The most straightforward reading of each of these two texts is that God appears to the patriarch in theophany, just as we have seen in myriad

[21] Hamori 2008: 25.

THE GOD WHO BECAME HUMAN

other texts, and that in these two cases, the form of theophany is human.'[22]

However, it must be noted that on the surface Hosea 12 with its reference to Jacob appears to tell a different story to that of Hamori. What is straightforward in Genesis 32 becomes not so much so given Hosea 12:3–5:

> In the womb he grasped his brother's heel;
>   as a man he struggled with God.
> He struggled with the angel and overcame him;
>   he wept and begged for his favour.
> He found him at Bethel
>   and talked with him there –
> the LORD God Almighty,
>   the LORD is his name!

Unsurprisingly then Jewish commentators have taken the Genesis 32 encounter to be one between Jacob and an angel. J. D. Levenson sums up the Jewish tradition of interpretation:

> [Most] traditional Jewish commentators have taken him [Jacob's opponent] to be angelic. A well-known midrash [*Gen. Rab.* 77.3] sees him as the 'patron angel of Esau' and thus interprets this episode as a warning to all future enemies of the Jewish people: 'Your patron angel could not withstand him [i.e. Jacob/Israel] and you seek to attack his descendants?'[23]

How then is the challenge posed by Hosea 12:3–5 to be addressed? Hamori deals with the challenge by suggesting that the word for 'angel' in the text (*mal'āḥ*) is a gloss.[24] W. Kaiser, Jr., takes a different tack:

> Hosea 12:4 describes the antagonist, then, as an 'angel.' But since Old Testament appearances of God, or theophanies, are routinely

---

[22] Ibid. In her taxonomy of anthropomorphisms Gen. 18 and 32 present 'concrete anthropomorphisms'. Medieval Jewish thinker Moses Maimonides (1995: 146) cannot accept any physicality in the event. In his view, 'All this wrestling and conversation took place in prophetic vision.' However, there is no textual evidence to support his contention. In contrast a contemporary Jewish scholar, James Kugel (2007: 161), describes the story as 'a narrative that seems to bespeak a most real encounter that took place long, long ago'.

[23] Levenson 2004: 67–68, note on Gen. 32:25.

[24] Hamori 2008: 110–111. However, the LXX has 'angel' (*angelou*) in its translation.

described as involving the 'angel of the Lord,' it should not surprise us that the Lord of glory took the guise or form of an angel. In fact, that is exactly what God would do later on in his enfleshment, or incarnation. He would take on flesh; in his coming as a babe to Bethlehem, however, he took on human flesh forever. But what really clinches the argument for this identification is the fact that in verse 3 of Hosea 12, the parallel clause equates this 'angel' with God himself. Jacob struggled with an 'angel,' yes, but he also 'struggled with God.'[25]

Reconciling the Genesis account and Hosea's interpretation is not easy for the interpreter but Kaiser, Jr., offers the most promising way forward.

Turning to early church reflection upon Genesis 32 once more, we find a consistent reading of the text in Christological terms. Clement of Alexandria provides a serviceable example. He writes, 'Furthermore, Jacob is said to have wrestled with Him. . . . Jacob called the place, "Face of God." . . . The "face of God" is the Word by whom God is manifested and made known. Then also was Jacob given the name Israel, because he saw God the Lord. It was God the Word.'[26] Some modern commentators are not as sure, with suggestions that include the following: an angel, a river spirit, a river demon, a river guardian, spirit of a dead man and even Esau's alter ego or Esau's patron angel.[27] However, as Paul R. House contends, 'He [Jacob] has not encountered a river demon in his opinion. He has encountered one who knows his past, present and future. Only God fits this description in the book of Genesis.'[28]

The Mosaic story and the 'embodied' God

There are a number of theophanic moments in the book of Exodus that are of interest. The burning bush in Exodus 3 is the most famous. God has remembered his covenant commitment to the children of

---

[25] Kaiser, Jr., et al. 2001, comment on Gen. 32.

[26] Quoted in Bercot 2002: 643.

[27] For a discussion of the range of suggestions past and present as to the identity of the wrestler see Kaiser, Jr., et al. 2001, and for a more recent survey see Hamori 2008: 13–23.

[28] House 1998: 80. Calvin 2002a, comment on Gen. 32:24, likewise understands the encounter as between God and Jacob. However, he also regards it as a 'nocturnal vision', though there is nothing in the text that suggests it was such (ibid., comment on Gen. 32:26). For a contrary opinion that the figure in view in the text is an angel see Sailhamer 1997, comment on Gen. 32:23–32.

Israel (Exod. 2:24). He meets Moses in the desert at Horeb, the mountain of God (Exod. 3:2–4):

> There the angel of the LORD appeared to him in flames of fire from within a bush. Moses saw that though the bush was on fire it did not burn up. So Moses thought, 'I will go over and see this strange sight – why the bush does not burn up.'
> When the LORD saw that he had gone over to look, God called to him from within the bush, 'Moses! Moses!'
> And Moses said, 'Here I am.'

All the elements of a theophany are present: the language of appearance, visible phenomena and the divine voice. In Fretheim's categories this is a theophany of 'God as Bearer of the Word'.[29] What is not present is any suggestion that this was an anthropomorphic theophany.

Once Israel is gathered at Sinai, however, anthropomorphic theophany comes into view. The description is curious. In Exodus 24:9–11 we read:

> Moses and Aaron, Nadab and Abihu, and the seventy elders of Israel went up and saw the God of Israel. Under his feet was something like a pavement made of lapis lazuli, as bright blue as the sky. But God did not raise his hand against these leaders of the Israelites; they saw God, and they ate and drank.

The divine becomes visible.[30] There is a reference to the sight of God, the feet of God and the hand of God. The reference to feet suggests a human form, whereas the reference to hand is more easily understood as metaphor.[31]

---

[29] Fretheim 1984: 81.

[30] Kaiser, Jr., et al. 2001, in reference to Exod. 24:9–11 draw attention to the way the LXX sought to moderate the force of the anthropomorphic descriptors: 'The translators who compiled the Greek version of the Old Testament, the Septuagint, were so concerned about any wrong connotations in Exodus 24:9 that they added "in the place where he stood" to the words "they saw the God of Israel." There is no basis for such an addition, however, except the tendency of this translation to avoid any descriptions of God in terms that are used of human beings (the so-called antianthropomorphic trend of the LXX).' The LXX translators appear to have seen correctly the force of the anthropomorphic language and were disturbed by it.

[31] Tigay (2003: 163) cautiously suggests, 'By focusing on what was *under His feet*, it seems to suggest that the leaders did not see God directly but from below' (original italics). However, unless they saw something more directly, how did the text make the spatial judgment that related the 'pavement' and the feet?

Israel's failure at Sinai is a well-known story. While Moses receives the Ten Commandments on the mountain top, Israel below indulges in breaking them with the idolatry of the golden calf (cf. Exod. 31:18; 32:7–8). Moses as covenant mediator pleads with God not to abandon his people (Exod. 32:11–14). Judgment follows but is mitigated by Mosaic intercession (Exod. 32:33–35). Moses seeks further reassurance that the divine presence will be with God's people and asks to see the divine glory (Exod. 33:18). God accedes to his servant's request and the divine glory is displayed (Exod. 33:19–23):

And the LORD said, 'I will cause all my goodness to pass in front of you, and I will proclaim my name, the LORD, in your presence. I will have mercy on whom I will have mercy, and I will have compassion on whom I will have compassion. But,' he said, 'you cannot see my face, for no one may see me and live.'
Then the LORD said, 'There is a place near me where you may stand on a rock. When my glory passes by, I will put you in a cleft in the rock and cover you with my hand until I have passed by. Then I will remove my hand and you will see my back; but my face must not be seen.'

This too is an anthropomorphic theophany with its references to back, face and hand. However, this account introduces important qualifications. This is no surprise given the divine statement in Exodus 33:20 above: '"But," he said, "you cannot see my face, for no one may see me and live."'[32]
What then did Moses see? Terence E. Fretheim perceptively comments regarding the reference to Moses' seeing the back of God: 'This suggests, not only that even Moses was granted less than a full sensorial view of God, but that what he was given had the lineaments of a human form.'[33] Richard Elliot Friedman accurately describes this encounter between Yahweh and Moses on Sinai as 'the ultimate, exceptional experience of God by anyone in the Bible [by which he means the Hebrew Bible], Moses seeing the actual form of God on Mount Sinai (Exod. 34). It is arguably the culminating moment of

[32] This statement is puzzling given Deut. 34:10: 'no prophet has risen in Israel like Moses, whom the LORD knew face to face [*pānîm bĕpānîm*]'. Most probably 'face to face' is an idiomatic way of asserting that Moses knew God with an unrivalled intimacy. Hamori (2008: 31) suggests, 'the thrust of the idiom once again relates to the intimacy of the communication, not to literal faces'.
[33] Fretheim 1984: 186, n. 42.

human history since Adam and Eve in this narrative, and it is as mysterious as anything in the Bible.'[34] Friedman's comment is accurate as long as only the Hebrew Bible is in view.

Jeffrey S. Niehaus correctly observes that in the biblical presentation theophany involves both a veiling and an unveiling.[35] It is as though outside Eden human ontology cannot bear the sight of the divine glory in its plenitude. A variety of commentators underline the point. For example, Jewish scholar Jeffrey H. Tigay comments, 'Although the Bible assumes that God has a physical (usually humanlike) form, many passages suggest that seeing him would be too awesome for humans to survive.'[36] Evangelical Walter Kaiser, Jr., helpfully suggests, 'That this is a figure of speech [Exod. 33:23] is clear from the double effect of God passing by while simultaneously protecting Moses with the divine "hand." Only after his glory, or presence, had passed by would God remove his gracious, protecting "hand." Then Moses would view what God had permitted.'[37] He then asks, 'But what was left for Moses to see? The translators say God's "back." But since God is spirit (Is 31:3; Jn 4:24) and formless, what would this refer to?'[38] Kaiser, Jr., answers his own questions: 'The word *back* can as easily be rendered the "after effects" of the glory that had passed by. This would fit the context as well as the range of meanings for the Hebrew word used. Moses did not see the glory of God directly, but once it had gone past, God did allow him to view the results, the afterglow, that his presence had produced.'[39]

One further account is of great interest in this part of the canonical unfolding. The setting is post-Sinai and Israel are on the march in the wilderness. Miriam and Aaron display a deep jealousy of their brother as God's chosen mouthpiece, and the Lord is displeased. We read in Numbers 12:4–8:

At once the LORD said to Moses, Aaron and Miriam, 'Come out to the tent of meeting, all three of you.' So the three of them went

[34] Friedman 1995: 16. I am grateful to Dr John Momson for drawing my attention to this book.
[35] Niehaus 1997.
[36] Tigay 2003: 111. The evidence he adduces for this claim includes Exod. 33:20–23 as well as Gen. 32:31; Exod. 19:21; Judg. 13:22; Isa. 6:5. I would qualify Tigay's comment as follows: 'Although the Bible takes for granted that God can assume a physical (usually humanlike) form . . .'.
[37] Kaiser, Jr., et al. 2001, in reference to Exod. 33:23.
[38] Ibid.
[39] Ibid.

out. Then the LORD came down in a pillar of cloud; he stood at the entrance to the tent and summoned Aaron and Miriam. When the two of them stepped forward, he said, 'Listen to my words:

> 'When there is a prophet among you,
>   I, the LORD, reveal myself to them in visions,
>   I speak to them in dreams.
> But this is not true of my servant Moses;
>   he is faithful in all my house.
> With him I speak face to face,
>   clearly and not in riddles;
>   he sees the form of the LORD.
> Why then were you not afraid
>   to speak against my servant Moses?'

Moses is a privileged person as he sees the form of God. He is a prophet, yes, but more than that as he is God's conversation partner at an unrivalled depth ('face to face'). Jewish scholar Nili S. Fox rightly comments, 'God distinguishes Moses' prophetic privileges from those accorded any other prophet. Moses can speak to God directly, in live dialogue rather than in dreams or visions. God is at his most anthropomorphic in these verses.'[40]

The picture of the 'embodied' God of anthropomorphic theophany is further complicated in the Mosaic materials by the witness of Deuteronomy. Moses preaches to Israel gathered on the plains of Moab just prior to their entry into the land of promise (Deut. 4:10–13):

Remember the day you stood before the LORD your God at Horeb, when he said to me, 'Assemble the people before me to hear my words so that they may learn to revere me as long as they live in the land and may teach them to their children.' You came near and stood at the foot of the mountain while it blazed with fire to the very heavens, with black clouds and deep darkness. Then the LORD spoke to you out of the fire. You heard the sound of words but saw no form; there was only a voice. He declared to you his covenant, the Ten Commandments, which he commanded you to follow and then wrote them on two stone tablets.

---

[40] Fox 2003: 308.

Israel experience a theophany as a gathered people. They hear the divine voice. They witness theophanic phenomena: fire, clouds and deep darkness. However they see no form.[41] Anthropopraxism is in evidence. Moses refers to God's speaking out of the fire and writing on the two stone tablets.

These Mosaic stories reveal two lines of important evidence. On the one hand there is anthropomorphic theophany albeit with qualifications as discussed above. On the other hand there is theophany but no sighting of God in human form. As in the patriarchal accounts, anthropomorphic theophany appears to be for the few (Moses or Moses and Aaron, Nadab and Abihu, and the seventy elders of Israel), and of the few for Moses even more so, and theophany for the many (gathered Israel). Importantly, however, theophany for Israel per se apparently comes to an end at Sinai. The experience was too much for them (Exod. 20:18–19): 'When the people saw the thunder and lightning and heard the trumpet and saw the mountain in smoke, they trembled with fear. They stayed at a distance and said to Moses, "Speak to us yourself and we will listen. But do not let God speak to us or we will die."' As Friedman contends, Sinai represents the high point in God's manifest presence to a community: 'After this scene in the bible, Yahweh never again speaks directly to an entire community Himself.'[42] He observes, 'Prophecy is mentioned

[41] Christensen 2004, comment on Deut. 4:11–24, asserts, 'The text is careful to specify that the voice of God was heard speaking from the midst of the burning fire, but no form was seen. Since no form was seen on the occasion of that awesome theophany, the people were commanded to make no images.' Kugel (2003: 92–93) notes, 'To date, not a single anthropomorphic statue of Israel's God has turned up at any of the numerous cultic sites excavated within the confines of biblical Israel (or outside of it, for that matter). . . . This is hardly a negligible piece of information, especially since it puts ancient Israel in such contrast with Mesopotamia.' This is one area of obedience that Israel seems to have got right.

[42] Friedman 1995: 16. Friedman mounts a novel argument that merits attention. He argues that as the storyline unfolds, God disappears as a direct and manifest actor in the Hebrew Bible. He sets out the story's unfolding in eight steps:

1. Moses sees God at Sinai.
2. Moses, the one man who has seen God, wears a veil.
3. God tells Moses, 'I shall hide my face from them.'
4. The last time God is said to be 'revealed' to a human: the prophet Samuel.
5. The last time God is said to have 'appeared' to a human king: King Solomon.
6. The last public miracle: the divine fire for Elijah at Mount Carmel; followed by God's refusal to appear to Elijah at Horeb/Sinai.
7. The last personal miracle: the shadow reverses before Isaiah and Hezekiah.
8. God is not mentioned in Esther.

Friedman argues that God is allowing human freedom and the taking of responsibility by so disappearing. But there may be a stronger answer, which he himself gives but

in passing in the book of Genesis (20:7), but prophecy in this formal sense of divine messages mediated through individuals begins here in Exodus at Sinai.'[43] It seems that God takes the plea of Israel seriously.

The Judges story and the 'embodied' God

The book of Judges does not make for pleasant reading. Abraham's children are in the land of promise but they are also caught up in a cyclical existence of periods of obedience, periods of disobedience, divine judgment in the form of consequent oppression from nations round about them, desperate cries to the Lord for deliverance, the divine provision of a judge as the bearer of Yahweh's rule and a subsequent period of *šālôm* before the cycle starts up again.

The Gideon narrative provides an interesting example. Judges 6 opens with the Israelites doing evil in the Lord's sight and the divine judgment being Midianite oppression. The situation is desperate (Judg. 6:2): 'Because the power of Midian was so oppressive, the Israelites prepared shelters for themselves in mountain clefts, caves and strongholds.' Israel calls upon the lord (Judg. 6:6): 'Midian so impoverished the Israelites that they cried out to the LORD for help.' God acts. The angel of the Lord visits Gideon. The divine message is brief and to the point (Judg. 6:14): 'The LORD turned to him and said, "Go in the strength you have and save Israel out of Midian's hand."' Gideon's diffidence is soon apparent (Judg. 6:15): '"Pardon me, my lord," Gideon replied, "but how can I save Israel? My clan is the weakest in Manasseh, and I am the least in my family."' He seeks a sign and is given graciously more than one. After the first sign (the fire flaring from the rock and consuming the meat and bread), Gideon realizes that the stranger is no ordinary visitor (Judg. 6:22): 'When Gideon realized that it was the angel of the LORD [*mal'āḥ YHWH*], he exclaimed, "Alas, Sovereign LORD! I have seen the angel of the LORD face to face!"' At this point, with the angel of the Lord absent,

---

does not sufficiently develop. He writes (140), 'Instead of contact with God directly, there was contact with His church. Instead of God directly, contact with His book. Instead of the God who acts (i.e., who acts publicly, visibly, identifiably), God who speaks; or, perhaps: who has spoken.' Mutatis mutandis does this not also apply to the New Testament revelation regarding Christ? The publicly, visibly, identifiably acting Christ is now the ascended Christ who acts by word and Spirit (cf. 82 and 140). In other words theophany in the Old Testament gives way to progressive inscripturation, and Christophany in the New Testament gives way to progressive inscripturation.
43 Ibid. 17.

the Lord speaks (Judg. 6:23): 'But the LORD said to him, "Peace! Do not be afraid. You are not going to die."'

Gideon's encounter with the mysterious angel of the Lord in Judges 6:1–40 brings an important set of questions into sharp relief. Who is this angel of the Lord? How is the angel of the Lord related to Yahweh? The angel of the Lord is introduced as such by the narrator in Judges 6:11. The language is anthropopraxic. The angel of the Lord comes and sits under the oak (Judg. 6:11). The angel speaks to Gideon (Judg. 6:12). However, the speaker becomes the Lord (Judg. 6:14, 16, 18) before the narrative returns briefly to the angel as Gideon's conversation partner and before the angel disappears (Judg. 6:20–21). There is no further reference to the angel of the Lord in the Gideon cycle, though there are references to the Lord as speaker (Judg. 6:23, 25; 7:4, 7).

Charles H. H. Scobie rightly maintains, 'In a number of passages it is not easy to distinguish the angel of the Lord from the Lord himself.'[44] Judges 6:1–40 is a good example. Early in the account the angel of the Lord appears to be simply a divine messenger in human form (e.g. Judg. 6:11). Angels in the biblical narratives do indeed appear in human form, as we found in the story of Abraham's three visitors and in the Hagar and Ishmael story (e.g. Gen. 18:2). However, in Gideon's case there are puzzling turns. Walter Kaiser, Jr., states the puzzle well: 'If Gideon only saw an angel, why did he fear that he might die?'[45] The angel of the Lord appears to transcend the mere angelic category. Because it is an encounter with the angel of the Lord he is then given divine assurance that he will not die (Judg. 6:23). In Judges 6:24 we find that Gideon is assured and builds an altar in response, which he calls 'The LORD Is Peace' (Hebr. *šālôm*).

Some interpreters, for example Susan Niditch, see the angel of the Lord in the Judges passage as 'an intermediary messenger who appears at first to be a human being'.[46] So what does she do with the change of speaker in the text? She argues, 'having experienced the power of God through an intermediary, Gideon now receives messages directly from the Lord'.[47] Certainly angels do function as divine messengers

---

[44] Scobie 2003: 113. Earlier in this chapter we saw this with regard to the burning bush in Exod. 3:2–6. In this passage it is the angel of the Lord who is first thematized (v. 2) as appearing within the bush, but next we read that it is God who calls him from within the bush (v. 4). In the patriarchal account of Hagar and Ishmael (Gen. 16:13) Hagar identifies the angel of the Lord as 'You are the God who sees me,' for she said, 'I have now seen the One who sees me.'

[45] Kaiser, Jr., et al. 2001, in reference to Judg. 6:22–23.

[46] Niditch 2001: 182.

[47] Ibid.

in both Old Testament and New Testament. Scobie captures this idea well: 'The Hebrew *mal'ākh*, from the root *l'k* = "send," means one who is sent, a messenger. The LXX and NT Greek equivalent *angelos* provides the English word "angel."'[48] Gerald Bray concurs and points out the difference between patristic and contemporary exegetes on the matter of interpreting these sorts of biblical materials:

> The real point of difference between ancient and (most) modern commentators is to be found in the ways in which they generally assess the relationship between the Old Testament to the new. It was standard practice in ancient times to look for typological and prophetic foreshadowings of the coming of Christ in the Old Testament, and so we find that the Fathers saw nothing wrong in regarding epiphanies of angels, for example, as preincarnational appearances of the Son of God.[49]

He adds, 'This would not meet with general acceptance today.'[50]

Bray is right to claim that most of today's exegetes would not see preincarnational appearances of Christ in the Old Testament. There are exceptions however that need to be noted. For example, Walter Kaiser, Jr., is emphatic:

> It is clear from this abundance of evidence that the angel of the Lord in the Old Testament was a preincarnate form of our Lord Jesus Christ, who would later permanently take on flesh when he came as a babe in Bethlehem. But mark it well: the one who came after John had already been before – he was that angel of the Lord. His full deity was always observed and yet he presented the same mystery of the Trinity that would later be observed in 'I and the Father are one' (Jn 10:30) and 'my other witness is the Father, who sent me' (Jn 8:18). It is that word *sent* that ties together the angel, messenger or sent one into an Old Testament theology of christophanies, appearances of God in human form.[51]

Kaiser, Jr., is confident – too confident? – about the clarity of the Old Testament regarding Christophanies. However, whether the anthropomorphic theophanies of the Old Testament are in fact Christophanies

---

[48] Scobie 2003: 113.
[49] Bray 2002: 164.
[50] Ibid.
[51] Kaiser, Jr., et al. 2001, in reference to Judg. 6:22–23, original emphasis.

is an important question to which we shall return at this chapter's end. The question is important because if these anthropomorphic theophanies are appearances of the pre-incarnate Christ, then there are indeed anticipations of the incarnation in the Old Testament.

The former prophets and the 'embodied' God

In the unfolding biblical plotline we are now with Israel settled in the land of promise.[52] Once more, as we shall see, God is rendered as 'embodied'. There are examples of anthropomorphism, anthropopathism and anthropopraxism. In contrast to the earlier biblical accounts, what we do not see are any "*is*" theophanies. Two accounts from this period are particularly instructive for our purposes: those concerning Samuel and those involving Solomon.

Samuel

Samuel is an outstanding player in the drama of Scripture. He was a prophet, priest and judge. His threefold 'office' (*munus triplex*) in many ways anticipates that of the Christ to come. He first experienced a theophany of God the bearer of the Word as a child. His mother Hannah had dedicated him to God and he served at Shiloh under Eli the priest (1 Sam. 1:1 – 2:11). It was a period in Israel's history in which 'in those days the word of the LORD was rare; there were not many visions' (1 Sam. 3:1). Then God spoke to Samuel (1 Sam. 3:2–10):

> One night Eli, whose eyes were becoming so weak that he could barely see, was lying down in his usual place. The lamp of God had not yet gone out, and Samuel was lying down in the house of the LORD, where the ark of God was. Then the LORD called Samuel.
> Samuel answered, 'Here I am.' And he ran to Eli and said, 'Here I am; you called me.'

---

[52] Friedman (1995: 80) comments interestingly, 'Even books and courses on "the Bible as literature" rarely speak of plot. As I said earlier, most of us are accustomed to studying the small passage or single biblical book. After all, who would have guessed that a work with so many authors, spread out over so many years, would have so continuous a story? We would have expected an anthology of stories, arranged roughly in chronological order, but in fact we have a coherent story. (I must admit that my fundamentalist students give me a knowing wink at this point.)' Friedman's (95) explanation for this phenomenon will not convince anyone with a robust view of biblical inspiration: 'It appears to be a side effect of the Bible's singular history. A fortuitous side effect.'

But Eli said, 'I did not call; go back and lie down.' So he went and lay down.

Again the LORD called, 'Samuel!' And Samuel got up and went to Eli and said, 'Here I am; you called me.'

'My son,' Eli said, 'I did not call; go back and lie down.'

Now Samuel did not yet know the LORD: the word of the LORD had not yet been revealed to him.

A third time the LORD called, 'Samuel!' And Samuel got up and went to Eli and said, 'Here I am; you called me.'

Then Eli realized that the LORD was calling the boy. So Eli told Samuel, 'Go and lie down, and if he calls you, say, "Speak, LORD, for your servant is listening."' So Samuel went and lay down in his place.

The LORD came and stood there, calling as at the other times, 'Samuel! Samuel!'

Then Samuel said, 'Speak, for your servant is listening.'

This theophany proved to be no isolated episode. The account goes on to assert in 1 Samuel 3:21, 'The LORD continued to appear at Shiloh, and there he revealed himself to Samuel through his word.' This claim is highly significant for Friedman. He observes this is 'The last time God is said to be "revealed" to a human: the prophet Samuel.'[53] Moreover the text affirms that God appeared to Samuel. There is no fulsome elaboration however. We simply do not know what form the appearance assumed in any detail. Even so, there may be a clue in 1 Samuel 3:10: 'The LORD came and stood there.' James Barr sees here 'a trace of the common picture of theophany in erect human form'.[54] In other words here is another anthropomorphic theophany.[55] One further observation is in order. There is now a clear nexus between revelation and word in 1 Samuel 3:21: 'there he revealed himself to Samuel through his word'.

Solomon

King Solomon is the last person in the Old Testament to whom God is said to have appeared. The first revelatory account concerns a dream

[53] Ibid. 82. For comparative material see Gen. 18:2; 28:13; Amos 7:7; 9:1. Also see n. 36 above.

[54] Barr 1960: 32.

[55] Klein (2004) in his section on 'Samuel and the Word of Yahweh (3:1–21 [4:1a])' describes it as an 'auditory message dream theophany', but I prefer 'anthropomorphic theophany'.

(1 Kgs 3:5): 'At Gibeon the LORD appeared to Solomon during the night in a dream, and God said, "Ask for whatever you want me to give you."' Solomon famously asks for wisdom (1 Kgs 3:9): 'So give your servant a discerning heart to govern your people and to distinguish between right and wrong.' Solomon's wisdom is soon demonstrated in the story of the two prostitutes and the baby boy (1 Kgs 3:16–28). His fame spreads. Even the queen of Sheba comes visiting to see that wisdom for herself and is suitably impressed. This is the high point of the undivided kingdom, as 1 Kings 10:23–25 shows:

> King Solomon was greater in riches and wisdom than all the other kings of the earth. The whole world sought audience with Solomon to hear the wisdom God had put in his heart. Year after year, everyone who came brought a gift – articles of silver and gold, robes, weapons and spices, and horses and mules.

However, ancient Near Eastern *realpolitik* sets in: foreign alliances made firm by marriage. In the very next chapter we read (1 Kgs 11:1–2), 'King Solomon, however, loved many foreign women besides Pharaoh's daughter – Moabites, Ammonites, Edomites, Sidonians and Hittites. They were from nations about which the LORD had told the Israelites, "You must not intermarry with them, because they will surely turn your hearts after their gods."' And turn his heart they did. The divine response is anger (1 Kgs 11:9): 'The LORD became angry with Solomon because his heart had turned away from the LORD, the God of Israel, who had appeared to him twice.' Those two appearances are referred to first in 1 Kings 3:5, and then in 1 Kings 9:2 (which mentions 'a second time').

The very fact that God had appeared to Solomon on two occasions and spoke to him makes Solomon's turning away from God to follow after idols all the more blameworthy. Indeed it appears an 'axiom' of biblical thought that knowledge brings responsibility, and the greater the knowledge the greater the responsibility and accountability (cf. Amos 3:2; Luke 12:47–48). Solomon had been privileged to experience theophanies of God as bearer of the Word. He had not merely received the divine word as in 1 Kings 6:11 but had seen something in a dream. As Fretheim comments, 'the appearance would have impressed the word upon Solomon in a way that just words would not have'.[56] But what did Solomon see on those two occasions? We are not told. An

---

[56] Fretheim 1984: 85.

anthropomorphic theophany is a possibility. What is clear though is the anthropopraxism of a speaking God with whom one may converse in a dialogue (e.g. in 1 Kgs 3:5–15 there is dialogue, whereas in 1 Kgs 9:3–9 there is only monologue).[57]

The latter prophets and the 'embodied' God

In the latter prophets there are no accounts of an earthly encounter with the 'embodied' God. There are no analogues to Abraham at the Oaks of Mamre or to Jacob at the Jabbok. There are however accounts of sightings of God. These sightings take place in visionary experience. These are theophanies of God as bearer of the Word and can be best categorized as visionary anthropomorphic theophanies. Three prophets in particular will occupy our attention. First we shall consider Isaiah, then Amos and finally Hosea.

Isaiah's vision

In the eighth century Isaiah has an extraordinary vision of God in the temple in Jerusalem. He not only has a vision of God but also of the divine retinue of seraphim. He also hears the divine voice commissioning him to take a message of judgment to Judah.[58] We read in Isaiah 6:1–9:

> In the year that King Uzziah died, I saw the Lord, high and exalted, seated on a throne; and the train of his robe filled the temple. Above him were seraphim, each with six wings: with two wings they covered their faces, with two they covered their feet, and with two they were flying. And they were calling to one another:

> > 'Holy, holy, holy is the LORD Almighty;
> > the whole earth is full of his glory.'

> At the sound of their voices the doorposts and thresholds shook and the temple was filled with smoke.

[57] Taking into account all the relevant references, 1 Kings relates how God appeared twice to Solomon and spoke to him four times, including on the occasion of the two appearances (1 Kgs 3:5–15; 6:11–13; 9:1–9; and 11:11–13, which is a word of judgment).

[58] Coggins (2001: 443) points out the parallels with the commissioning of Ezekiel as presented in Ezek. 1. He suggests 'the possibility that the accounts are based on some known form of commissioning'. If so, here again is an example of divine accommodation by which God meets us, where we are placed in history in the form of life that we know.

'Woe to me!' I cried. 'I am ruined! For I am a man of unclean lips, and I live among a people of unclean lips, and my eyes have seen the King, the Lord Almighty.'

Then one of the seraphim flew to me with a live coal in his hand, which he had taken with tongs from the altar. With it he touched my mouth and said, 'See, this has touched your lips; your guilt is taken away and your sin atoned for.'

Then I heard the voice of the Lord saying, 'Whom shall I send? And who will go for us?'

And I said, 'Here am I. Send me!'

He said, 'Go and tell this people:

> "Be ever hearing, but never understanding;
> be ever seeing, but never perceiving."'

The Lord is rendered as an immense presence: 'the train of his robe filled the temple'. The phenomena of theophany are in evidence: smoke, shaking and the human response of expressed unworthiness. The Lord sits in divine council and speaks.[59] These are the traces of anthropomorphic theophany, albeit in visionary form.[60]

Also in Isaiah 6 we see the typical feature of the human response to theophany as one of fear and dread: 'Woe to me.' As Kuntz points out, 'In theophany, the God of Israel draws near as one whose ways are supremely holy and utterly mysterious. Man is overawed by the self-manifestation of the *mysterium tremendum.*'[61] He elaborates:

> Biblical man hides his face (so Moses in Ex. 3:6 and Elijah in 1 Kings 19:13), falls backwards toward the ground (so Abraham in Gen. 17:3 and Ezekiel in Ezek. 1:28), or utters a word of awful exposure

---

[59] On the divine council motif in the passage see Kugel 2007: 545–546. Also see 1 Kgs 22:19–20: 'Micaiah continued, "Therefore hear the word of the Lord: I saw the Lord sitting on his throne with all the multitudes of heaven standing round him on his right and on his left. And the Lord said, 'Who will entice Ahab into attacking Ramoth Gilead and going to his death there?'"' The God of the Bible is presented not only as the King who decrees, but also as the one who deliberates in divine council.

[60] Sommer (2004: 796) goes too far to suggest, 'This is one of many passages indicating that some biblical authors conceive of God as a physical being whom a few people can see.' If Isa. 6 is read in the context of the entire book, the God of Isaiah is transcendent in an unrivalled way. For example, Isa. 31:3 informs the reader that 'But the Egyptians are mere mortals and not God; / their horses are flesh and not spirit'. The Hebrew synonymous parallelism is illuminating here. Interestingly Sommer has no comment on this claim. In contradistinction see Grogan 1997, comment on Isa. 31:3, for an insightful recognition of the ontological differences expressed in this text.

[61] Kuntz 1967: 43.

(so Isaiah of Jerusalem in Isa. 6:6, 'Woe is me! For I am undone')
or dismay (so Jacob in Gen. 28:17, 'How awesome is this place!').[62]

Sometimes one hears the statement 'If only God would show himself,
then I would believe.' In the light of the human response to God in
the biblical account of theophany, such a challenge is to ask for much
more than is bargained for.[63]

Amos's vision

Another eighth-century prophet, Amos, also had a visionary experience (Amos 1:1): 'The words of Amos, one of the shepherds of Tekoa
– the vision he saw [*ḥāzâ* is typically used of prophecy] concerning
Israel two years before the earthquake, when Uzziah was king of Judah
and Jeroboam son of Jehoash was king of Israel.'

Two elements in the vision are of a particular interest. The first is
in Amos 7:7–8:

> This is what he showed me: the Lord was standing by a wall that
> had been built true to plumb, with a plumb-line in his hand. And
> the LORD asked me, 'What do you see, Amos?'
> 'A plumb-line,' I replied.
> Then the Lord said, 'Look, I am setting a plumb-line among my
> people Israel; I will spare them no longer.'

The vision presents the Lord as a standing figure holding a plumb
line like a builder.[64] The second element is in Amos 9:1:

> I saw the Lord standing by the altar, and he said:
>
> 'Strike the tops of the pillars
> so that the thresholds shake.

---

[62] Ibid.

[63] It is no accident that in the New Testament we find that the *visio Dei* (vision of
God) is predicated on the necessity of human transformation at the ontological level.
We need to be glorified to see the glorious God (cf. Rom. 8:30; 1 Cor. 15:35–57; 2 Cor.
5:1–5; Phil. 3:20–21; 1 John 3:1–3). The ancient principle of connaturality (like knows
like; like can reveal like) underlies the need for such a glorious transformation.

[64] The Hebrew is difficult. Some commentators see no reference to a plumb line in
the text but to a tin wall (e.g. Dines [2001: 583] and Stuart [2004] comment on Amos
7:7). And some commentators see no reference to Yahweh as the standing figure. Stuart
(2004), for example, does not, but in his comment on Amos 9:1 sees Yahweh presented
as a standing figure. However, all the major translations – NRSV, NIV, ESV and *JSB* –
translate *'ānāk* as 'plumb line'.

> Bring them down on the heads of all the people;
>> those who are left I will kill with the sword.
> Not one will get away,
>> none will escape.'

In this part of the prophecy God again is a standing figure and a speaking one. In both elements there are traces of anthropomorphic theophany in visionary expression. As Barr maintains in relation to Amos, 'There is little direct description of the theophanic appearance although an erect figure of human likeness seems clearly implied.'[65]

Hosea's vision

The eighth-century prophecy of Hosea stands as a witness against any Marcionite attempt to posit a wrathful, unfeeling God of the Old Testament against the loving one of the New Testament. In a remarkable passage in Hosea 11:8–9 we find that God's holiness becomes the grounds for divine compassion and not divine wrath. God saves his people because he is the holy God. He looks upon his broken people in Hosea 11 and, filled with compassion for their plight although undeserved, declares:

> How can I give you up, Ephraim?
>> How can I hand you over, Israel?
> How can I treat you like Admah?
>> How can I make you like Zeboyim?
> My heart is changed within me;
>> all my compassion is aroused.
> I will not carry out my fierce anger,
>> nor will I devastate Ephraim again.
> For I am God, and not a man –
>> the Holy One among you.
>> I will not come against their cities.

John Day rightly observes, 'In vv. 8–9, one of the most moving passages in the OT, YHWH struggles with himself, and the anguish of his love dictates that he cannot totally destroy Israel.'[66] Verse 8 speaks of God's heart and God's compassion. This passage in Hosea

---

[65] Barr 1960: 36. Also see Ezek. 1:26 for another trace of anthropomorphic theophany: 'Above the vault over their heads was what looked like a throne of lapis lazuli, and high above on the throne was a figure like that of a man.'
[66] Day 2001: 577.

is the high point of Old Testament anthropopathism, a veritable 'window into the heart of God', as Leon J. Wood suggests.[67] The God revealed in the Old Testament is a feeling God and not reducible to Mind, albeit with an upper case 'M'. This is not a God like Aristotle's 'thought thinking itself'.

The theomorphic life of the prophet

Terrence E. Fretheim offers an interesting line of inquiry concerning theophany and the life of the Old Testament prophet. He argues that 'The prophet's life was reflective of the divine life.'[68] Moses provides one of his examples. Twice in the book of Exodus Moses is described 'as God'. In Exodus 4:16 Aaron is to speak for Moses and Moses is to be as God to him, and in Exodus 7:16 Moses will be as God to Pharaoh and Aaron shall be his prophet. This is God's doing. Fretheim concludes, 'Moses became a vehicle for divine immanence.'[69] I would add 'and concomitance'.

Fretheim also draws attention to how Old Testament figures on occasion are said to be clothed with God's Spirit. He suggests, 'In these cases [e.g. Judg. 6:34; 1 Chr. 12:18; 2 Chr. 24:20; Mic. 3:8; Isa. 61:1], God becomes so active within the life of an individual that he can be said to be an embodiment of God.'[70] In interpreting the ingesting of the Word of God by Ezekiel in Ezekiel 3:1–3, Fretheim quotes Samuel Terrien with approval, describing the prophet as a 'living incarnator of divinity'.[71] Passages which speak of the prophet's suffering in the light of the people's sins and parlous state and God's own attitudes are such that it is hard to distinguish the two, as in Jeremiah 8:18 – 9:1.[72] Fretheim contends, 'At the least, Jeremiah's mourning [Jer. 8:18 – 9:1] is an embodiment of the anguish of God, showing forth to the people the genuine pain God feels over the hurt that his people are experiencing,' and, 'Yet, it seems best to understand the mourning of God and prophet as so symbiotic that in everything we hear the anguish of both.'[73] In the light of this evidence Fretheim argues, 'The people thus not only hear the Word of God from the

[67] Wood 1997, comment on Hos. 11:8–9.
[68] Fretheim 1984: 149.
[69] Ibid. 151.
[70] Ibid. Fretheim is less convincing here. Gideon in Judg. 6:34 is clothed with the Spirit, as the ESV has it (contra NIV). However, Mic. 3:8, which refers to the prophet's being filled with the Spirit, is a stretch on Fretheim's part.
[71] Ibid. 153. Terrien (1978: 241) is speaking in particular of Amos.
[72] Ibid. 160–162.
[73] Ibid. 161.

prophet, they *see* the Word enfleshed in their midst.'[74] Fretheim's reading of these texts is highly suggestive. He contends, 'The prophet's life is . . . Theomorphic.'[75]

However, he is aware that he needs to be cautious lest he read too much anachronistically back into texts that predate Christ: 'Finally, we should note that the prophet's life as embodied Word of God is partial and broken. The OT does not finally come to the conclusion that God was incarnate in a human life in complete unbrokenness or in its entirety. . . . Yet, in the prophet we see decisive continuities with what occurs in the Christ-event.'[76]

Conclusion

In this chapter we have been exploring – albeit briefly and selectively – the theophanic language of the patriarchal, Mosaic, former and latter prophetic periods. God is rendered as a person who speaks, acts and feels. We have seen evidences in these texts of anthropomorphism, anthropopathism and anthropopraxism. In two places the Lord is rendered in human terms as someone who eats and wrestles, and does so in history (Gen. 18 and 32 respectively). In other places the experience is visionary, more fragmentary and heavenly. Such renderings are best described, following James Barr, as anthropomorphic theophanies. Traces of these anthropomorphic theophanies are found along the unfolding biblical plotline. However *Deus revelatus* (God revealed) needs the balance of *Deus absconditus* (God concealed or hidden). The divine appearance is not to be presumed on and cannot be controlled or manipulated by the creature. A surprising number of Jewish scholars I have referenced argue that the God of the Hebrew Bible is assumed by many of the biblical authors to be 'embodied'. However, we have seen no incarnation of deity as such even though the life of a prophet might be accurately described as theomorphic in some instances. Next we shall consider whether an incarnation of 'the embodied' God was part of Israel's hope. However, before we do so, there is a question that has been tabled as to whether or not these Old Testament anthropomorphic theophanies were in fact Christophanies. To that question we shall turn in a subsequent chapter by way of an excursus.

---

[74] Ibid. 165, original emphasis.
[75] Ibid.
[76] Ibid. 166.

Chapter Three

God prepares the way in Israel's hope

The ancient people of Israel knew changes in their fortunes. Oppression under Pharaoh gave way to life under God in a land of promise (Exodus to Joshua). In that land and because of Israel's unfaithfulness, before long new cycles of oppression began. These cycles were broken only by God's oppressed people calling on the name of the Lord, and that Lord responded by raising up judges to deliver them (Judges). Then came Solomon's glorious kingdom, the high-water mark of Israel's national fortune. Even the queen of Sheba was impressed (1 Kgs 10). However, once more a people, starting with their king, descended into disobedience and fracture. The northern part of the subsequent split is overwhelmed by Assyria in 722 BC (2 Kgs 17) and then the southern definitively by the Babylonians in 586 BC (2 Kgs 25). But in that land of promise and even in exile in Babylon there were those who never ceased to wait on the Lord with expectation. Indeed in Old Testament terms to wait on the Lord is to hope in him, as in Isaiah 40:30–31:

> Even youths grow tired and weary,
>   and young men stumble and fall;
> but those who hope [*qāwâ*, 'wait', as in the ESV] in the LORD
>   will renew their strength.
> They will soar on wings like eagles;
>   they will run and not grow weary,
>   they will walk and not be faint.[1]

However, what exactly was the content of that hope?

One way of summing up the hope of Israel as presented in the canon of the Old Testament is that it was the hope for a new (*ḥādāš*) state of affairs, whether a new song on the lips of God's people, as in Psalm

---

[1] J. D. W. Watts 2002b, comments on Isa. 40:31: 'They are *those waiting* on Yahweh. The word *qāwâ* may mean "wait" or "hope." Here the ideas overlap: "waiting hope" or "hopeful waiting"' (original emphasis).

40:3, or a new covenant, as in Jeremiah 31:31, or a new spirit and a new heart within God's people, as in Ezekiel 36:26, or a new heavens and a new earth, as in Isaiah 65:17.[2] Indeed there was hope that God himself would come to set the world right (Ps. 96). The God of the Bible is the God who can do a new thing.[3] A new state of affairs is needful at personal, societal and environmental levels because of the corruption and disorder the primordial disobedience has introduced into the sphere of creation. Israel is very much aware – to adapt the title of one of Cornelius Plantinga's books – that things are not the way they're supposed to be.[4] Charles H. H. Scobie captures the point admirably: 'Amid the chaos and darkness caused by Israel's rebellion and disobedience, and indeed the rebellion and disobedience of all human kind, again and again the OT sees the only hope as lying in some future action of God on behalf of his people and of his world.'[5]

The question is, however, whether God's Old Testament people expected a divine-human incarnation as the way in which their hope would be realized? As stated above, they were looking for Yahweh to come himself. But to come in the flesh? In this chapter we shall consider recent treatments of Israel's hope that contend that no incarnation is in view in the Hebrew Bible. Next we shall turn our attention to B. B. Warfield's contrasting argument that the Old Testament in fact expected a divine Messiah to come to Israel's aid, and shall look at some contemporary support for it. Next we shall explore Israel's hope as found in certain key Old Testament texts and their import. We shall also briefly explore intertestamental expectations and a recent development in the typological reading of Scripture.

The hope for a divine Messiah

We begin on a negative note. First, some recent scholarship that says the Old Testament betrays no notion of a coming divine Messiah, is

---

[2] Gowan 2006: 149–150.

[3] If this chapter were on Israel's hope more generally speaking, I would suggest five concentric circles as a heuristic device for a fruitful reading of Old Testament Scripture. The outermost circle is hope for the cosmos, as in Isa. 65 – 66, with the new heavens and the new earth; the next circle would be hope for the nations, with even Assyria and Egypt given a future with God, as in Isa. 19; then hope for Israel itself, as in Jer. 31 and the new covenant; next hope for agents of the divine purpose to come, as in Mal. 4 and Elijah, to name only one such; and finally and innermost the hope for Yahweh himself to come, as in Ps. 96.

[4] That disobedience cannot be reduced to the merely human level given the biblical testimony. Christianity has classically observed disorder begun first in the angelic realm. Also see C. Plantinga 1995: 93–95.

[5] Scobie 2003: 92.

unclear on the question or at least says very little on the subject. Indeed, leaving aside the question of the expectation of a divine Messiah, some scholars see little in the Old Testament by way of messianic hope per se.[6] We shall then turn to scholarship of a previous generation and some in our own that is far more positive.

As mentioned above, for much recent scholarship there is no expectation whatever of a divine Messiah to be found in the Old Testament witness, nor is any clarity to be had there concerning the question. For example, J. Andrew Dearman acknowledges that patristic interpreters found references to the pre-incarnate logos in the Old Testament that prepared the way for the coming of Christ,[7] but concludes his study of theophany, anthropomorphism and *imago Dei* in the Old Testament with the statement that 'There is no line of thought which leads inevitably from the OT to the Christian doctrine of the incarnation.'[8] Even so, he contends:

> And although no line of thought in the OT leads inevitably to the doctrine of the incarnation (because of the difference between anticipation and reality, seed-bed and flower), when interpreters work back to the OT from the claim that 'whoever has seen me has seen the Father' (John 14:9), they find themselves in mysteriously familiar territory.[9]

He is not alone in this judgment. Alan F. Segal argues that there is in Judaism some background to ideas like resurrection and Trinity. But that unique relation of Spirit and matter, which the church has labelled 'incarnation', is much harder to find.[10] He notes that the divine presence is presented in a variety of ways in the Old Testament (e.g. theophany per se, the angel of the Lord, the temple). However, he maintains concerning this variety, 'None of them precisely fits the Christian use of the term incarnation.'[11] N. T. Wright sums up the common view of the academy – a view he challenges – in these terms: 'no first-century Jew could think of a human being, far less than

---

[6] For example, Terrien 1978: 227: 'Traditionally, the prophets of Israel have been viewed as the announcers of the Messiah. In fact, however, very few of their utterances were concerned with messianic hope, even when they hailed the advent of God upon a new earth.'

[7] Dearman 2002: 32.

[8] Ibid. 45.

[9] Ibid. 46.

[10] Segal 2002: 130.

[11] Ibid. 136.

himself, as the incarnation of God. Jewish monotheism prohibits it; and even if it didn't . . . There is no actual model for it within Judaism.'[12]

Some scholars of a previous generation would not be at all convinced by some recent scholarship. One of the doyens of the evangelical tradition, Princeton theologian B. B. Warfield, writing in the opening decades of the twentieth century, posed the matter in the following terms: 'The question whether the Old Testament has any testimony to give as to the Deity of our Lord, when strictly taken, resolves itself into the question whether the Old Testament holds out the promise of a Divine Messiah.'[13] His answer to the question is entirely affirmative. He maintains that Psalm 45:6, Isaiah 9:6 and Daniel 7:13 rightly understood show that the Old Testament expected a divine Messiah. Furthermore the Old Testament expectation that Yahweh himself was coming coalesces with the figures of the promised child of Isaiah 9:6 and the Son of Man of Daniel 7:13.[14] The relevant texts read:

> Let the heavens rejoice, let the earth be glad;
>> let the sea resound, and all that is in it.
> Let the fields be jubilant, and everything in them;
>> let all the trees of the forest sing for joy.
> Let all creation rejoice before the LORD, for he comes,
>> he comes to judge the earth.
> He will judge the world in righteousness
>> and the peoples in his faithfulness.
>>> (Ps. 96:11–13)

> Your throne, O God, will last for ever and ever;
>> a scepter of justice will be the scepter of your kingdom.
>>> (Ps. 45:6)

> For to us a child is born,
>> to us a son is given,
>>> and the government will be on his shoulders.

[12] N. T. Wright 2002a: 50.
[13] Warfield 1968: 79. This quotation is taken from an article that first appeared in 1916.
[14] Ibid. 86, 88, 102 and 116 respectively. There is an able examination in Zaspel (2010: 214–220) of Warfield's argument for an Old Testament expectation of a divine Messiah.

> And he will be called
> Wonderful Counsellor, Mighty God,
> Everlasting Father, Prince of Peace.
> (Isa. 9:6)

In my vision at night I looked, and there before me was one like a son of man, coming with the clouds of heaven. He approached the Ancient of Days and was led into his presence. (Dan. 7:13)

For Warfield Psalm 45:6, Isaiah 9:6 and Daniel 7:13 viewed together with Psalm 96:11–13 bear witness to a hope for a figure that transcends the merely human. He concludes his discussion of the divine Messiah in the Old Testament with the words of another scholar, F. Godet:

> There was in the whole of the Old Testament from the patriarchal theophanies down to the latest prophetic visions, a constant current towards the incarnation as the goal of all these revelations. The appearance of the Messiah presents itself more clearly to the view of the prophets as the perfect theophany, the final coming of Jehovah.[15]

Regarding the coming of God as Ruler and King, Warfield contends that the parallel between the coming of God in those roles and the expectation of a human who is the Saviour in those same roles is 'very complete'.[16] Warfield seeks to capture the coming of Yahweh motif and its parallel with the coming of a human Saviour in a quote he takes from a work by Ernst Sellin:

> He too is the ruler over the peoples (Gen. xlix. 10; Ps. lxxii. 11), to the ends of the earth (Deut. xxxiii. 17; Mic. v. 3; Zech. ix. 10 f.), the scepter-bearer over the nations (Num. xxiv. 17–19; Ps. xlv. 17) to whose dominion there are no limits (Is. ix. 6), etc.; he too bears sometimes but not often the title of 'King' (Ps. xlv. 2; lxxii. 1; Zech. ix. 9; Jer. xxiii. 5), elsewhere those of 'Judge' (Mic. v. 1), 'Father' (Is. ix. 5), 'Anointed' or 'Son of Jehovah' (Ps. li. 2, 7). Precisely as the activity of the one, so that of the other is three-fold: it is his to destroy the enemies (Num. xxiv. 17b; Deut. xxxiii. 17; Ps. li. 9 [sic]; xlv. 6; cx. 1, 2, 5); he has to judge (Is. ix. 6b; xi. 3; Jer. xxiii. 5b; Ps.

---

[15] Warfield 1968: 126.
[16] Ibid. 96–97.

lxxii. 6); and finally he has to 'save' (Zech. lx. 9 [*sic*]; Jer. xxiii. 6; Ps. lxxii. 4, 12), above all by bringing social betterment, Paradise, and universal peace (Gen. xlix. 11, 12; Is. vii. 15; xi. 4, 6–9; Mic. iv. 4a, 5b; Zech. lii. 9b, 10 [*sic*]; Ps. lxxii. 12, 16). . . . Moreover he is given a name. 'Emmanuel,' by which his appearance is notified as the fulfillment of Balaam's prophecy of the end of days, 'Jahve, his God is with him'; and he is further designated as 'Star' (Num. xxiv. 17), as 'God-Hero' (Is. ix. 5), as 'God's Son' (Ps. li. 7); . . . [and] exegesis is continually bringing us back to the idea that Is. vii. 14, Mic. v. 2 assume thoroughly a miraculous birth of a man; . . . [and] there is the promise to him when scarcely born, the dominion of the world (Gen. xlix. 10; Is. ix. 5; Mic. v. 3).[17]

For Warfield what Sellin encapsulates is 'the correlation of the hope of the coming Savior, with the hope of what we have been accustomed to speak of as "the advent of Jehovah"'.[18] What others of his day endeavoured to keep distinct – the coming of a saviour and the coming of Yahweh – Warfield wanted to synthesize. For him the ultimate synthesis was to be found in one person alone, namely Jesus who was yet to come.[19]

Almost a hundred years after Warfield wrote, Raymond C. Ortlund, Jr., who stands in the same tradition as Warfield, has revisited the question of whether the deity of the Christ is part of Old Testament faith. His careful discussion merits serious attention.

Ortlund, Jr., distinguishes three categories of texts. The first category he argues consists of texts that are inaccurately construed by some to reveal the deity of Christ. Psalm 2 centres on a personage who is the Lord's Anointed (v. 2), his king (v. 6), and his Son (vv. 7, 12). He contends that the interpretative crux is verse 7, as per the ESV:

> I will tell of the decree:
> The LORD said to me, 'You are my Son;
> today I have begotten you.'

Does 'today' refer to a day that is always today, namely eternity as Augustine argued? Or is it referring to the coronation day of the Davidic king? With regard to this text he concludes, 'Psalm 2 says

---

17 Ibid. 97. Correct references at [*sic*] are Ps. ii.9, Zech. ix.9, Zech. iii.9b, 10.
18 Ibid. 99.
19 Ibid. 100.

much about the Christ – his unique role in God's plan for history, his inevitable judgment of the nations, all fulfilled in Jesus as the final son of David. But Psalm 2 does not reveal his deity.'[20]

The second category of texts consists of those, according to Ortlund, Jr., that can accurately be construed as revealing the deity of the Christ. According to Ortlund, Jr., there are four Old Testament texts that can accurately be construed to reveal the deity of Christ. Three are ones that Warfield majored on (Ps. 45; Isa. 9; Dan. 7). The other is Psalm 110.

Ortlund, Jr., embraces translations of Psalm 45:6 that render the verse as addressed to God in terms of 'Your throne, O God' will be eternal or everlasting. He sees support for this rendering in the LXX, an Aramaic Targum, Jerome's Latin translation and Hebrews 1:8. The superscription attached to the psalm describes it as a wedding song intended for royal nuptials; but as the language is so extravagant, how can it apply to any ordinary Davidic king? He is convinced that Psalm 45:6 'foresees a divine-human king – divine because of "O God" in verse 6, human because of "God, your God" in verse 7'.[21] He quotes Derek Kidner with approval that the verse is '*consistent with* the incarnation, but mystifying in any other contexts'.[22] However, his own conclusion is stronger: 'Psalm 45, if allowed to speak for itself, *demands recognition* as a prophecy of a divine-human Messiah and the joy of his ultimate glories with his people.'[23] Isaiah 9:6, Ortlund, Jr., maintains, is best understood as affirming the deity of the promised 'human child', the 'Mighty God' upon whose shoulders rests the government that never ends. He argues, 'And Hezekiah cannot be the king Isaiah is referring to, because the endless triumph of verse 7 goes far beyond the accomplishment of any historic son of David.'[24] Daniel 7's vision of the one like the Son of Man' is best interpreted as rendering '[a] human-like figure presented at the heavenly court . . . at a level fit for deity.'[25] Ortlund, Jr., acknowledges that Psalm 110 poses exegetical difficulties. Even so, verse 1 is striking:

[20] Ortlund, Jr., 2011: 40–42, esp. 42. He also considers Prov. 8, a text beloved by the ancient Arians, and argues (42–44) that it is not germane to the deity of Christ question despite the labours of patristic writers such as Gregory Nazianzen.

[21] Ibid. 46.

[22] Ibid. 47, my emphasis.

[23] Ibid., my emphasis.

[24] Ibid. 51.

[25] Ibid. 54. Interestingly Ortlund, Jr., quotes with approval Warfield's discussion of the divine Messiah with regard to this verse.

The LORD says to my Lord:

'Sit at my right hand
until I make your enemies
a footstool for your feet.'

Ortlund, Jr., contends that the figure of whom David writes in verse 1, who is the Lord seated at the right hand of the Lord, cannot be reduced to any ordinary king of Israel. This figure clearly goes beyond David himself. Moreover this figure has a unique priesthood, according to verse 4: 'in the order of Melchizedek'. Ortlund, Jr., contends, 'Unlike the ancient kings of Israel, the Messiah is a king-priest – and forever, after the analogy of Melchizedek.'[26] For him Psalm 45:6, Isaiah 9:6, Daniel 7:13 and Psalm 110:1 provide firm evidence that the Old Testament held out the promise of a divine-human Messiah.

The third category includes Old Testament texts that are not clear enough to be certain one way or the other on the question of the deity of Christ. There are two such texts that some interpret as describing a divine-human Messiah, but Ortlund, Jr., is not so convinced. Regarding Isaiah 7:14 he maintains, 'But if Matthew saw in Isaiah 7:14 an indirect foreshadowing of Jesus, then the divine element in the name Immanuel does not necessarily identify the nature of the child.'[27] In fact it could be argued that the promised child is the *mahēr šālāl ḥāš baz* ('quick to plunder, swift to spoil', NIV footnote) of Isaiah 8:1–4. He concludes that Isaiah 7:14 is consistent with an affirmation of the deity of the Messiah but that interpretation is not demanded. He views Micah 5:2 similarly, which speaks of a ruler coming out of Bethlehem as someone who is 'from ancient days' (ESV). He believes that although, with its time reference, there is a case for the verse's referring to eternity, it is on balance more likely to be about 'the antiquity of the Messiah's Davidic roots'.[28]

The discussion by Ortlund, Jr., raises a very important hermeneutical point. Is an interpretation demanded by the text in view, or is the interpretation under discussion simply consistent with that text of Scripture? The issue is not whether a New Testament writer or Jesus himself as presented in the Gospels interpreted the Old Testament text correctly when seeing it as messianic or prophetic. A robust doctrine of the inspiration of Scripture does not reduce the

---

[26] Ibid. 49.
[27] Ibid. 56.
[28] Ibid. 58.

text merely to what the human authors intended. There is the divine author. The story of Scripture is a story of double agency. There can be a fuller meaning in canonical perspective that later events clarify.

Interestingly present-day Jewish scholars Adele Berlin and Marc Zvi Brettler, writing in *The Jewish Study Bible*, lend some independent albeit guarded support to Warfield's reading of Psalm 45:6. They write that verse 7 (v. 6 in the NIV) could be read as presenting the king as divine. However, although this would have ancient Near Eastern parallels, in the Hebrew Bible it would be the only occurrence.[29] In the same volume Lawrence M. Wills argues that the author of Daniel 7:1–14 is 'most likely' presenting a 'celestial being'.[30]

What then was Israel hoping for according to the texts under discussion (Ps. 45:6, Isa. 9:6 and Dan. 7:13 viewed together with Ps. 96:11–13)?

Israel's hope and the incarnation: key texts revisited

Expressing oneself in language can take a variety of forms. The British are famous for their understatement. Points are made subtly with an economy of words but a wealth of implication. There is a story of Oscar Wilde, the British playwright and wit, told at a party by someone he did not care for that this particular gentleman had driven by Wilde's house on a previous day but did not have the time to call in. Wilde's reply was just two words, 'Thank you!' At the other end there is hyperbole. Jesus famously said that it was easier for a camel to go through the eye of a needle than for a rich man to enter the kingdom of God (Matt. 19:24). Funny but hardly subtle. The question is whether the language found in Psalm 45:6, Isaiah 9:6, Daniel 7:13 and Psalm 110:1 is similarly hyperbolic. We shall consider each of these texts in turn.

Psalm 45:6

Psalm 45 is a wedding song and a royal one at that. In the ESV and NRSV translations the psalm addressed to the king becomes in verse 6 an address to God: 'Your throne, O God'. As C. S. Rodd points out, the meaning of verse 6 is a matter of much debate. He references some

---

[29] Berlin and Brettler 2004: 1332.
[30] Wills 2004: 1656.

of the other possibilities; for example, 'Your throne is everlasting like that of God', as in the NRSV margin. However, he rightly says that the most natural way to take the Hebrew is to render it as an address to God.[31] Derek Kidner comments on verse 6, '*Throne* and *sceptre* introduce the array of formal splendours and symbols of the king, for whose honour and retinue no rarity is too costly and no person too exalted.'[32] He adds, as Ortlund, Jr., noted, 'This paradox [he is referring to the phrase 'God, your God'] is consistent with the incarnation, but mystifying in any other context. It is an example of Old Testament language bursting its banks, to demand a more than human fulfilment (as did Ps. 110:1, according to our Lord).'[33] Peter C. Craigie expands the picture:

> Psalm 45 is a superb example of what C. S. Lewis has called 'second meanings in the Psalms' (*Reflections on the Psalms*, 101–15). The primary meaning of the psalm is clear; it is a wedding song, celebrating the marriage of a king to a princess. **In its original sense and context, it is not in any sense a messianic psalm.** And yet within the context of early Christianity (and in Judaism before that), it becomes a messianic psalm par excellence.[34]

Psalm 45:6 provides an excellent example of how an Old Testament text takes on a valence that was unseen in its own time but with the unfolding of salvation history its depth of meaning becomes patent.[35] Dots were being laid down in the Old Testament scriptures but lay unjoined.

---

[31] Rodd 2001: 380. What drives the quest for an alternative reading? George H. Guthrie (2007: 937) helps to answer the question: 'Such an address would not have been out of place in ancient Egypt but in Israel it is the sole example.'

[32] Kidner 1973, comment on Ps. 45:6.

[33] Ibid., comment on Ps. 45:7.

[34] Craigie 2002, comment on Ps. 45:3–9 (my emphasis in bold). In fact arguably the psalm taken as a whole undermines the notion of a divine-human Messiah as the primary referent. For in Ps. 45:8–17 we read of the king's consort and their progeny. Interestingly Roman Catholics see the queen here as a reference to Mary (e.g. Broderick 1987: 374). Similarly 2 Sam. 7:14, with its reference to divine forgiveness for the Davidic king, disqualifies the primary referent as a divine-human Messiah. Typologically considered, however, both Ps. 45 and 2 Sam. 7 betray trajectories that legitimately point to the divine-human Christ who indeed came. I owe these insights to D. A. Carson in private correspondence.

[35] For an excellent treatment of Ps. 45:6–7 in both its Old Testament context and in its New Testament recontextualization as found in Heb. 1:8–9 see G. H. Guthrie 2007: 936–939.

Isaiah 9:6

Some scholars are very confident that Isaiah 9:6 speaks of a divine Messiah to come (e.g. as we saw in Warfield and in Ortlund, Jr.). The context is the fall of the northern kingdom, and the hope for both a future restoration and the overthrow of the enemies of God's people. In view is the birth of a Davidic king or perhaps the coronation of such. However, given that so many extravagant names (throne names) are predicated of this child – 'Wonderful Counsellor, Mighty God, Everlasting Father, Prince of Peace' – it is a puzzle how any merely human king could be so named. The name 'Mighty God' (*'ēl gibbôr*) is of particular importance in this view.[36] Geoffrey W. Grogan comments:

> If the child of Isaiah 7:14–16 . . . typifies the ultimate divine Christ, the child of these verses is that Christ. It is true that monarchs of the Near East often received exaggerated adulation from their subjects, especially at their enthronement and at subsequent kingdom renewal ceremonies. This is not Mesopotamia, however, but Judah, and Hebrew prophecy was founded on truth, not flattery . . . To speak to monarchs words that could not be taken at their face value was hardly consistent with their calling.[37]

Alec Motyer argues similarly: '*Mighty God*: the repetition of this title in 10:21, referring to the Lord himself, establishes its meaning here. Translations like "Godlike Hero" are linguistically improbable, side-stepping the implication that the Old Testament looked forward to a divine Messiah.'[38] For Motyer 'Mighty God' refers to the person and power of the child.

Other scholars will have none of this. Benjamin D. Sommer in *The Jewish Study Bible* rejects any suggestion that Isaiah 9:5 (v. 6 in the NIV) has a divine Messiah in view: 'These names do not describe that person who holds them but the god whom parents worship.'[39] Indeed this translation renders the Hebrew of Isaiah 9:5 (v. 6 in the NIV) as follows: 'He has been named "The Mighty God is planning grace; The Eternal Father, a peaceable ruler.' His argument is that these are

---

[36] On throne names see Matthews, Chavalas and Walton 2000, comment on Isa. 9:6. Also see the excursus on throne names in J. D. W. Watts 2002a, comment on Isa. 9:6–7.

[37] Grogan 1997, comment on Isa. 9:6.

[38] Motyer 1999, comment on Isa. 9:6.

[39] Sommer 2004: 802.

throne names that need to be read in the light of how names were understood in ancient Israel. He gives examples: 'thus the name Isaiah in Hebrew means "The Lord saves"; Hezekiah, "The Lord strengthens"'.[40] Another Jewish scholar, James L. Kugel, renders the Hebrew in a slightly different way but again in complete sentences: 'He has been named "Mighty-God-counsels-wondrous-things," "Eternal-father-is-a-peaceful-ruler."'[41] How then is the exalted language to be explained? Kugel argues:

> In the ancient world, it went without saying that a new golden age could be brought about only by a new golden ruler . . . life worked from the top down. Only a great new ruler could change things, but if such a ruler did arrive, he might indeed cause everything to be different: righteousness and justice and peace would all come about as a result of his rule.[42]

Traditional Judaism interpreted Isaiah 9:6 as applying to Hezekiah.[43] These early exegetes saw then no divine Messiah implications in 'Mighty God'.

On balance Isaiah 9:6 is consistent with the coming of a divine Messiah but does not demand that reading. R. Coggins provides a cautious but in my view sound comment: '"Mighty God" may imply divine kingship, for which there is some evidence in ancient Israel (cf. Psalm 45:6), or "God" here may be a kind of superlative.'[44] Indeed if 'Mighty God' refers to the person and power of the child (so Motyer) then why not 'Everlasting Father'? Of course if that were so, then the incarnation of the Father would be in view and not that of the Son. The way around this for Motyer is to distinguish between person and role. Motyer argues that 'Everlasting Father' refers to this King's relation to his subjects.[45] In other words this throne name embodies the hope of kingly care. However, if so, why not argue that 'Mighty God' is the hope for a king mighty enough to defeat enemies in a Godlike way? I do not hold this view myself; I wish only to point out that the interpretation of the throne names of Isaiah 9:6 is not quite as straightforward as some think. Coggins's caution is warranted.

---

[40] Ibid.
[41] Kugel 2007: 552.
[42] Ibid.
[43] Coggins 2001, comment on Isa. 9:6.
[44] Ibid.
[45] Motyer 1999.

Therefore I would move this text from Ortlund, Jr.'s accurately construed to reveal the deity of Christ category but not to his not clear enough to be certain one way or the other category.[46] Instead another category is needed, that of the 'Quite plausible'.

Daniel 7:13

In this apocalyptic work, Daniel 7:13 speaks of 'one like a son of man' (*bar 'ĕnāš* in Aramaic). However, to whom does the phrase refer? Rikki E. Watts captures the debate well: 'is the figure concrete or symbolic, celestial or human, individual or corporate' or some combination?[47] Charles H. H. Scobie discusses only one option. The figure of the Son of Man in Daniel 7 refers to '*a collective figure symbolizing* "the holy ones of the Most High," i.e., God's faithful people'.[48] He rejects the notion that the text is referring 'to an individual figure, whether the Davidic messiah, personified Wisdom, or an angel'.[49] Lawrence M. Wills, however, as a Jewish scholar is attracted to the proposition that an angelic figure such as Michael is in view.[50] G. L. Archer, Jr., will have none of this. He contends:

> The personage who now appears before God in the form of a human being is of heavenly origin. He has come to this place of coronation accompanied by the clouds of heaven and is clearly no mere human being in essence. The expression 'like a son of man' (*kebar enas*) identifies the appearance of this final Ruler of the world not only as a man, in contrast to the beasts (the four world empires), but also as *the heavenly Sovereign incarnate*.[51]

Archer, Jr., sees the incarnation per se in the text. This contention goes beyond the evidence and prematurely forecloses on the interpretative options.

In the light of the above diversity of opinion Watts is right to describe the identification of the Son of Man in Daniel 7 as 'hotly

---

[46] Interestingly Isa. 9:6 is not quoted in any New Testament document. Matt. 4:12–17 does quote Isa. 9:1–2 in relation to Jesus' beginning his preaching ministry in Galilee. In view is Christ's ministry though and not his divinity. See Blomberg 2007: 18–19. Blomberg (2007) argues that in its Old Testament context Isa. 9:6 envisions 'no mere mortal'.

[47] R. E. Watts 2007: 134.

[48] Scobie 2003: 340, original emphasis.

[49] Ibid.

[50] Wills 2004: 1656–1657.

[51] Archer, Jr., 1997, comment on Dan. 7:13–14, my emphasis.

contested'.[52] Indeed he argues that 'no resolution' is in sight.[53] My point in parading this diversity of scholarly opinion is a simple one. Leaving to one side the way Jesus used the phrase of himself, the identity of the Son of Man in Daniel 7 when considered within the confines of the Old Testament canon is not transparent. Little wonder then, as Christopher J. H. Wright can write, 'Most scholars are agreed that the "Son of Man" was not a messianic title or figure in the inter-testamental Jewish writings. That is, the people of Jesus's day, whatever else they were hoping for in the way of a messiah, were not on the lookout for a "Son of Man." '[54] Therefore I would move this text from Ortlund, Jr.'s accurately construed to reveal the deity of Christ category to his not clear enough to be certain one way or the other category.

Psalm 110:1

Psalm 110:1 is the most quoted or alluded to Old Testament text to be found in the New Testament.[55] The text is intriguing:

> The LORD says to my lord:
>
> 'Sit at my right hand
> until I make your enemies
> a footstool for your feet.'

However, is Ortlund, Jr., correct to see this royal psalm as revealing the deity of the Christ? On the one hand if David is the speaker, then the identity of the two lords is the crucial question. 'The right hand' (*yāmîn*) is the place of greatest power or dignity next to that of the monarch. Normally this was where the second-in-command would sit.[56] Interestingly Bathsheba was given that honour by Solomon (1 Kgs 2:19). Derek Kidner comments, 'What is unique is the royal speaker, addressing this more-than-royal person.'[57] On this reading clearly a greater than David is in view. On the other hand if the speaker is a court prophet, then one of the lords is Yahweh and the other is the Israelite king. In fact, although pre-Christian Jewish interpretation

---

[52] R. E. Watts 2007: 134.
[53] Ibid. 133.
[54] C. J. H. Wright 1992: 149.
[55] G. H. Guthrie 2007: 943. According to Guthrie, Ps. 110:1 is cited twenty-two times in the New Testament.
[56] Berlin and Brettler 2004: 1284.
[57] Kidner 1995, comment on Ps. 110:1.

on occasion understood the psalm as messianic, these interpreters did not regard the psalm as necessarily referring to a divine Messiah.[58] Therefore yet again I would move this text from the accurately construed to reveal the deity of Christ category to the not clear enough to be certain one way or the other category. Remembering, of course, that at this stage we are moving within the horizon of Israel's ancient text, not that of the complete biblical canon.

The reference above to the completed biblical canon raises an important consideration. At this point someone reading this analysis may be somewhat frustrated. After all, for example, does not Hebrews 1:12 employ Psalm 110:1 – and Psalm 45:6 for that matter – as a key element in establishing the superiority of Jesus to angels? Indeed the New Testament writer does. However, the useful discussion of Ortlund, Jr., as to whether the deity of Christ is to be found revealed in the Old Testament appears to assume that the reader who may accurately or inaccurately construe the Old Testament text with regard to the question is the Christian who believes the Nicene Creed.[59] Our concern is different if we are reading the Old Testament with our New Testament shut at this stage. We are endeavouring to understand what ancient Israel hoped for before the revelatory light of Christ became available. This, of course, does not preclude the fact that in the light of Christ such Old Testament texts take on a legitimate depth of significance that may not have been apparent to the original writer.[60]

Intertestamental hopes

Jewish intertestamental hopes took a variety of forms. Donald E. Gowan sums these expectations up in an admirable way. I quote *in extenso*:

Hope for the ideal future could be expressed very nicely in post-OT Judaism without a Messiah. No such figure appears in the

---

[58] Longenecker (1994: 376–377) states that it was not until AD 260 that rabbis understood Ps. 110:1 as messianic. Up until then they viewed the text as referring to God's speaking to Abraham, to David or to Hezekiah.

[59] Ortlund, Jr., 2011: 39.

[60] For an excellent nuanced treatment of this greater significance see Beale in Beale 1994: 392–393. He points out how 'the latter parts of biblical history function as the broader context to interpret earlier parts because they all have the same, ultimate divine author who inspires the various human authors, and one deduction from this premise is that Christ as the center of history is the *key to interpreting the earlier portions of the Old Testament and its promises*' (original emphasis).

eschatology of *Jubilees*; *1 Enoch* 1–36; 91–104; *Assumption of Moses*; *2 Enoch*; *Sibylline Oracles IV*; the War Scroll; Psalms Scroll, or Habakkuk Commentary of Qumran; or in any of the books of the Apocrypha except 2 Esdras. Messiah does appear in other documents from Qumran, but does not play a major role in them (1QSa II. 11–22; The Patriarchal Blessings; 1QS IX.11). A royal figure who might fairly be said to represent the messianic hope, although the word itself is not used, appears in the *Testaments of the Twelve Patriarchs* (*T. Sim.* 7:2; *T. Jud.* 24:1–6; *Dan.* 5:10–13; *T. Jos.* 19:8–11) in company with an eschatological priest. A white bull who presumably represents the Messiah appears in the dream-vision of Enoch (*1 Enoch* 90:37), but plays no significant role.[61]

He acknowledges that there is one, extensive, pre-Christian delineation of the Messiah to be found in *Psalms of Solomon* 17, which is a mid-first-century BC document. The figure portrayed is that of a Davidic king who defeats the enemies of God's people, regathers Israel and settles them in the land of promise under his judgeship. He will rule the nations. However, he 'is still a purely human figure'.[62]

Gowan's picture of Second Temple expectations needs nuancing. As Darrell L. Bock points out, *1 Enoch* 33–34, one of the texts Gowan refers to, presents a 'transcendent figure of divinely bestowed authority'.[63] Moreover Bock judiciously quotes *Psalms of Solomon* 17.4 to reveal how deeply Davidic its expectations are: 'Lord, you chose David to be king over Israel, and swore to him about his descendants forever, that his kingdom should not fall before you.'[64] Even more apposite though is *Psalms of Solomon* 17.33–36:

> And he shall purge Jerusalem, making it holy as of old:
> So that nations shall come from the ends of the earth to
> see his glory,
> Bringing as gifts her sons who had fainted,
> And to see the glory of the Lord, wherewith God hath
> glorified her.
> And he [shall be] a righteous king, taught of God over
> them.

---

[61] Gowan 2006: 39.
[62] Ibid. Gowan rightly contends that Roman occupation fuelled such a hope.
[63] Bock 2005: 504.
[64] Ibid.

And there shall be no unrighteousness in his days in
    their midst,
For all shall be holy and their king the anointed [Messiah]
    of the Lord.[65]

Bock also reviews the Qumran materials. His conclusions are worth
stating: 'So we see four major figures of the end time expected by Jews
of one sort or the another; a regal David-like figure [*Psalms of
Solomon*]; a transcendent figure described as one like a son of man
[*1 Enoch*]; a priestly figure [1QS 9.11]; and a prophetic teacher [CD
6.11 and 4QFlor].'[66]

What is clear is that the intertestamental hopes for a deliverer of
some kind were highly diverse. No synthesis is on offer, much like the
Old Testament testimony itself. As Walther Eichrodt says of the Old
Testament literature:

> *Thus at the close of its career the form of the Old Testament hope
> cries out for a critique and a reconstruction* which will be able to
> reach out and grasp the unchanging truth hidden under its bewil-
> dering diversity, and set this in the very center where it can dominate
> all else, while at the same time unifying its struggling contra-
> dictions, its resting in a timeless present and its tense waiting for a
> consummation at the end of history. Both needs are fully met in
> the NT confession of Jesus as the Messiah.[67]

Importantly for our purposes no expectation of an incarnation is
plainly in view in the pages of the Old Testament. But is that all that
can be said? Recent work in the area of typology suggests no.

Typology and incarnation

The human mind looks for patterns. This is part of the human
endeavour to make sense of our environment. Ideally both reason and
imagination are involved. Imagination posits a hidden likeness
between things that are at first sight unalike. Reason assesses claims
that a pattern has been discovered and not merely imposed. When
only imagination is involved we get the bizarre – such as the woman

---

[65] Quoted in Kee 1980: 174.
[66] Bock 2005: 504.
[67] Quoted in Dyrness 1998: 200, original emphasis.

THE GOD WHO BECAME HUMAN

trying to sell a half-eaten piece of toast on eBay, while claiming that
an image of the Virgin Mary is on it.[68]

Any attempt at a typological reading of Scripture can invite the
criticism that reason has been left behind and the religious imagination has triumphed. And yet the imagination is vital to human
knowing, even theological knowing – as Karl Barth maintained. He
wrote, 'But human possibility of knowing is not exhausted by the
ability to perceive and comprehend. Imagination, too, belongs no
less legitimately in its way to the human possibility of knowing. A
man without imagination is more of an invalid than one who lacks
a leg.'[69] Walter Brueggemann helpfully describes this use of the
religious imagination as 'good-faith extrapolation'.[70] Caution is
needed though because imagination may work in unconvincing ways.
I recall a sermon that allegorized the colours of the curtains of the
tabernacle. One colour stood for the deity of Christ and another for
his humanity. This is not typology but allegory. What the preacher
said was true but not true to the passage in view. What distinguishes
typology from allegory? A. T. Hanson describes the difference well:
'If used excessively or indiscriminately, typology can pass over into
allegory. Allegory means using any person or event, or object in the
Old Testament *arbitrarily* to signify a corresponding event or thing
in the New Testament.'[71]

Caution should not mean timidity. After all, there is precedent
within special revelation for the typological reading of Scripture that
starts with the Old Testament itself. Isaiah looks back to the exodus
from Egypt and sees a pattern relevant to God's future dealings with
Israel (cf. Exod. 1 – 15; Isa. 43:1–19; 51:9–11). So too in the New
Testament Matthew's Gospel looks back to the Egyptian captivity
of God's people and subsequent escape as interpreted by Hosea,
and applies that pattern to Jesus (cf. Hos. 11:1; Matt. 1:14–15). A. T.
Hanson captures the essence of a typological reading of Scripture:
'The practice in the New Testament and the early church whereby a
person or a series of events occurring in the Old Testament is inter-
preted as a type or foreshadowing of some person (almost invariably
Christ) or feature in the Christian dispensation.'[72] Helpfully Hanson's

[68] 'Woman "Blessed by the Holy Toast"' <http://www.hotspotsz.com/Woman_
blessed_By_The_Holy_Toast_(Article-13486).html>, accessed 4 Dec. 2010.
[69] Barth, *CD* III/1: 91.
[70] Brueggemann 2002: 16.
[71] Hanson 1993: 784, my emphasis.
[72] Ibid. 783–784.

phrase 'feature in the Christian dispensation' is broad enough to cover both an event (e.g. exodus) and an institution (e.g. priesthood).

The attentive reader will have noticed that very little has been made of typology in the present study. This is not because I have an issue with a typological reading of Scripture. Far from it![73] The question is not whether there is a typological preparation in the providence of God for Christology in general. I would argue there most definitely is such a preparation in relation to Christ's prophethood (a greater than Moses), kingship (a greater than David and Solomon), priesthood (a greater than Levi) and sacrifice (a greater than any tabernacle- or temple-offered precursor) *inter alia*. But the incarnation? Recent work on typology may indeed answer that question, albeit in a finely finessed way that respects both reason and imagination.

In his work *Jesus the Son of God* D. A. Carson writes of trajectories found in Old Testament texts that lead ultimately to Christ as the Son of God who is both human and divine. In particular the texts that speak of David and the hope connected with his house provide a case in point. A text such as 2 Samuel 7:14 in the first instance 'certainly' applies to Solomon.[74] Another key text, Psalm 2:7, first 'probably' applies to David and his immediate successors, and a third one, Psalm 45:6–7, 'certainly applies, initially, to kings who had their heirs who replaced their fathers, not to Jesus'.[75] Even so, for Carson the significance of these texts cannot be left there: 'Yet in all three cases the context drops hints of a fulfillment that outstrips local petty monarchs.'[76] He acknowledges that 'this Davidic trajectory is subtle'.[77] Subtle, yes, but also crucially important. He argues, 'If these trajectories are not identified and understood, however, we will be at a loss to understand how the Old Testament texts that are said to be fulfilled in Jesus actually "work." '[78] By 'trajectory' he means, 'to use the more traditional terminology, this Davidic typology'.[79] In his view such Davidic texts are 'inherently forward looking'.[80] Because the writer to the Hebrews is aware of this Davidic trajectory in the Old Testament he can legitimately apply Psalms 2:7 and 45:6–7 to Jesus. Another

---

[73] For a first-rate discussion of typology as a method of interpretation see Hugenberger 1994: 331–341.

[74] Carson 2012: 75.

[75] Ibid.

[76] Ibid.

[77] Ibid.

[78] Ibid.

[79] Ibid. 49.

[80] Ibid.

example for Carson is provided by Ezekiel 34, which twenty-five times refers to Yahweh as coming to be the shepherd of his people in the face of the failure of their human shepherds (leaders), and yet the chapter ends with David as the shepherd. He concludes, 'The visitation of the Lord and the coming of his servant David become more than a little blended' (Ezek. 34:23–24).[81]

Given this approach one can see how the Old Testament provides anticipatory texts whose deeper significance in the light of the incarnation event can be both seen and drawn out in a way that is neither fanciful nor arbitrary. Again Hebrews 1 is the case in point. Carson is aware of what such subtlety means:

> It takes some hard work to uncover how these trajectories, these typologies, actually work. But when we take the time and effort to examine them, we are hushed in awe at the wisdom of God in weaving together intricate patterns that are *simultaneously so well hidden in their development* [in the Old Testament] and so magnificently obvious in their fulfillment [in the New Testament].[82]

The emphasized words are important because, as we shall see in the next chapter, Christ's appearing in the flesh is described as a mystery in the Pauline sense of something hidden in the plan of God but now revealed. This subtle typological argument does not undermine that Pauline claim, although an argument that the Old Testament explicitly expects an incarnation would subvert it. To that discussion we now turn.

Conclusion

When arguing whether or not the idea of the Trinity was to be found in the Old Testament, B. B. Warfield asserted that the Old Testament was like a dimly lit room:

> This is not an illegitimate reading of New Testament ideas [trinitarian ideas] back into the text of the Old Testament; it is only

---

[81] Ibid. 37. Carson's language 'more than a little blended' is a tad too strong. The sequence in Ezek. 34 of first the derelict shepherds, Yahweh's intention to rescue, his judging between lean and fat sheep and then the setting up of a Davidic prince as a ruler after the rescue and judgment suggest more a juxtaposing of images than their blending.

[82] Ibid. 75–76, my emphasis.

reading the text of the Old Testament under the illumination of the New Testament revelation. The Old Testament may be likened to a chamber richly furnished but dimly lit; the introduction of light brings into it nothing which was not in it before; but it brings out into clearer view much of what was in it but was only dimly or even not at all perceived before.[83]

Point taken! However, in contrast Warfield had no such reticence in relation to what he believed was a *clear* expectation in the Old Testament that a divine Messiah would come. I am unable to follow either Warfield or Ortlund, Jr., all the way in this. There are Old Testament texts that prima facie when read together are consistent with that idea but do not demand it (e.g. Ps. 45:6; Isa. 9:6; Dan. 7:13). There are other readings of these texts that are also defensible. Significantly, though, when other texts that are relevant to Israel's messianic hope are considered, the picture becomes much more problematical for the Warfield and Ortlund, Jr., thesis. For example, on any reckoning 2 Samuel 7:14a is salient for Israel's messianic hopes: 'I will be his father, and he will be my son.' However, the next part of the verse, 14b, shows that the figure in view is all too human: 'When he does wrong, I will punish him with a rod wielded by men, with floggings inflicted by human hands.' And as for Psalm 45:6, the psalm goes on to describe the king's queen (Ps. 45:9–17).

The results yielded in this chapter then may appear limited. The Old Testament expected human agents or even divine agents of the divine purpose to come to Israel's aid at some juncture in its future: a prophet like Moses, a Davidic king, the Son of Man, the child born bearing the name 'Mighty God', and the Old Testament writers also expected God himself to come. But an incarnate divine-human deliverer? On the surface of it there seem then to have been two distinct but unsynthesized lines of expectation – one concerning God and another concerning a human agent – that constituted the mainsprings of Israel's hope. How then can this chapter be dealing with the preparation for the incarnation in Israel's hope? Recent developments in the typological reading of Scripture help us address that question. And that question will be further addressed in the next chapter when I shall draw on Nicholas Wolterstorff's fertile idea of data-background beliefs as we consider the New Testament testimony to the Word who became flesh.

---

[83] Warfield 1968: 30.

Chapter Four

The great mystery

In this chapter we begin our discussion of the epicentre of the divine project to restore to its rights the created order. To do so, first we explore how Jesus, as delineated in the Gospels, saw himself in the light of the testimony of the Old Testament, and then examine how the New Testament writers in retrospect saw in Jesus the fulfilment of Old Testament promise and prediction. With regard to the latter we shall examine some key claims in Matthew, Mark, Paul, Hebrews and John. Even so, I shall contend the Old Testament Scriptures per se did not offer the prospect of an incarnation as part of the hope of Israel. It was a mystery in the sense of 'revelation that is in some sense "there" in the [Old Testament] Scriptures but hidden until the time of God-appointed disclosure'.[1] No surprise then that 1 Timothy 3:16 can state, 'Beyond all question, the mystery from which true godliness springs is great: He appeared in the flesh.' (This text will play a pivotal role in this chapter.) Importantly there is another way that the Old Testament may have prepared the way for the incarnation. Drawing on Nicholas Wolterstorff's theory of theories, a suggestion of how this is so will be offered. Regarding this back story preparation, the anthropomorphisms, anthropopathisms and anthropopraxisms of the Old Testament take on particular relevance.

In retrospect

There is nothing like looking in retrospect to see connections, implications and entailments that otherwise would be hard to discern. The Monday-morning quarterback can see it all: the play that should have been made or completed, the tactic that should have been employed, the tackle that turned the game. The New Testament writers had a

---

[1] Beale and Carson 2007: xxvii. They contend that this idea of mystery is one that pervades the New Testament more than the twenty-seven or twenty-eight explicit uses of *mystērion* (mystery) might at first suggest. Dunn (2009: 185) takes a contrary view in arguing that 'In biblical texts, *mystery* does not refer to undisclosed secrets, but rather to divine secrets now revealed by divine agency' (original emphasis). This is puzzling. What is the difference between something undisclosed until revealed, and a secret now being an open one?

source of epistemological aid that no Monday-morning quarterback can know. The Holy Spirit has come. In the upper room before the crucifixion Jesus said, 'But when he, the Spirit of truth, comes, he will guide you [the apostles] into all the truth' (John 16:13). I shall canvas only five examples of what was discerned when the time had fully come (*hote de ēlthen to plērōma tou chronou*), to borrow the Pauline phrase from Galatians 4:4.

According to Jesus

In dialogue and debate with others Jesus often grounded his self-understanding on the testimony of the Old Testament Scriptures. Craig L. Blomberg sums up the New Testament witness in an admirable way:

> When it comes to the inspiration, truthfulness, authority and relevance of the Bible of his world, Jesus could scarcely have held to higher views. The central theological and moral truths of Scripture – monotheism, the double love-commandment, the frequent rebellion of humanity (including God's own people), the promises of eschatological judgment and blessing beginning with a Messianic age of God's beneficent reign on earth through that Messiah – all proved central to Jesus' own thinking as well. He acknowledged Scripture's divine origin as God's word and words. He quoted from the Bible extensively and intensively. He affirmed the inviolability of its contents down to the smallest details. To whatever degree the contents of the Hebrew canon had solidified by his day, Jesus affirmed their unity but also their tripartite division. He interpreted the historical narratives in ways that suggest he believed that at least most (and probably all) of the events narrated really happened. *He saw the collection of scriptural writings as open-ended, however, pointing forward to a time when God would fulfill his complete salvation-historical purposes for the ages. He believed that such an era had been inaugurated with his ministry. As a result, he mined the Scriptures for predictions and patterns that so closely paralleled events in and surrounding his life that the faithful Jew should have been able to see God's providential hand of guidance in them, fulfilling or filling full his word of old.*[2]

---

[2] Blomberg, 'Further Reflections on Jesus' View of the Old Testament', unpublished paper (2010), 35, my emphasis. According to Blomberg (36), 'Jesus *is* credited in the four Gospels with quoting from Deuteronomy 22 times, Psalms 19 times, Exodus 14 times, Isaiah 11 times, Leviticus 7 times, Genesis 6 times, Daniel 5 times, Hosea 3 times, Numbers, Malachi and Zechariah twice each, and Micah and Jonah once each' (original emphasis).

Blomberg rightly sees that Jesus is presented in the Gospels as the supreme hermeneutist or interpreter of the sacred writings.[3]

Luke's Gospel in particular gives insight into Jesus as the hermeneutist. Luke 24 is especially instructive. In Luke 24:25–27 the risen Christ appears on the road to Emmaus teaching Cleopas and one other disciple that the Old Testament's *leitmotiv* (main idea) was Jesus himself. First he chides them, 'He said to them, "How foolish you are, and how slow to believe all that the prophets have spoken! Did not the Messiah have to suffer these things and then enter his glory?"' Then he instructs them, 'And beginning with Moses and all the Prophets, he explained [*diermēneuein*, 'to translate', 'to interpret', 'to explain'] to them what was said in all the Scriptures concerning himself' (Luke 24:27). Later in the same chapter the scene shifts to Jerusalem. Cleopas and the other disciple bring the news of their encounter with Jesus to the Eleven (Luke 24:33). Jesus appears once more and the disciples are frightened (Luke 24:37). He reassures them in Luke 24:44, 'This is what I told you while I was still with you: everything must be fulfilled that is written about me in the Law of Moses, the Prophets and the Psalms.' Being so informed is necessary but not sufficient. Next we read, 'Then he opened [*dianoichein*, 'to open'] their minds so they could understand the Scriptures' (v. 45). In systematic categories this is a classic instance of the revelatory word and the illuminated mind.[4]

Luke 24 has further significance for our purposes. According to David W. Pao and Eckhardt J. Schnabel with reference to Luke 24:25, 'Later Christians understood Jesus' statement as a model for the "global reading of the OT as *praeparatio evangelica*" [preparation for the gospel].'[5] As C. J. H. Wright explains, 'But for those with eyes and ears and memories, the Hebrew scriptures had already provided the patterns and models by which he [Jesus] could be understood, and by which he could understand and explain himself and his goals to others.'[6] In that light we now turn our attention to examples of such

---

[3] A case in point is how Jesus creatively applied to himself and his context both Daniel and a psalm (cf. Dan. 7:13; Ps. 110:1; Mark 14:62). For an insightful discussion see R. E. Watts 2007: 112, 233–235.

[4] Acts 16:14 provides a parallel with reference to Lydia's hearing Paul's gospel message: 'One of those listening was a woman from the city of Thyatira named Lydia, a dealer in purple cloth. She was a worshipper of God. The Lord opened [*dianoichein*] her heart to respond to Paul's message.' The reference to the heart (*kardia*) in this text and the reference to the mind (*nous*) in Luke 24:45 strongly suggests that 'open' rather than 'interpret' or 'translate' is the best way to render the Greek.

[5] Pao and Schnabel 2007: 400.

[6] C. J. H. Wright 1992: 110.

readings of the Old Testament from Matthew, Mark, Hebrews and John that appear to have the incarnation in view.

According to Matthew

It is unsurprising that the early church made Matthew's Gospel the beginning of the New Testament canon.[7] As Craig L. Blomberg argues, 'Why then was Matthew put first when the canonical sequence of the four Gospels, and eventually of the entire New Testament, was crystallized? Doubtless one answer is because of Matthew's clearest and most frequent links to the Old Testament.'[8] Those clear links begin in Mathew's first chapter. In that chapter as we shall see, not only is its Jewishness patent, but the genealogy that begins it explicitly takes the reader back in the history of God's dealings to Abraham, the father of the faithful.

The Matthean genealogy provides a natural bridge to the Old Testament testimony.[9] According to Matthew 1:1, 'This is the genealogy of Jesus the Messiah the son of David, the son of Abraham.' The three names in reverse order – Abraham, David and Jesus – become the structural key to what follows. In a highly stylized and selective way in three series of fourteen names each Matthew covers salvation history from Abraham to Jesus. The first series canvasses Abraham to David (Matt. 1:2–6a), the second one David to the Babylonian exile (Matt. 1:6b–11), and the last one from the exile to the birth of Jesus (Matt. 1:12–16). Matthew 1:17 sums it up: 'Thus there were fourteen generations in all from Abraham to David, fourteen from David to the exile to Babylon, and fourteen from the exile to the Messiah.' At this juncture in the Matthean account there is no hint that Jesus is God incarnate. The Christology in view is from below.

What follows next in the account (Matt. 1:18–23) adds another dimension to this picture.

---

[7] In my view the early church did not confer authority on the books of the New Testament. Books were included because their inherent authority was recognized. However, the early Christians were clearly responsible for sequencing the books of the New Testament. Someone wisely put Matthew first and Revelation last. The fact that the early church ordered the canon can easily become the idea that the early church created the authority of the canon. But this is a mistake, I'd argue.

[8] Blomberg 2007: 1.

[9] The genealogy in Luke 3:23–38 provides an illuminating contrast. Luke begins with Joseph and climaxes with Adam, the son of God. The Lucan account places the Jesus story in the framework of universal history, while the Matthean one sets Jesus within the history of Abraham and his descendants. Although it needs pointing out that the Matthean account ultimately has the whole world in view (cf. Gen. 12:1–3 and Matt. 28:18–20).

This is how the birth of Jesus the Messiah came about: his mother Mary was pledged to be married to Joseph, but before they came together, she was found to be pregnant through the Holy Spirit. Because Joseph her husband was faithful to the law, and yet did not want to expose her to public disgrace, he had in mind to divorce her quietly.

But after he had considered this, an angel of the Lord appeared to him in a dream and said, 'Joseph son of David, do not be afraid to take Mary home as your wife, because what is conceived in her is from the Holy Spirit. She will give birth to a son, and you are to give him the name Jesus, because he will save his people from their sins.'

All this took place to fulfil what the Lord had said through the prophet: 'The virgin will conceive and give birth to a son, and they will call him Immanuel' (which means 'God with us').

This is no ordinary birth. The Holy Spirit is involved in a way without precedent in the canonical presentation. The surprising reference to the four women in the genealogy anticipates this to a degree. Tamar (v. 3), Rahab (v. 5), Ruth (v. 5) and Bathsheba (v. 5) were not Israelites and their pregnancies were atypical, each in their own way. (Theologically these women also point to the fact that the Abrahamic promise is for the Gentiles and not just the Jews, as the Great Commission of Matthew 28:18–20 with its reference to 'all nations' underlines.) Mary's pregnancy was likewise atypical but in an even more extraordinary fashion.[10]

In fact, according to Matthew this child fulfils Old Testament Scripture (v. 22). Isaiah 7:14 has come to pass. For some the prediction of Isaiah 7:14, quoted in Matthew 1:23, is now realized: 'God with us.'[11] For others Matthew has misunderstood the Old Testament text,

---

[10] Allison, Jr. (2001: 849), favours the view that the Gentile status of the women, rather than the atypical circumstances of their conceiving children, was the reason for their Matthean inclusion. I'd argue that this is not an either–or but a both–and.

[11] Ibid. Allison, Jr. (ibid.), takes the view that the use of the title 'Emmanuel' drawn from Isa. 7:14 'does not entail that Jesus is God'. The homage (*prosekynēsan*, 'they worshipped') offered by the Magi suggests otherwise (Matt. 2:11). When worship is offered to apostles and angels it is rejected as inappropriate, as worship should be directed only towards God (cf. Matt. 2:11 and Acts 14:8–18, where the idea is present; and Rev. 22:8–9, where *proskynein* is actually used twice). Having said that, the language of *proskynein* may simply in places mean the protocol one adopts before a great one (e.g. Matt. 8:2, which both the NIV and ESV translate more literally as 'knelt'). However, the next use of *proskynein* after the Magi story is in Matt. 4:8–10, in the context of the devil's attempt to persuade Jesus to abandon his obedience to his messianic task. France

which most probably in its original context referred to the birth of Isaiah's own son Maher-Shalal-Hash-Baz (cf. Isa. 7:14; 8:8, 10). Craig L. Blomberg illuminatingly suggests that a double fulfilment is quite possible. The birth of Maher-Shalal-Hash-Baz did not exhaust the fulfilment. In the light of descriptors that come after in Isaiah, 'Almighty God', 'Eternal Father' and 'Prince of Peace', Blomberg argues that these are 'prophecies that scarcely could have been fulfilled in a mere earthly king'.[12] The worship of this child by the Magi in the very next chapter (Matt. 2:8, 11) and the quotation from Micah 5:2 (Matt. 2:5–6) reinforce the view that here is king who transcends the merely human.[13]

Matthew's Gospel does not say in so many words that this Jesus is God incarnate – unlike John's Gospel, which is quite explicit on the matter, as we shall soon see – but that idea appears to be implicit in the account.

According to Mark

Compared to Matthew's Gospel Mark's account of Jesus makes fewer explicit references to the Old Testament Scriptures, but where it does it orients the entire narrative and does so from the start.[14]

Mark's Gospel begins on a new exodus note. According to Thorsten Moritz, and he acknowledges the seminal work of Rikki E. Watts here, Mark 1:1–3 is an important hermeneutical key to understanding the Marcan narrative.[15] The text reads as follows:

> The beginning of the good news about Jesus the Messiah, the Son of God, as it is written in Isaiah the prophet:

(1985: 87) offers this comment: 'The verb *worship* (*proskyneō*) need mean no more than to pay homage to a human dignitary, but Matthew frequently uses it in contexts where Jesus' more-than-human status is recognized (e.g. 14:33; 28:9, 17), and the same implication may be present here.' On balance then 'worship' makes the better sense in Matt. 2:2, 11.

[12] Blomberg 2007: 4.

[13] For the substance of this paragraph I am indebted to ibid. 3–7. Jesus is fully human but not merely human. He is essentially human but not commonly human. (I owe these distinctions to T. V. Morris 2001.) Like Jesus, Adam and Eve had no human father and yet their essential humanity is never under debate in Scripture.

[14] Compare Matthew's fifty-five quotations of the Old Testament (twenty of which are in Matthew alone and twice as many as Mark's) with a relatively fewer number of Old Testament quotations in Mark's account (see Blomberg 2007: 1). How quotations and allusions are reckoned is a debatable point.

[15] Moritz 2005: 481. For the substance of this paragraph I am indebted to Moritz's fine discussion.

'I will send my messenger ahead of you,
  who will prepare your way' –
'a voice of one calling in the wilderness,
  "Prepare the way for the Lord,
    make straight paths for him."'

Mark creatively brings Isaiah 40:3, Malachi 3:1 and Exodus 23:20 together to make at least three points. God is coming to Zion to restore his people (Isa. 40). The Lord's coming to his temple will mean judgment (Mal. 3). God will ensure that the way is prepared (Exod. 23:20).

John the Baptist is the promised Elijah, and Jesus is – as Rikki E. Watts suggests – 'identified not merely as Yahweh's agent, but in some mysterious way with Yahweh's very presence'.[16] Mortiz is more explicit: 'Mark consciously sets the appearance and ministry of Jesus in the context of the NE [New Exodus]. For him, this is the story of the beginning of the renewal of God's people, and Jesus is revealed not just as a protagonist in the NE story, but as Israel's returning God.'[17]

The next chapter in Mark provides a story that illustrates Moritz's claim (Mark 2:1–12). The setting is Capernaum. Jesus is teaching in a home. Teachers of the law are present. Four friends carrying a paralysed friend cannot access the home because of the crowd. Famously they make an opening in the roof and lower their friend down. Jesus, impressed with their faith, in verse 5 pronounces to the paralysed man, 'Son, your sins are forgiven.' The teachers of the law are alarmed (vv. 6–7): 'Now some teachers of the law were sitting there, thinking to themselves, "Why does this fellow talk like that? He's blaspheming! Who can forgive sins but God alone?"' They rightly understand that forgiving sins is not a human prerogative. It belongs to God alone. To them Jesus appears to have slandered the God of Israel and usurped his place.[18] Jesus, however, is unfazed at their thinking (Mark 2:8–11):

Immediately Jesus knew in his spirit that this was what they were thinking in their hearts, and he said to them, 'Why are you thinking

---

[16] R. E. Watts 2007: 122.

[17] Moritz 2005: 482.

[18] Tuckett (2001: 891) argues that 'strictly Jesus does no more than declare God's forgiveness'. This is unconvincing given the scribes' reaction to Jesus. Keener's (1993) comment on Mark 2:5 suggests, 'Strictly speaking, therefore, these legal scholars would have been mistaken in interpreting Jesus' words as blasphemy, even by their own rules. But the term was used much more broadly in popular parlance in this period, and they may apply it in the general sense of dishonoring the divine name.'

these things? Which is easier: to say to this paralysed man, "Your sins are forgiven," or to say, "Get up, take your mat and walk"? But I want you to know that the Son of Man has authority on earth to forgive sins.' So he said to the man, 'I tell you, get up, take your mat and go home.'

The formerly paralysed man did just that and those there were amazed (v. 12). God is on his way to Zion in Mark's account and yet this Jesus is clearly human. The self-referencing title 'the Son of Man' has enough ambiguity to cover both the human and the divine.

Mortiz is right to speak of Mark's '*implied* Jesus incarnational theology'.[19] As in Matthew's account, incarnational theology is present but not explicit. There is no attempt in either Gospel to prove in some sense that this Jesus is both God and human, and that the Old Testament predicted as much. The interests of both Gospels lie elsewhere.

According to Hebrews

In Hebrews the implied incarnational theology of Matthew and Mark gives way to an explicit one. In fact, by the time the reader has completed the reading or hearing of Hebrews 1:5 – 2:18 he or she has learnt that this Jesus is truly God and truly human. Further, the reader learns that with regard to his humanity the Son became human. It was not always the case. An event has taken place that has made it so. The Old Testament testimonies and the fact of the Christ's coming are creatively brought together in a way that no Old Testament writer appears to have imagined. Harold W. Attridge rightly describes Hebrews as 'a masterpiece of early Christian homiletics, weaving creative scriptural exegesis with effective exhortation'.[20] To these opening chapters we now turn.

Hebrews opens on a revelatory note in Hebrews 1:1–2: 'In the past God spoke to our ancestors through the prophets at many times and in various ways, but in these last days he has spoken to us by his Son, whom he appointed heir of all things, and through whom also he made the universe.' The nature of this Son is next thematized in verse 3: 'The Son is the radiance of God's glory and the exact representation of his being, sustaining all things by his powerful word.' This Son is divine. What follows surprises (v. 4): 'After he had provided purification for

[19] Moritz 2005: 484, my emphasis.
[20] Attridge 2001: 1236.

sins, he sat down at the right hand of the Majesty in heaven. So he became as much superior [*kreittōn*, 'better' or 'higher ranked'] to the angels as the name he has inherited is superior to theirs.' Creation (v. 3) and redemption (v. 4) have been conjoined in the person of this Son whose superiority has been made patent.[21]

No angel can match this Son, as the catena (*ḥārûz*, 'string of pearls') of Old Testament quotations makes plain: Psalm 2:7 (v. 5); 2 Samuel 7:14 (v. 5); Deuteronomy 32:43 (v. 6); Psalm 104:4 (v. 7); Psalm 45:6–7 (vv. 8–9); Psalm 102:25–27 (vv. 10–12); Psalm 110:1 (v. 13).[22] Angels are divine beings but are not God. This Son is both a divine being and God. Angels worship the Son (v. 6). The Son does not worship angels.

The very next chapter of Hebrews makes it clear that this Son is also truly human. He fulfils the divine expectations of humanity as Psalm 8:6–8 portrays it (Heb. 2:6–8). But who is this remarkable person to whom the world to come is subject (v. 5)? Hebrews 2:9 gives his human name: 'Jesus'. There is purpose at work here (Heb. 2:9–10):

> But we do see Jesus, who was made lower than the angels for a little while, now crowned with glory and honour because he suffered death, so that by the grace of God he might taste death for everyone.
> In bringing many sons and daughters to glory, it was fitting that God, for whom and through whom everything exists, should make the pioneer of their salvation perfect through what he suffered.

Once more 'salvation' (*sōtēria*) is the key term (cf. Heb. 1:14; 2:3; 2:10).[23]

Jesus the Son is the agent of this salvation. He provided purification for sins (Heb. 1:3) and tasted death for everyone (Heb. 2:9). But there is even more to the story and the more is incarnation (Heb. 2:14–18):

---

[21] The superiority (*kreittōn*) of the Son is the thesis of the letter. He is superior not only to angels but is a better priest than the Levitical order could provide, and he provides a better sacrifice and ushers in a better covenant than the Mosaic one, which leads to a better country informed by better promises. Jewish Christians in danger of letting go their Christian distinctives in the face of outside pressures needed to be reminded of this superiority and should not drift from the message they had first embraced (Heb. 2:1).

[22] For a discussion of how the writer of Hebrews uses Old Testament Scripture and of the nature of the *ḥārûz* method see G. H. Guthrie 2007: 923. Also see the fine discussion of how the writer to the Hebrews uses Ps. 45:6–7 in application to Jesus in a way that goes beyond but not against the psalm when set in its Old Testament context, where in that context it applied to the Davidic king's acting in a Godlike way with a Godlike character. See Harris 1992: esp. 200, 202, n. 73, and 227.

[23] The NIV has 'salvation' twice in Heb. 2:3 but actually it occurs only once. The NRSV and ESV are to be preferred here.

Since the children have flesh and blood, he too shared in [*kekoinōnē-ken*, 'shared', 'partook of'] their humanity so that by his death he might break the power of him who holds the power of death – that is, the devil – and free those who all their lives were held in slavery by their fear of death. For surely it is not angels he helps, but Abraham's descendants. For this reason he had to be made like them, fully human in every way, in order that he might become a merciful and faithful high priest in service to God, and that he might make atonement for the sins of the people. Because he himself suffered when he was tempted, he is able to help those who are being tempted.

This passage makes explicit what was implicit in Hebrews 1:3. Jesus the Son has assumed a role – 'a merciful and faithful high priest' – that presupposes a genuine human nature and he carried out that role definitively as the reference in Hebrews 1:3 to sitting down (*ekathisen*) at the right hand of God suggests.[24]

By the time the first-century hearer or reader of this exhortation (*tou logou tēs paraklēseōs*, 'the word of exhortation') had been exposed to the first two chapters, the idea of both the deity and humanity of Jesus the Son would have been encountered in the context of concerned pastoral exhortation (Heb. 2:1, 'so that we do not drift away'). The idea of incarnation is firmly grounded in such New Testament testimonies.[25]

According to John

Richard Elliot Friedman makes this general statement concerning the presentation of Christ in the Christian Gospels:

Against the backdrop of the Hebrew Bible, one reads in the first four books of the New Testament – Matthew, Mark, Luke, and John, the four Gospels – a narrative in which, after centuries of hiddenness, the deity once again manifests His presence visibly in human form. There had been nothing like this since the Genesis accounts of Eden and Jacob's struggle with god. Over a millennium had passed since, according to the Hebrew Bible, the creator told

---

[24] In the next chapter we shall explore this important passage further with reference to the rationale of the incarnation.

[25] Both G. H. Guthrie (2007: 944) and Attridge (2001: 1239) recognize that Hebrews presents the incarnation. Jewish scholar Eisenbaum (2011: 409) likewise: 'For Hebrews, Jesus is both fully human and fully divine.'

Moses, 'I shall hide My face from them,' and then in one moment, there is the most immediate expression of the divine presence on earth since Sinai.[26]

Although Friedman's academic discipline is in Hebrew and comparative literature, he is aware that

> [t]here is scholarly controversy over when the doctrine that Jesus was an incarnation of God took hold. Whatever doubt there is of incarnation in Matthew, Mark, and Luke – known as the Synoptic Gospels – it appears to be explicit in the Gospel of John, both in the passages that identify Jesus as 'Lord and "God"' (John 20:18, 28) and in the famous opening of the book . . .[27]

To that opening we now give attention.

The Prologue to John's Gospel is magisterial (John 1:1–18). Indeed David Brown and Ann Loades claim, 'it is arguable that this is John's most revolutionary contribution to Christian theology. The Word has ceased to be the medium that keeps God and the world apart; instead, it has become that which binds world and God together.'[28] The Prologue appears to work recursively. If you read the rest of the Fourth Gospel in its light you get oriented to its themes (e.g. light versus darkness, life versus death). Then upon rereading the Prologue more of its depth can be seen and so even more may be gained by rereading the rest of the narrative.[29] John 1:1 begins in eternity with the Word, and climaxes with this Word's becoming flesh (*sarx egeneto*) in time in verse 14. The opening verse runs, 'In the beginning was the Word [*logos*], and the Word was with God, and the Word was God.' Identity and yet distinction.[30] Here is a puzzle to which a trinitarian theology brings light. This Word is the agent through whom creation happened (v. 3). In this Word is found life and light for humanity (v. 4). John the Baptist bore witness to this light (vv. 6–9). However, in words that are programmatic for the main narrative (vv. 10–13):

---

[26] Friedman 1995: 126.

[27] Ibid.

[28] Brown and Loades 1996: 3.

[29] Carson (2010: 113) says, 'We are *supposed* to read it both ways. That is the way the Gospel of John has been written: the more we read it, the more we see new connections that are there in the text' (original emphasis).

[30] An excellent discussion of this point is found in Bauckham 1998: 74–75 of how the story of Jesus becomes part of the identity of the God of Israel. He calls (78) his position a 'Christology of divine identity'.

He was in the world, and though the world was made through him, the world did not recognize him. He came to that which was his own, but his own did not receive him. [Broadly speaking, chs. 1–12.] Yet to all who did receive him, to those who believed in his name, he gave the right to become children of God – children born not of natural descent, nor of human decision or a husband's will, but born of God. [Broadly speaking, chs. 13–20.]

John 1:14 adds a further descriptor to this picture. The Word become flesh is the Father's unique Son in whom the great covenant values (Hebr. *ḥesed*, 'grace', 'loving kindness', and *'ĕmet*, 'truth') announced in the revealing of the divine name at Sinai (Exod. 34:6–7) have their embodiment: 'The Word became flesh and made his dwelling among us. We have seen his glory, the glory of the one and only [*monogenous*, 'unique'] Son, who came from the Father, full of grace and truth.'[31] As Andreas J. Köstenberger comments, 'The reference in 1:14 to Jesus taking up residence among God's people resulting in the revelation of God's glory (the first occurrence of *doxa* in this Gospel) also harks back to OT references to the manifestation of the presence and glory (*kābôd*) of God, be it in theophanies, the tabernacle, or the temple.'[32] James D. G. Dunn adds to the picture when he contends that the Fourth Gospel makes an epochal claim in verse 14 concerning this manifestation of the divine presence: 'something quite new is being claimed here. Not simply a dwelling among, an appearance to, a temporary visitation, but "became" – incarnation'.[33] The Prologue does not stop there though. We read in John 1:17 that the Word who is the Son has a human name that anchors him securely in human history. The Word become flesh is Jesus Christ. As such he stands in contrast to Moses in this respect: 'For the law was given through Moses; grace and truth came through Jesus Christ.' Thus by John 1:17 we have learned that the abstract Logos now bears a personal

---

[31] With reference to John 1:14–18 Bauckham (ibid. 74) argues, 'All these terms ['glory', 'grace' and 'truth'] allude to the story of God's self revelation of himself to Moses in Exodus 33–34, in which the central character description of God occurs.' On the importance of Exod. 33 – 34 for the doctrine of God see Cole 2008: 24–36.

[32] Köstenberger 2007: 422.

[33] Dunn 2008: III, 37. Dunn (2009: 37) argues that John 1:14 is 'the definitive statement of the Christian understanding of incarnation'. How the language of 'definitive' squares with an earlier statement of his (31) is not obvious: 'But if so, the danger is that we forget that *incarnation* is at best a heuristic term, a term seeking definition even while offering definition, and try to give it a precision that is not possible' (37, original emphasis).

name.[34] The implication is staggering and well articulated by R. T. France: 'Now Jesus, as the Word made flesh, is a thoroughly concrete embodiment of the very nature of God. He is a *living anthropomorphism*, God expressed in human form.'[35]

An incident related in the next chapter of John's Gospel throws more light on the nature of the divine presence now enfleshed. Jesus clears the temple – the place where the divine presence is supposed to be found – of those selling animals and birds for sacrifice as well as the money changers (John 2:13–22). When challenged, he replies in verse 19, 'Destroy this temple, and I will raise it again in three days.' His hearers are astonished (v. 20): 'It has taken forty-six years to build this temple, and you are going to raise it in three days?' In retrospect the evangelist knows the true import of Jesus' words (vv. 21–22): 'But the temple he had spoken of was his body. After he was raised from the dead, his disciples recalled what he had said. Then they believed the Scripture and the words that Jesus had spoken.'

This is no Jesus 'meek and mild'. Understandably he is challenged by the vested interests. The Jews demand a sign. By what authority is Jesus permitted to behave so outrageously? In the light of the resurrection the disciples could fathom what Jesus was saying so puzzlingly on this dramatic occasion. Köstenberger sums up John's thesis – and the temple cleansing is some of the evidence for it – in the following illuminating way:

> In essence, the thrust of John's presentation of Jesus as the new temple is the conviction that instead of the old sanctuary, it is now Jesus who has become the proper place of worship for God's people. This marks all previous places of worship, and all manifestations of God's presence and glory with his people, as preliminary anticipations of his final and definitive revelation in the Lord Jesus Christ. Just as Jesus, as the new Israel, is the vine and his followers the branches, he is to be the center of all God's

---

[34] Some see in the Prologue a wisdom story with Jewish parallels. For example, *1 Enoch* 42.1–2 (the dating of this work is difficult) combines a descending and an ascending personified wisdom in narrative form. Wisdom looks for a place to dwell with humankind but is unsuccessful and returns to the heavens. However, this contention is effectively critiqued by Elbert IV (2011: 51), who concludes, 'To suggest that John had this type of Jewish Wisdom story [*1 Enoch* 42.1–2] in mind is not convincing. There are no substantive parallels in the Jewish literature for the incarnation. In John's prologue, we are moving well beyond anything ever said of Wisdom.' For a contrary view on the Prologue and Jesus as the personification of wisdom incarnate see Treier 2005: 845.

[35] France 1970: 47, my emphasis.

activity and of all worship directed to God. It is readily apparent, then, that John presents Jesus as divine, for worship is to be rendered to no one but God alone.[36]

Jesus is the temple presence of the God of Israel. John 1:14, which speaks of the Word's having tented or tabernacled (*eskēnōsen*) among us, with all its resonances of the tabernacle as the place of the divine presence in the wilderness, is now amplified in John 2 in concrete action within the precincts of the Jerusalem temple.[37] G. K. Beale draws John 1:14 and John 2 together and rightly concludes, 'The special revelatory presence of God, formerly contained in the holy of holies of the tabernacle and temple, has now burst forth into the world in the form of the incarnate God, Jesus Christ.'[38]

The unfolding Johannine narrative also makes plain the real humanity of this Word incarnate. A journey makes him weary by the time he reaches Jacob's well at Sychar in Samaria (John 4:6). At Bethany in Judea the death of his friend Lazarus makes him weep, and moves and troubles him (John 11:33–35). In the Johannine account this Jesus is no phantom but the God who wept human tears.

But incarnation?

Nothing reviewed thus far suggests that the New Testament believed that their Old Testament forebears were expecting an incarnation. Even John's Gospel, which has the most explicit incarnational theology, has no suggestion of such an expectation. With reference to the testimony of the Fourth Gospel Richard Bauckham rightly says, 'Thus God's gracious love, central to the identity of the God of Israel, now takes

[36] Köstenberger 2011: 109. N. T. Wright 2008: 96 adds to the point, 'This is the plan that throughout the Bible is articulated in terms of God's choice of Israel as the means of redemption and then, after the long and checkered story of God and Israel, God's sending of his son, Jesus. Incarnation – already adumbrated in the Jewish tradition in terms not least of the Temple as the place where God chooses to live on earth – is not a category mistake, as Platonists ancient and modern imagine. It is the center and fulfillment of the long-term plan of the good and wise creator.'

[37] These resonances, or, to use Köstenberger's phrase, 'preliminary anticipations', suggest that the tabernacle and temple were types of Christ as the antitype. Typologically there is a better case for the church as temple of the Holy Spirit – note, not the temple of Christ – as the antitype. See the discussion in McKelvey 2001: 806–811: 'The church is the temple of God, or of God's Spirit, and never the temple of Christ.'

[38] Beale 2004: 195. John 1:51 could usefully be discussed at this point but will be left to the next chapter.

the radically new form of a *human life* in which the divine self-giving happens. **This could not have been expected**, but nor was it uncharacteristic. **It is novel** but appropriate to the identity of the God of Israel.'[39] There is a very good reason for this. The incarnation was a mystery, as noted in the opening paragraph of this chapter. Speaking generally, David Hill captures the relevant sense of New Testament mystery well: 'In the New Testament, therefore, *mystērion* signifies a divine secret that is being (or has been) revealed in God's good time, an open secret in some sense.'[40] H. H. D. Williams III amplifies the content of the mystery: 'In the New Testament a revealed mystery involves Jesus Christ and his place within God's plan of salvation.'[41]

The key text for exploring the mystery for our purposes is found in 1 Timothy 3:14–16. However, it is not the only text in 1 Timothy that thematizes 'mystery'.[42] In 1 Timothy 3:9 we read in the ESV, 'They must hold the mystery [*mystērion*] of the faith with a clear conscience.' The NIV is more an interpretation at this point but a defensible one: 'They must keep hold of the deep truths of the faith with a clear conscience.' 'Mystery' has been rendered 'the deep truths of the faith'. P. T. O'Brien concurs when he comments, 'it is best to understand the phrase as referring to the corpus of Christian teaching'.[43] Our key text needs to be read with the earlier reference in mind.

According to Philip H. Towner, the term 'mystery' in these verses (which are hymnic in form) 'denotes the appearance of Christ in history as the hidden salvation plan of God'.[44] Paul writes to Timothy (1 Tim. 3:14–16):

---

[39] Bauckham 1998: 74. The italics are original. The bold is my emphasis.

[40] Hill 1993: 538.

[41] Williams III 2001.

[42] O'Brien (1993: 621) points out, '*Mystērion* appears twenty-one times in Paul's letters out of a total of twenty-seven NT occurrences. Usually it points not to some future event hidden in God's plan, but to his decisive action in Christ here and now. Paul normally employs the term with reference to its disclosure or its being revealed (Rom 16:25–26; 1 Cor 2:10; Col 1:26–27; Eph 1:9; 3:3, 5).' The text in view in 1 Tim. 3 is the only one in which the Pauline use of the term 'mystery' includes the incarnation. Some might argue in that light that too much is being asked of one text. However, there is only one text that tells the story of the tower of Babel (Gen. 11) and there is only one account of the day of Pentecost (Acts 2). 1 Tim. 3:16 appears in hymnic material that presumably had wide currency in early Christianity.

[43] Ibid.

[44] Towner 1994: 97. O'Brien (1993: 621) usefully comments, 'In 1 Timothy 3:16 the unusual expression "the mystery (*mystērion*) of godliness" ("our religion," NRSV) appears. "Godliness," a favorite term in 1 Timothy, which usually refers to "the duty which people owe to God," is here understood in an objective way to refer to the content or basis of Christianity.'

Although I hope to come to you soon, I am writing you these instructions so that, if I am delayed, you will know how people ought to conduct themselves in God's household, which is the church of the living God, the pillar and foundation of the truth. Beyond all question, the mystery from which true godliness springs is great:

> He appeared [*ephanerōthē*, 'was manifested'] in the flesh,
> > was vindicated by the Spirit,
> was seen by angels,
> > was preached among the nations,
> was believed on in the world,
> > was taken up in glory.[45]

As far as the structure of the hymn is concerned, there are three main views among scholars.[46]

Significantly for our purpose, whichever view is embraced, the first line of the hymn is seen to refer to the incarnation and that the incarnation is a part of the divine mystery.[47] As I. H. Marshall argues, 'Although no subject is expressed . . . The language is based on that used elsewhere to describe how the Son of God was incarnate. The thought is of an epiphany in human form, and that a divine or heavenly subject is intended. The reference is certainly to the earthly life of Jesus and not his resurrection appearances.'[48] In other words the incarnation is a datum of salvation history (*Heilsgeschichte*) that hither to had not been made known. Vladimir Lossky captures the sense of mystery well: 'The work of Christ is a "dispensation of the mystery which from all ages has been hidden in God", as St. Paul said, an "eternal purpose which was realized in Jesus Christ". However,

---

[45] Pauline authorship of 1 Timothy is widely rejected in scholarship. However, for a spirited defence of Pauline authorship – the position adopted in this study – see Schnabel 2012: 383–403.

[46] For a canvassing of the options see Mounce 2002, comment on 1 Tim. 3:14–16. The first view that Mounce covers on how to structure the hymn can be found in Barrett 1963: 65–66, comment on 1 Tim. 3:14–16. The third view that Mounce treats can be seen in Drury 2001: 1225, comment on 1 Tim. 3:14–16. This is the chiastic approach. Mounce (2002) himself argues for what he describes as the second one.

[47] Mounce 2002. Mounce 2002, comment on 1 Tim. 3:14–16, points out that 'Most agree that the first line of the hymn refers to Christ's incarnation.' Interestingly when O'Brien (1993: 621) discusses the hymn, he argues, 'The hymn's focus is upon Christ's humiliation and exaltation, and Christians' ongoing praise of him as the exalted and glorified One.' True, but the first line – 'He appeared in the flesh' – is not to be passed over without comment if justice is to be done to the hymn.

[48] Marshall 1982: 10.

there is no necessity of nature in the incarnation. . . . It is the work of the will, the mystery of divine love.'[49]

Given the mystery referred to in 1 Timothy 3:16 it is no surprise then that the Old Testament contains no explicit presentation of an incarnation as part of the hope of Israel. A returning Elijah? Yes! A coming Son of Man? Yes! A coming Davidic messiah? Yes! A God-man? No! If this is so, how could the Old Testament text and story have prepared the way, as this study is arguing? Is the incarnation one theme that arises *de novo* once the New Testament era has arrived? Thus a biblical theology of incarnation can start only with the New Testament text, unlike other themes such as convent, election and sacrifice, to name just a few. To answer these questions, help can be found in a surprising place, namely in a theory about theory.

Nicholas Wolterstorff, the eminent Christian philosopher, offers a fascinating account of the nature of theorizing. In every theory some pattern is present. To determine whether the pattern is truly present, theories need to be weighed. Weighing theories requires beliefs. Some beliefs have to do with the data. He writes, 'At the center of all weighing of theory with respect to the presence or absence of the pattern claimed is a *decision* to take certain of one's beliefs about the entities within the theory's scope as data for one's weighing of the theory.'[50] However, what is acceptable data is in turn contingent upon other beliefs that Wolterstorff calls 'data-background beliefs'.[51] He gives an example. He takes as a datum that the desk is brown because he believes that his sense of sight is working properly and that the light in the room is not distorting the colour. Importantly data-background beliefs are 'a condition of one's accepting as data that which one does'.[52]

How is Wolterstorff's theory about theorizing relevant to the question of incarnation? In my view, without the Old Testament accounts of theophany – especially the *'îš* ones – and depictions of God in anthropomorphic (e.g. depicted with ears, eyes, arms, hands, fingers), anthropopathic (depicted as angry, afflicted, grieving) and anthropopraxic ways (depicted as standing, sitting, ruling, fighting, walking) there would not have been the possibility of data-background

---

[49] Lossky 1976: 138. For a fine discussion of 'mystery' in Pauline usage see Carson 2004: 393–436. Carson argues (424) that 'The occurrence in 1 Timothy 3:16 is clearly bound up with the incarnation, in so far as the incarnation is tied to the heart of the gospel.'

[50] Wolterstorff 1984: 66, original emphasis.

[51] Ibid. 67.

[52] Ibid.

beliefs that were crucial for the intelligibility of an actual incarnation – for example, the belief that God was coming to Zion and the belief that a Davidic king, who by definition was human, was also coming. And the idea that implicit in certain key Davidic texts the figure in view resists being reduced to the merely human adds to the picture. Without these data-background beliefs who would have been able to combine the biblical ideas of God and humanity into the notion of God incarnate? Or again data-background beliefs about the Logos, the tabernacling presence of God, and creaturely flesh make the claim that 'The Word became flesh and tabernacled among us' plausible in a first-century setting.

An older writer, H. P. Liddon, captures something of the significance of such data-background belief preparation in the following way. Of course, Wolterstorff's language was unavailable to him at his time of writing in the nineteenth century:

Whether in them [Old Testament theophanies] the Word or Son actually appeared, or whether God made a created angel the absolutely perfect exponent of His Thought and Will, do they not point in either case to a purpose in the Divine Mind which could only be realized when man had been admitted to a nearer and more palpable contact with God than was possible under the Patriarchal or Jewish dispensations? Do they not suggest, as their natural climax and explanation, some Personal Self-unveiling of God before the eyes of His creatures? Would not God appear to have been training His people, by this long and mysterious series of communications, at length to recognize and to worship Him when hidden under, and indissolubly one with a created nature? Apart from the specific circumstances which may seem to explain each Theophany at the time of its taking place, and considering them as a series of phenomena, is there any other account of them so much in harmony with the general scope of Holy Scripture, as that they were successive lessons addressed to the eye and to the ear of ancient piety, in anticipation of a coming Incarnation of God?[53]

He describes the role of theophanies as 'This preparatory service'.[54] My argument is that anthropomorphisms, anthropopathisms and anthropopraxisms similarly prepare the way for what Friedman

[53] Liddon 1908: 59–60. These words first appeared in print in 1866.
[54] Ibid. 60.

describes as the 'ultimate anthropomorphism . . . God in the form of a man, yet still the one and only God. Cosmic yet personal. The *logos* yet flesh. People could walk and talk with an incarnation of an infinite being beyond the universe.'[55]

Conclusion

Biblical theology as a discipline traces the great themes of Scripture from their first appearance in the canon to the last, whether the key term (or terms) appears or the idea does. Key ideas such as covenant, election, sacrifice, kingdom, the land, inheritance and presence, among many others, become the lens through which the unfolding biblical story is viewed. Old Testament believers would have found foregoing terms in Hebrew (or Aramaic) and the ideas instantiated by them familiar. 'Covenant' (*běrît*) and the idea of it, for example, would have been familiar to Abraham, Isaac, Jacob, Moses, Samuel, David, Isaiah, Ezekiel, Malachi and the psalmist, but incarnation? Not even the notion of the divine presence, whether resident in tabernacle or temple, would necessarily have implied incarnation. It is true that the trajectory of key texts relating to David and his house were suggestive of a more than merely human figure in view. But that trajectory was subtle, not easily perceived before the actual coming of Christ.

With the incarnation comes a newness in God's dealings with humankind that early church fathers appreciated. Anthony Tyrell Hanson captures the newness well:

> The newness came through the incarnation, not through the revelation of the Son as such. What was new was not grace, or faith, or rejection, or love, or Son, or Word, but God the Word incarnate, God the Son incarnate. . . . It was the taking of flesh as such, the act, the event in history, culminating of course in death and resurrection, that was unique, supreme, new.[56]

---

[55] Friedman 1995: 136, original emphasis. Writing from a Jewish perspective, Friedman shows remarkable insight into what can be read in the New Testament literature. This should not surprise. He knows how to read a book. The noetic effects of sin do not mean that the New Testament cannot be understood without regeneration. What it means rather is that there is no affection for that testimony without the work of the Spirit (see 1 Cor. 2:11–14). Jesus both expected Nicodemus to understand the doctrine of the new birth and told him of the need to be born again (cf. John 3:7, where the 'you' is plural, and 3:10).

[56] Hanson 1965: 170. Hanson quotes (169) from Ignatius and Irenaeus to show that the early church recognized the newness in God's dealings that the coming of Jesus into the world represented.

Paul made the same point: 'Beyond all question, the mystery from which true godliness springs is great: He appeared in the flesh' (1 Tim. 3:16). And for Paul the one who appeared in the flesh is he in whom the fullness of deity dwells, as his letter to the Colossians makes plain: 'For in Christ all the fullness of the Deity [*theotēs*, 'deity'] lives in bodily form' (Col. 2:9).[57]

But why incarnation per se and not some other way? What was the rationale for the incarnation? To that question we shall soon turn but next is an excursus dealing with a contemporary debate.

Excursus: the pre-incarnate Christ, theophany and the Old Testament debate

As we saw in previous chapters, the early church fathers (e.g. Clement of Alexandria) and some modern commentators (e.g. Walter Kaiser, Jr.) see in the Old Testament anthropomorphic theophanies appearances of the pre-incarnate Logos or Son. A robust trinitarian faith would make the suggestion all the more plausible. For the trinitarian Christian, following Augustine, *omnia opera trinitatis ad extra indivisa sunt* (the works of the Trinity outward are undivided),[58] the Father, Son and Holy Spirit are in every divine action but not necessarily in exactly the same way. And therefore any anthropomorphic theophany in the OT *ex hypothesi* involved the second Person of the triune Godhead. Furthermore, if there is merit in Fretheim's distinction between 'Theophanies of God as Warrior' and 'Theophanies of God as Bearer of the Word' – and I believe there is – then the idea that it is the Word who is the actor in these Old Testament anthropomorphic theophanies is strengthened. This proposition is further buttressed if the doctrine of appropriation is brought into play. This doctrine assigned a particular work especially to one of the triune Godhead: creation to the Father, revelation and redemption to the Son, and sanctification to the Holy Spirit, although the Trinity is involved in every divine action in some way.

---

[57] This Pauline claim expresses the highest of Christologies. Not only is the full deity of Christ affirmed but so is his real humanity. As N. T. Wright (1986: 171) comments, 'We should not, however, drive a wedge between the two [Col. 1:19; 2:9]. Part of Paul's point is that the incarnation, the taking of "bodily" form by God, was and is the "solid reality" in which were fulfilled all the earlier foreshadowings, all the ancient promises that God would dwell with his people. The word *theotēs*, translated "the Deity", is to be distinguished from *theiotēs*, "divinity" – an attribute that might conceivably be possessed by a being of lesser standing than God himself.'

[58] Quoted in Colle 1994: 96.

I have argued that once Christ came, in retrospect the New Testament writers and early church fathers could see in the Old Testament connections, implications and entailments hitherto hidden from view. However, recently a different view has been championed. In this view those who experienced such anthropomorphic theophanies in Old Testament times knew they were seeing Christ. Controversially Paul Blackham argues so.[59] According to Blackham not only are there Christophanies in the Old Testament, but that testament also teaches the doctrine of the Trinity.[60] He rejects conservative scholarship that has notions of progressive revelation that deny that Old Testament saints such as Abraham explicitly put their trust in Christ. He also rejects critical scholarship that attempts to see some kind of Christian development of the Hebrew understanding of God. Margaret Barker illustrates his point:

> The Trinitarian faith of the Church had grown from the older Hebrew belief in a pluriform deity, and so the earliest Christian exegetes had not been innovators when they understood the Lord of the Hebrew Scriptures as the second God, the Son of El Elyon. The One whom they recognized in Jesus had been the Lord, and so they declared 'Jesus is Lord'.[61]

Blackham draws attention to that Old Testament strand of evidence that affirms that God cannot be seen, and yet some do see God (e.g. cf. Exod. 24:9–11; 33:18–23 *inter alia*). Next he examines the use of such scriptural evidence by second-century fathers. In particular he explores how Justin Martyr and Irenaeus drew a trinitarian understanding of God from Old Testament evidence, with the Father as the hidden One and the Son as the appearing One, especially in the guise of the angel of the Lord. He maintains that, theologically speaking, God is not known without a mediator and that mediator is the Son. He further argues, following Colin E. Gunton, it was Augustine who decisively broke from this tradition of the theological interpretation of Old Testament Scripture. In other treatments of Christophany he appeals to some of the luminaries in

---

[59] Blackham 2001a.
[60] Blackham 2005: 35–47. The substance of this paragraph is indebted to this article.
[61] Quoted in ibid. 37.

the Christian past such as Luther, Calvin, John Owen and Jonathan Edwards.[62]

There is little doubt that New Testament characters and writers saw Christ at work in the Old Testament. In John's Gospel we find these words on the lips of Jesus himself:

> Your father Abraham rejoiced at the thought of seeing my day; he saw it and was glad.
>
> 'You are not yet fifty years old,' they said to him, 'and you have seen Abraham!' (John 8:56–57)

Even after Jesus had performed so many signs in their presence, they still would not believe in him. This was to fulfil the word of Isaiah the prophet:

> 'Lord, who has believed our message
> and to whom has the arm of the Lord been revealed?'

For this reason they could not believe, because, as Isaiah says elsewhere:

> 'He has blinded their eyes
> and hardened their hearts,
> so they can neither see with their eyes,
> nor understand with their hearts,
> nor turn – and I would heal them.'
> (John 12:37–40)

Isaiah said this because he saw Jesus' glory and spoke about him. Likewise Paul argues in 1 Corinthians 10:1–4 that Christ was active in the time of Moses:

---

[62] Blackham 2001b. Malone (2005) is critical of Blackham's use of historical sources, especially of Owen. Malone points out the restraint that Owen exhibited regarding Christophanies: 'Owen arguably finds fewer christophanies than do some christophanist scholars' and 'neither is he [Owen] comfortable speculating about biblical events without sufficient warrant'. I might add that in this Owen truly followed the spirit of Calvin. Greidanus (1999: 197) makes a similar point about contemporary scholars and preachers who are quick to see Christophanies in Old Testament figures such as the Angel of Yahweh, the Commander of the Lord's army and the Wisdom of God. He writes with particular reference to preaching from the Old Testament, 'Not only does the speculation involved put the sermon on a shaky footing, but this identification of Christ with Old Testament figures short-circuits the task of preaching Christ as the fullness of God's self-revelation in his incarnate Son, Jesus.'

> For I do not want you to be ignorant of the fact, brothers and sisters, that our ancestors were all under the cloud and that they all passed through the sea. They were all baptized into Moses in the cloud and in the sea. They all ate the same spiritual food and drank the same spiritual drink; for they drank from the spiritual rock that accompanied them, and that rock was Christ.

Peter adds to the Pauline picture by referring to the prophets. 1 Peter 1:10–12 states:

> Concerning this salvation, the prophets, who spoke of the grace that was to come to you, searched intently and with the greatest care, trying to find out the time and circumstances to which the Spirit of Christ in them was pointing when he predicted the sufferings of the Messiah and the glories that would follow. It was revealed to them that they were not serving themselves but you, when they spoke of the things that have now been told you by those who have preached the gospel to you by the Holy Spirit sent from heaven. Even angels long to look into these things.

However, the question is not whether Christ was at work in the Old Testament but whether Old Testament saints consciously believed in him. On this latter issue Blackham is less convincing.[63] It is one thing to say that the Old Testament saints were saved by Christ. It is quite another to say that they knew Christ was their saviour.

As Graeme Goldsworthy contends, Blackham appears to be interpreting the New Testament primarily through the lens of the Old Testament, whereas primarily the Old Testament should be interpreted through the lens of the New. Justice needs to be done to the incarnation as 'the final revelation of God'. Or, put another way, there is more merit in a more traditional understanding of progressive revelation than Blackham allows. Moreover Blackham does not appear to feel the weight of opposing arguments and alternative exegeses. This attitude Goldsworthy labels 'exegetical authoritarianism', and not without some justification.[64]

Despite the arguments above, a caveat is in order. I have argued that the idea that these Old Testament anthropomorphic theophanies

---

[63] For a sympathetic and accurate exposition of Blackham's position see Saville n.d.
[64] For the substance of this paragraph see Goldsworthy 2001.

are appearances of the pre-incarnate Christ needs to be weighed carefully. Calvin has wisdom to offer on this point:

> I willingly accept what the old writers teach, that when Christ appeared in those early times in the form of a man, it was a prelude of the mystery which was revealed when God manifested in the flesh. But we must beware of imaging, that Christ then was incarnate; for we do not read that Christ was incarnate; for we do not read that God sent his Son in the flesh before the fullness of time.[65]

The suggestion that the anthropomorphic theophanies were actually appearances of the pre-incarnate Son of God is plausible and the idea is defensible. However, it must be observed that even though this proposition is consistent with the biblical testimony it is not demanded by it.

What an extraordinary person Jesus was to have caused such a searching for Old Testament language, personages, events and institutions in the attempt to construe his identity and significance. His own reading of the Old Testament as the back story to his own identity and mission led the way to reading those Scriptures in a way that may have eluded – and in the case of the incarnation I have contended did – even the Old Testament writers and readers.[66] Some contemporary proposals for Jesus' identity hardly begin to explain this phenomenon of so reading the ancient Scriptures, whether that of Jesus as the cynic sage or as the wandering Jewish charismatic healer, to name just two. These proposals concerning Jesus are just too small. There is an explanation large enough, however, and it is the classic one articulated at Chalcedon in AD 451. This Jesus is one Person who is truly God and truly human. The Word became incarnate. The secret is out. Now it is an open secret or a 'mystery', in the Pauline sense of the term.

---

[65] Quoted in Greidanus 1999: 142.
[66] A point recognized by Beale and Carson (2007: xxvii).

Chapter Five

Cur Deus homo

Søren Kierkegaard (1813–55) was a Christian genius, albeit an eccentric one. He is widely regarded as 'the father of existentialism'.[1] This nineteenth-century Danish thinker saw his role as one of reintroducing Christ to Christendom. He believed, for example, that the clergy in Denmark were 'little more than a branch of the civil service'.[2] He knew how to write in a way that would startle his readers. For him the incarnation represented an absolute paradox that posited the Eternal's entering time.[3] He famously and provocatively wrote of the incarnation in the following way:

> If the contemporary generation had left nothing behind them but these words: 'We have believed that in such and such a year the God appeared among us in the humble figure of a servant, that he lived and taught in our community, and finally died,' it would be more than enough. The contemporary generation would have done all that was necessary; for this little advertisement, this *nota bene* on a page of universal history, would be sufficient to afford an occasion for a successor [future believers], and the most voluminous account can in all eternity do nothing.[4]

Kierkegaard captures the wonder of an incarnation in these words but such minimalism leaves the believer in an epistemological vacuum. 'More than enough'? Hardly! Happily the New Testament writers did not think so. So then why, according to the New Testament writers, did God become human, or, to use the famous title of Anselm's classic work, *cur Deus homo*?[5]

[1] Law 2000: 303.

[2] Ibid. 302.

[3] Kierkegaard (1941a: 528) says, 'The paradox consists principally in the fact that God, the Eternal, came into existence in time as a particular man.'

[4] Kierkegaard 1936, emphasis original.

[5] Anselm intentionally wrote his work as though he knew nothing of Christ. He expounds what he sees as the human predicament and how an incarnation and atonement provided by a God-man can remedy the problem that reason has uncovered. It contrasts then with the present one that seeks to discover how the Bible itself answers his question. The methodology could not be more different. For a useful treatment of Anselm's appeal to reason see González 1987: 158–167.

New Testament answers

In general terms the incarnation qualified Jesus to be what Adam failed to be and what Israel failed to be: the true image of God walking the earth and exercising dominion. He proved to be the faithful son in contrast to Adam and Israel.[6] Thomas Oden finely sums up the rationale of the incarnation as found in the biblical testimony. He offers five biblically defensible reasons for the incarnation:[7]

> *To reveal God to humanity (John 1:18; 14:7–11)*
> *To provide a high priest interceding for us able to sympathize with human weaknesses (Heb. 4:14–16)*
> *To offer a pattern of the fullness of human life (1 Pet. 2:21; 1 John 2:6)*
> *To provide a substitutionary sacrifice for the sins of all humanity (Heb. 10:1–10)*
> *To bind up the demonic powers (1 John 3:8)*

I would add a sixth: to redeem those under law (Gal. 4:4). Let's now examine these, although not necessarily in Oden's order.

To reveal the Father to us

The revelatory importance of the incarnation is in view in John's Gospel to a degree that no other New Testament document can rival. From the Prologue (John 1:18) we learn that the Word who became flesh without ceasing to be the Word is the exegete of the invisible Father: 'No one has ever seen God; the only God, who is at the Father's side [*kolpos*, lit. 'bosom', 'breast', 'chest'], he has made him known [*exēgēsato*]' (ESV).[8] René Kieffer comments insightfully, 'The prologue now makes it explicit that the Word is identical with Jesus, the Messiah, v. 18, in contrast to Moses who could not see God without dying (Ex 33:20), Jesus is said to be in the Father's bosom and is himself "God" (probably the original reading, attested already in P[66] and P[75]).'[9] Kieffer points out, 'The "bosom" expresses the

---

[6] I elaborate on these claims in Cole 2009b: 103–119, and so shall not expand on them here.

[7] Oden 1992: 271, original emphasis. By 'biblically defensible' I mean claims that have exegetical grounding rather than are the products of theological speculation.

[8] I prefer the ESV to the NIV here as the ESV follows the more difficult reading (*lectio difficilior*). The NIV renders the Greek, 'No one has ever seen God, but the one and only Son, who is himself God and is in the closest relationship with the Father, has made him known.'

[9] Kieffer 2001: 963.

intimacy Jesus shares with his Father (see 13:25 on the beloved disciple), in his pre-existence, his mission on earth, and his return to the Father (cf. 17:5). He is therefore the proper revealer of God.'[10] John 1:18 appears to follow the ancient epistemological principle of connaturality (like knows like).[11]

The encounter between Jesus and Nathaniel at the end of the first chapter of John throws further light on the revelation Jesus brings. Nathaniel is astonished at Jesus' knowledge of him, as related in John 1:47–48:

> When Jesus saw Nathanael approaching, he said of him, 'Here truly is an Israelite in whom there is no deceit.'
> 'How do you know me?' Nathanael asked.
> Jesus answered, 'I saw you while you were still under the fig-tree before Philip called you.'

This revelation elicits a confession of faith from Nathanael in verse 49: 'Then Nathanael declared, "Rabbi, you are the Son of God; you are the king of Israel."' Jesus' response is profound (John 1:50–51): 'Jesus said, "You believe because I told you I saw you under the fig-tree. You will see greater things than that." He then added, "Very truly I tell you, you will see 'heaven open, and the angels of God ascending and descending on' the Son of Man."' Hans Urs von Balthasar rightly draws out the significance of this claim: 'In the Son, therefore, heaven is open to the world. He has opened the way from the one to the other and made exchange between the two possible, first and foremost through his Incarnation (Jn 1:51).'[12] The temporary stairway between earth and heaven that Jacob witnessed in Old Testament times (Gen. 28:12) has given way to the permanence of the Word enfleshed as the link between the human and the divine. There is a bridge between heaven and earth that was not there before. In Pauline language the mediator (*mesitēs*) has come (1 Tim. 2:5).

A. M. Ramsey maintained, 'God is Christlike and in him there is no unChristlikeness at all.'[13] The famous scene set in the upper room in John's Gospel in which Jesus prepares his disciples for his return

---

[10] Ibid.

[11] Another example of connaturality is found in 1 Cor. 2:10b–11 in relation to the Spirit and the depths of God.

[12] Balthasar 1986: 52.

[13] Ramsey 1969: 98. Balthasar (1986: 67) strikingly says of Jesus, 'He is the Father's fragrance in the world.'

to the Father provides evidence for Jesus' contention (John 14:1–9). Jesus detects their alarm at the thought of his departure and in the light of their anxiety promises them a future with him (John 14:1–4):

> Do not let your hearts be troubled. You believe in God; believe also in me. My Father's house has many rooms; if that were not so, would I have told you that I am going there to prepare a place for you? And if I go and prepare a place for you, I will come back and take you to be with me that you also may be where I am. You know the way to the place where I am going.

Thomas is puzzled: 'Lord, we don't know where you are going, so how can we know the way?' (v. 5). Jesus responds with another one of the famous emphatic 'I am' statements found in this Gospel: 'I am [egō eimi] the way and the truth and the life. No one comes to the Father except through me. If you really know me, you will know my Father as well. From now on, you do know him and have seen him' (vv. 6–7). This time it is Philip asking the questions: 'Lord, show us the Father and that will be enough for us' (v. 8). Jesus' answer is striking. To see him at work is to see the Father at work: 'Don't you know me, Philip, even after I have been among you such a long time? Anyone who has seen me has seen the Father. How can you say, "Show us the Father"?' (v. 9). Indeed shortly after this, in the narrative flow of the Fourth Gospel, Jesus is presented in prayer to the Father in a garden setting. In that prayer he sums up his mission in revelatory terms (John 17:6 ESV): 'I have manifested your name to the people whom you gave me out of the world.'[14] According to Andreas J. Köstenberger, 'The notion that Jesus reveals the Father in his whole Person, both works and words, is foundational to John's Gospel (e.g., 1:18; 8:19, 27; 10:38; 12:45; 14:9–11).'[15] Put another way, Jesus has made the divine nature known. D. A. Carson rightly suggests:

> Do you want to know what the character of God is like? Study Jesus. Do you want to know what the holiness of God is like? Study Jesus. Do you want to know what the wrath of God is like? Study Jesus. Do you want to know what the forgiveness of God is like? Study Jesus. Do you want to know what the glory

---

[14] I prefer the ESV here to the NIV. The reference to 'name' is freighted with revelatory significance that 'you' (NIV) simply does not capture: 'I have revealed you to those whom you gave me out of the world' (NIV). Happily the NIV does have 'name' in the footnotes.
[15] Köstenberger 2007: 498.

of God is like? Study Jesus all the way to that wretched cross. Study Jesus.[16]

Jesus has truly exegeted the Father by word and deed.[17]

To redeem us

Paul's letter to the Galatians contains deep Christology. In it Paul skilfully places his Christology in an eschatological framework of how the promises to Abraham are realized in Jesus Christ: 'If you belong to Christ, then you are Abraham's seed, and heirs according to the promise' (Gal. 3:29). He explains further by drawing attention to the problematic in Galatians 4:1–3, 'What I am saying is that as long as an heir is under age, he is no different from a slave, although he owns the whole estate. The heir is subject to guardians and trustees until the time set by his father. So also, when we were under age, we were in slavery under the elemental spiritual forces of the world.' However, there is a divine timetable. According to that timetable, 'when the set time had fully come, *God sent his Son, born of a woman*, born under the law, to redeem those under the law [*hina tous hypo nomon exagorasē*], that we might receive adoption to sonship' (Gal. 4:5, my emphasis). The idea of 'redemption' in this context may have a double background: Yahweh's redemption of his 'firstborn son' Israel in the Old Testament and the Greco-Roman slave market where slaves were purchased. Both ideas would have resonated with Galatian congregations that would have had a mixture of Jewish and Gentile believers in their membership. John Stott comments:

> What is emphasized in these verses is that the one whom God sent to accomplish our redemption was perfectly qualified to do so. He was God's Son. He was also born of a human mother, so that He was human as well as divine, the one and only God-man. And

[16] Carson 2010: 117.

[17] Kruse (2003: 75) helpfully comments on John 1:18, 'The word used for "making known" is *exēgeomai*, which means to "set forth in great detail" or "expound". Its cognate is *exēgēsis*, which in its anglicized form is used to mean "exegesis"/"exposition". The evangelist is saying, then, that the Word (Jesus), being God the one and only, at the Father's side, the only one who has seen God, has "expounded" him, made him known, through his person, words and works.' Even so, it is important to note that although revelation is a leading motif in the Christology of the Fourth Gospel it is not Gnosticism, as though salvation comes by enlightenment. Right from the very first chapter Jesus is presented as not only the Word become flesh who exegetes the Father but as the 'Lamb of God who takes away the sins of the world' (cf. John 1:1, 14, 18, 29).

He was born 'under the law', that is, of a Jewish mother, into the Jewish nation, subject to the Jewish law. Throughout His life He submitted to all the requirements of the law. He succeeded where all others before and since have failed: He perfectly fulfilled the righteousness of the law.[18]

Stott then draws out the theological implications of the Pauline text:

So the divinity of Christ, the humanity of Christ and the righteous-ness of Christ uniquely qualified Him to be man's redeemer. If He had not been man, He could not have redeemed men. If He had not been a righteous man, He could not have redeemed unrighteous men. And if He had not been God's Son, He could not have redeemed men for God or made them the sons of God.[19]

The divine largesse does not stop with the sending of the Son. The Spirit is also sent. Paul argues (Gal. 4:6–7), 'Because you are his sons, God sent the Spirit of his Son into our hearts, the Spirit who calls out, "*Abba*, Father." So you are no longer a slave, but God's child; and since you are his child, God has made you also an heir.' The sending of the Son secures our status of sonship. The sending of the Spirit of the Son secures our Jesus-like experience of sonship. We too pray '*abba* Father like he did'.[20]

To represent us as great high priest

The priest in Israel played a mediatorial role in representing the worshipper to God and God to the worshipper. None was more important in this role than Israel's high priest. The letter to the Hebrews with its Jewish orientation makes much of this role in presenting Jesus Christ as the High Priest. The letter contends in Hebrews 2:16–18:

For surely it is not angels he helps, but Abraham's descendants. For this reason he had to be made like them, fully human in every way, in order that he might become a merciful and faithful high priest in service to God, and that he might make atonement for the sins of the people. Because he himself suffered when he was tempted, he is able to help those who are being tempted.

[18] Stott 1986: 105.
[19] Ibid. Longenecker 2002, comment on Gal. 4:4, is much more reticent than Stott in seeing any reference to Christ's pre-existence in the sending-of-the-Son language.
[20] Stott 1986: 105. A point well made by Stott.

This text contains the first explicit reference in Hebrews of Jesus in the high priestly office, which is to play such an important role in subsequent chapters, especially 7–10.

Jesus in this role is the intercessor par excellence according to Hebrews 4:14–15: 'Therefore, since we have a great high priest who has ascended into heaven, Jesus the Son of God, let us hold firmly to the faith we profess. For we do not have a high priest who is unable to feel sympathy for our weaknesses, but we have one who has been tempted in every way, just as we are – yet he did not sin.' The reason why Jesus is able to so sympathize is because he is truly human. Thus the writer can confidently exhort the readership, 'Let us then approach God's throne of grace with confidence, so that we may receive mercy and find grace to help us in our time of need' (Heb. 4:16). His priesthood is not subject to the limitations death brings, where priest after priest is removed by it: 'Now there have been many of those priests, since death prevented them from continuing in office; but because Jesus lives for ever, he has a permanent priesthood. Therefore he is able to save completely those who come to God through him, because he always lives to intercede for them' (Heb. 7:23–25). His priesthood is Melchizedekian (Heb. 7:11–19). Moreover in this high priestly role he is credentialled to offer the definitive sacrifice for sins. Unlike the Levitical priesthood he is without sin, and therefore as both offerer and offering he has a purity the old order could never provide (Heb. 10:1–14). A point we shall return to shortly.

Jesus' humanity is a necessary condition for his carrying out not only his high priestly role as intercessor in Hebrews 2:16–18, as we have seen, but also for his being the liturgical leader, as in Hebrews 8:1–2: 'Now the main point of what we are saying is this: we do have such a high priest, who sat down at the right hand of the throne of the Majesty in heaven, and who serves in the sanctuary, the true tabernacle [*tōn hagiōn leitourgos kai tēs skēnēs*, lit. 'of the holy things servant and of the tent/tabernacle'] set up by the Lord, not by a mere human being.' If there had been no incarnation, there would have been no one qualified to so serve humankind. As Leon Morris says, 'The nature of the work Jesus came to accomplish [as high priest] demanded the Incarnation.'[21]

To substitute sacrificially for us

Both the letter to the Hebrews and the Pauline letters make clear the importance of Christ's righteous humanity as a prerequisite for his

---

[21] L. Morris 1997, comment on Heb. 2:17.

saving work. He could not have stood in our place as our substitute without it. Moreover without his righteousness we could not stand before a holy God as righteous unless in union with him. His righteousness becomes our own.

We begin with Hebrews and return to the theme of Jesus as our high priest. Hebrews 7:26–28 is of special relevance as it summarizes so much of Hebrews' presentation of Jesus' high priestly ministry:

> Such a high priest truly meets our need [*eprepen*, 'fitting'] – one who is holy, blameless, pure, set apart from sinners, exalted above the heavens. Unlike the other high priests, he does not need to offer sacrifices day after day, first for his own sins, and then for the sins of the people. He sacrificed for their sins once for all when he offered himself. For the law appoints as high priests men in all their weakness; but the oath, which came after the law, appointed the Son, who has been made perfect for ever.

As our high priest he perfectly represents us before God. Unlike the old Levitical order he does not have to offer a sacrifice for his own sins – he had none: 'one who is holy [*hosios*], blameless [*akakos*], pure [*amiantos*], set apart from sinners'. William L. Lane comments, 'The three terms are not descriptive of static moral qualities but of dispositions demonstrated by the incarnate Son in spite of his complete involvement in the life of common humanity.' This high priest now exalted to the heavens is 'the high priest appropriate to the Christian community . . . qualified by spiritual and moral perfection'.[22] And as the sacrifice itself he provides a perfection no bull or goat could give. Hebrews 9:14 draws out the latter point in a classic a fortiori argument: 'How much more [in comparison to bulls and goats], then, will the blood of Christ, who through the eternal Spirit *offered himself unblemished to God*, cleanse our consciences from acts that lead to death, so that we may serve the living God!' (my emphasis).

The accent of the superiority of Christ's sacrifice to those under the old order reaches its apogee in Hebrews 10:1–18. That superiority is articulated in three ways. Under the old order animal sacrifices were offered; under the new order Christ's own body was the offering. Under the old order an earthly setting was the location for sacrifice. Under the new it is the heavens. Under the old order sacrifices were daily affairs. Under the new only one affair – that of Christ offered

---

22 Lane 2002, comment on Heb. 7:26.

once for all time.[23] What is of striking interest is the writer's use of Psalm 40:6–8a in Hebrews 10:5–7:

Therefore, when Christ came into the world, he said:

'Sacrifice and offering you did not desire,
  but a body you prepared for me;
with burnt offerings and sin offerings
  you were not pleased.
Then I said, "Here I am – it is written about me in the scroll –
  I have come to do your will, my God."'

As Guthrie rightly argues, 'The use of kosmos ("world"), along with the context, suggests here that the incarnation is in mind.'[24] The writer of Hebrews then draws out the theological implications of Christ's coming into the created order. Christ came into the world to do away with the old order and to bring in a new one. A new covenant has come (Heb. 10:15–16). It took the sacrifice of himself to do so and what he did was definitive and final (v. 12, *eis to diēnekes*, 'for ever', 'uninterrupted'). Hence, having offered himself, 'he sat down at the right hand of God' (v. 12) and as per verse 13 fulfilled Psalm 110:1: 'waiting from that time until his enemies should be made a footstool for his feet' (ESV).

Paul too draws attention to the substitutionary nature of Christ's saving work.[25] Two texts for 2 Corinthians are of special importance here. We shall treat them in reverse order to their appearance in the letter and bring them into conversation with one another. The first is 2 Corinthians 8:9, 'For you know the grace of our Lord Jesus Christ, that though he was rich, yet for your sake he became poor, so that you through his poverty might become rich.' This wonderful Christology is posited by Paul for a very practical reason. He wants to motivate the Corinthians to give to the Jerusalem project: a collection from the Pauline churches to be taken to Jerusalem. The Macedonians

---

[23] G. H. Guthrie 2007: 975. I am indebted to Guthrie for the substance of this paragraph.

[24] Ibid. 977.

[25] The language of substitution used with reference to Christ's work is highly controversial, especially if the atonement is in view and penal substitution is being claimed. However, in my view, much of the debate is bedevilled by a category mistake. Sin is compared to crime. How can the innocent suffer for the guilty. But sin is a religious category. In the divine court it is the judge who is the offended party, not some impersonal law that a judge who has not been offended is to administer impartially. For an example of this category mistake see Crisp (2008: 208–227), who makes over a dozen references to 'crime' in his discussion of the logic of penal substitution.

have given generously to provide for the needs of the Jerusalem saints, but what of the Corinthians? Will they be generous too? If they act with Christlike generosity, they will be indeed.

In 2 Corinthians 8:9 Paul presents the great stooping as an 'incarnational event'.[26] Colin G. Kruse captures it well: 'It is most likely that what Paul had in mind was the whole drama of redemption, especially the incarnation.' Grace does what it does not have to do: give up the riches of heaven for our sakes. This is the nature of the divine largesse. But grace does not end the story there. The coming and cross of Christ – both incarnation and atonement are in view most probably – enrich us. This is one of the purposes of Christ's incarnation. What are these riches? To quote an earlier phrase from St Paul, they are 'an eternal weight of glory' (2 Cor. 4:17 ESV).

If both Jesus' coming and the cross are in view in 2 Corinthians 8:9, then Paul's powerful claim in 2 Corinthians 5:21, our second text, provides a lens through which to view just how 'poor' Christ was willing to become for our sakes: 'God made him who had no sin to be sin for us, so that in him we might become the righteousness of God.'[27] According to A. M. Hunter, in 2 Corinthians 5:21 'Paul declares that the crucified Christ, on our behalf, took the whole reality of sin upon himself, like the scapegoat: "For our sake [*hyper hēmōn*, 'on behalf of us'] he made him to be sin who knew no sin, so that in him we might become the righteousness of God."'[28] Our sin was exchanged for his righteousness. Hunter goes on to say, 'We are not fond nowadays of calling Christ's suffering "penal" or of styling him our "substitute"; but can we avoid using some such words as these to express Paul's view of the atonement?'[29]

---

[26] The phrase 'incarnational event' I owe to R. P. Martin 2002, comment on 2 Cor. 8:9.

[27] Bringing 2 Cor. 8:9 and 5:21 into conversation presupposes the integrity of 2 Cor. 1 – 9. I follow Carson and Moo 2005: 442 here. For the various arguments about the composition of 2 Corinthians see ibid. 429–442.

[28] Quoted in Cole 2009b: 139.

[29] Ibid. 140. Scholars do indeed attempt to avoid the language of substitution. For example, Margaret MacDonald (2001: 1141): 'The reference to the one who knew no sin having been made sin (v. 21) may refer to the sinless Christ taking on sin as a burden or being treated as a sinner for the sake of humanity (Gal. 3:13); sin may also refer to sin-offering here (Rom. 8:3; cf. Isa. 53:4–10).' This is too tepid given Gal. 3:13, where the language of substitution is strongly present: 'Christ redeemed us from the curse of the law by becoming a curse for us [*hyper hēmōn katara*, 'on behalf of us a curse'], for it is written: "Cursed is everyone who is hung on a pole."' N. T. Wright (in McCormack 2006: 252–253) provides another example. He argues that Paul is not talking soteriologically but vocationally. Paul becomes in Christ an embodiment of the righteousness or covenant faithfulness of God in his apostolic ministry of preaching reconciliation. This is far too subtle to be plausible in context.

To defeat the evil one

As we saw in an earlier chapter, in the biblical story of origins evil enters the human sphere through the serpent later identified in the canon of Scripture as the devil, the evil one (cf. Gen. 3:1 and Rev. 20:2). We also read of a promise made that the serpent will be overcome by the male seed of a woman:

> And I will put enmity
> between you and the woman,
> and between your offspring and hers;
> he will crush your head,
> and you will strike his heel.
>
> (Gen. 3:15)

However, for many Westerners to speak of the evil one is to enter the realm of fantasy. Modern materialism has banished the world of spirits. So much for the biblical view of what is real. Surprisingly spirits are fine for entertainment. Horror films and supernaturalistic television series have large followings. Significantly many Christians in the West are not immune from this Zeitgeist. Notional belief in the devil and his demons remains, but for all practical purposes life is lived as though there are only two realms of persons: God and us. One important contribution of the Pentecostal movement is to take the kingdom of darkness and spiritual warfare seriously.[30] Here is an area where Western Christians can learn from other believers in the majority world.

Christian anthropologist and missiologist Paul Hiebert especially drew attention to the need for the West to learn from other parts of the world. He describes his own experience in India in these terms:

> The reason for my uneasiness with the biblical and Indian worldviews should be clear: I had excluded the middle level of supernatural this-worldly beings and forces from my own worldview. As a scientist I had been trained to deal with the empirical world in naturalistic terms. As a theologian I was taught to answer ultimate questions in theistic terms. For me the middle zone did

---

[30] Tennent (2007: 179) writes of the expectations of Pentecostals concerning the Holy Spirit's present-day activity, including the Spirit's 'demonic deliverance of evil'. His ground-breaking study of systematic theology in dialogue with various world religions would have been enhanced if a whole chapter had been devoted to the subject of the devil and the demonic in, for example, Africa.

not really exist. Unlike Indian villagers, I had given little thought to spirits of this world, to local ancestors and ghosts, or to the souls of animals. For me these belonged to the realm of fairies, trolls, and other mythical beings.[31]

Hiebert describes the truncated universe that many a Western Christian lives in as 'the flaw of the excluded middle'.[32] The middle level of unseen spirits has been excluded.

Jesus did not embrace the flaw of the excluded middle. He had no difficulty in recognizing that evil cannot be reduced to the bad behavior of humankind. There is an enemy of God and humanity. In the parable of the weeds in Matthew 13:24–30 he speaks of an enemy who sows weeds among the wheat, and in his explanation in verses 36–43 identifies the enemy as 'the evil one', 'the devil' (esp. Matt. 13:38–39). In Mark's Gospel in response to a criticism that his power came from the dark side Jesus argued in classic *reductio ad absurdum* terms (Mark 3:23–27):

So Jesus called them over to him and began to speak to them in parables: 'How can Satan drive out Satan? If a kingdom is divided against itself, that kingdom cannot stand. If a house is divided against itself, that house cannot stand. And if Satan opposes himself and is divided, he cannot stand; his end has come. In fact, no one can enter a strong man's house without first tying him up. Then he can plunder the strong man's house.'

Thus he compared the devil to a strong man. Before a strong man can be despoiled he needs to be bound. Jesus saw his work in exorcism in those terms. He was despoiling the strong man by liberating those possessed from Satan's grip.[33]

The question though is whether any of the New Testament writers saw this combat against the devil as a rationale for the incarnation. Two important passages from two different New Testament writers come into view in answer to the question. The first is found in Hebrews 2:14–15: 'Since the children have flesh and blood, he too shared in

---

[31] Hiebert 1994: 196.

[32] Ibid. 189.

[33] In recent years it has become increasingly popular to present Jesus as committed to non-violence. Hence we see the rise of non-violent theories of the atonement; e.g. see Sanders 2006. However, how do Jesus' exorcisms fit into this picture of Jesus? Once more 'the flaw of the excluded middle' appears to be at work.

their humanity so that [with this purpose in mind: *hina* of purpose] by his death he might break the power [*katargeō*, 'to render inoperative or ineffective'] of him who holds the power of death – that is, the devil – and free those who all their lives were held in slavery by their fear of death.' The devil's power lies in the very human fear of death. But to quote the title of John Owen's famous Puritan work, the cross represents 'The Death of Death in the Death of Christ'. How the devil exercises his power is not explained but simply stated.[34] What is clear though is that in sharing our humanity Christ enters the sphere of the devil's rule and through his own death deprives the devil of his power.[35] George H. Guthrie comments, 'Since death was the prescription for victory in this case, the only way the Son could accomplish the needed task was to die, and the only way to die was to become human. This is, for our author, the logic of the Incarnation.'[36] Jesus thus comes before the reader in Hebrews 2:14–15 as humanity's champion who does battle on our behalf.[37]

The second text is found in the Johannine literature. There were those in the orbit of the first readers who were denying that a real incarnation had taken place. John would have none of it. In 1 John 3:7–8 we read, 'Dear children, do not let anyone lead you astray. The one who does what is right is righteous, just as he is righteous. The one who does what is sinful is of the devil, because the devil has been sinning from the beginning. The reason the Son of God appeared was to destroy the devil's work.' Stephen S. Smalley has it right when he comments:

> The aorist passive *ephanerōthē* (literally, 'he was manifested') indicates that . . . John is referring here to the Incarnation of Jesus in time and space. It was a *real* appearing, in history, with a specific

---

[34] Peterson 1994, comment on Heb. 2:14–15, offers an explanation in the light of the wider argument of Hebrews: 'We can only be released from Satan's power and freed to serve God by the forgiveness or cleansing made possible by Jesus' death (*cf.* 9:14–15, 27–28; 10:19–22). He removes the threat of judgment and condemnation for those who trust in him and gives the assurance of life in the world to come.'

[35] *Kratos* is translated as 'power' in Heb. 2:14 (NIV) but may also be rendered as 'rule'.

[36] G. H. Guthrie 1998: 110. D. Guthrie (1983: 96) argues, 'It is worth noting that in the Greek text the order is *blood and flesh*. It has been suggested that "blood" alludes to Christ's shedding of blood, which is then given as the reason for his becoming flesh, i.e. the atonement required the incarnation' (original emphasis). This is indeed suggestive but difficult to ground in the text.

[37] A point well made and developed by Lane 2002, comment on Heb. 2:14–15, in the light of the Old Testament presentation of God as warrior and intertestamental literature as well as Greek literature.

and salvific purpose in mind (in saying this, John is perhaps mindful of those heretics who were ready to claim that the Incarnation was merely an illusion).[38]

As for purpose, again Smalley's comments are helpful: 'John is thus saying here that the coming of Jesus, in flesh and blood, was concerned with unpicking the net of evil in which the devil has always attempted to trap human beings.'[39]

Given the testimonies of Hebrews 2:14–15 and 1 John 3:7–8 Calvin rightly sums up the nexus between the incarnation, the atonement and the Christus Victor theme in his famous *Institutes*:

> In short, since neither as God alone could he feel death, nor as man alone could he overcome it, *he coupled human nature with divine* that to atone for sin he might submit the weakness of the one to death; and that, wrestling with death by the power of the other nature, *he might win victory for us*. . . . But we should especially espouse what I have just explained: our common nature with Christ is the pledge of our fellowship with the Son of God; *and clothed with our flesh he vanquished death and sin together that the victory and triumph might be ours.*[40]

No incarnation, no atonement; but also no atonement, no victory over the evil one.

To model true humanity

In the New Testament the Old Testament concept of walking in the ways of Yahweh becomes walking in the ways of the Christ. As 1 John 2:6 says, 'Whoever claims to live in him must live as [*opheilei kathōs ekeinos periepatēsen*, 'ought to walk as that one'] Jesus did.'[41] In other words the *imitatio Dei* of the older revelation becomes overwhelmingly the *imitatio Christi* of the new one. Not that the *imitatio Dei* is missing from the New Testament, but generally the accent falls elsewhere. For example, 1 Peter has both ideas. In 1 Peter 1:15–16 the readers are exhorted to be holy as God is holy (cf. Lev. 19:2). Even so, when Peter

---

[38] Smalley 2002, comment on 1 John 3:8, original emphasis.
[39] Ibid.
[40] Calvin 2002b: 2.12.3, my emphases.
[41] I prefer the ESV here: 'whoever says he abides in him ought to walk in the same way in which he walked'. This preserves a fundamental idea in Jewish ethics, namely the walking in the ways of God.

addresses the matter of Christian slaves abused by their masters he appeals to the model Christ provided. Indeed in 1 Peter 2:21 the idea of walking in Christ's footsteps is made quite explicit: 'To this you were called, because Christ suffered for you, leaving you an example, that you should follow in his steps.'

The question though is not whether the New Testament writers exhort readers to be like Christ. They do. The issue is whether the New Testament explicitly states that a rationale for the incarnation was to provide an ethical model. Thomas Oden certainly thinks so in arguing that one of the purposes of the incarnation was '*To offer a pattern of the fullness of human life.*'[42] He brackets 1 Peter 2:21 and 1 John 2:6 as proof texts for his contention. Perhaps it would be more accurate to argue that both 1 Peter and 1 John draw a moral application out of the facts of the incarnate Son's life.

There is, however, a famous Pauline text that brings the incarnation to the fore and applies it to Christian behaviour. In Philippians 2:5–11 we find one of the richest Christological passages in all the New Testament and worth quoting in full:

> In your relationships with one another, have the same mindset as Christ Jesus:
>
> Who, being in very nature God,
>   did not consider equality with God something
>   to be used to his own advantage;
> rather, he made himself nothing [*ekenōsen*, lit. 'emptied'],
>   by taking the very nature of a servant [*doulos*, lit. 'slave'],
>   being made in human likeness.
> And being found in appearance as a man,
>   he humbled himself
>   by becoming obedient to death –
>   even death on a cross!
>
> Therefore God exalted him to the highest place
>   and gave him the name that is above every name,
> that at the name of Jesus every knee should bow,
>   in heaven and on earth and under the earth,
> and every tongue acknowledge that Jesus Christ is Lord,
>   to the glory of God the Father.

---

[42] Oden 1992: 271, original emphasis.

In this magnificent hymnic passage (vv. 6–11) Paul articulates the journey of Christ on our behalf from eternity into time and back to eternity.[43] In classic terms here are the two states of Christ: the state of humiliation (vv. 6–8, esp. the descent) and the state of glory (vv. 9–11, esp. the ascent).[44]

Paul's point is a pastoral one. There are problems at Philippi: 'Therefore if you have any encouragement from being united with Christ, if any comfort from his love, if any common sharing in the Spirit, if any tenderness and compassion, then make my joy complete by being like-minded, having the same love, being one in spirit and of one mind' (Phil. 2:1–2). Unity is needed. Perhaps Philippians 4:2–3 illustrates the problem: 'I plead with Euodia and I plead with Syntyche to be of the same mind in the Lord. Yes, and I ask you, my true companion, help these women since they have contended at my side in the cause of the gospel, along with Clement and the rest of my co-workers, whose names are in the book of life.' Understandably then Paul seeks a change in the Philippians' attitudes: 'Do nothing out of selfish ambition or vain conceit. Rather, in humility value others above yourselves, not looking to your own interests but each of you to the interests of the others' (Phil. 2:3–4). Informed by Christ's great

[43] There is much debate over whether Phil. 2:6–11 is a hymn. P. T. O'Brien argues yes, but G. D. Fee argues no. For a discussion of the debate see Carson and Moo 2005: 499–503, esp. 499, n. 1, which refers to O'Brien's and Fee's different stances. For a useful treatment of Phil. 2:6–11 in the context of other New Testament hymns, hymn fragments, songs and spiritual songs see Martin 2001. The journey metaphor I employ reflects the stimulating work of B. N. Fisk, who shows the illuminating parallels between early Greek novels with their V-shaped plot structure (high status gives way to humiliation before triumph and ultimate exaltation) and that of the Philippian hymn. He argues that the V-shaped plot pattern may have resonated with Paul's first readers, not that Paul was dependent upon such novels. See Fisk in C. S. Evans 2006: 45–73.

[44] The fact that the text speaks of Christ's emptying himself to enter the state of humiliation has spawned a whole school of Christological thought (kenotic Christologies). For a recent exploration see C. S. Evans 2006. Evans (4) explains the kenotic Christology of Phil. 2:6–11 in these terms: 'The Greek verb employed here, "kenoo", meaning to "empty oneself", inspired these theologians [kenoticists] to consider the idea that, in becoming a human being, God the Son in some way limited or temporarily divested himself of some of the properties thought to be divine prerogatives, and this act of self-emptying has become known as "kenosis".' Suffice it to say that much doctrinal and metaphysical speculation appears to have been built on a single word (v. 7, *ekenōsen*, 'emptied'). Gordon Fee would dispute this in ibid., ch. 2, where he argues that Hebrews and the Synoptic Gospels provide further evidence for the kenotic theory. One claim, however, that can safely be made in the light of John 17:5 is that the Christ for our sakes emptied himself of the glory [*doxa*] to which he was entitled: 'And now, Father, glorify me in your presence with the glory I had with you before the world began.' According to S. T. Davis and C. S. Evans (ibid. 314) this would make the writer 'a kenoticist in at least a limited sense'.

stooping, both in incarnation and atonement, the believer is to be like-minded: that is to say, humble and other-person centred (Phil. 2:5).[45] Paul illustrates what he means by way of a reference to his associate in ministry, Timothy. In Philippians 2:20–21 he refers to his co-worker Timothy, who exhibits the very Christlike mindset and practice that he is commending to the Philippians. He writes of Timothy, 'I have no one else like him, who will show genuine concern for your welfare. For everyone looks out for their own interests, not those of Jesus Christ.' Paul contrasts Timothy as someone 'who will genuinely care for the things concerning you [*ta peri hymōn*]' with those who 'seek the things of themselves' [*ta heautōn*]' (my tr.). Paul appears to be picking up the language of verse 4. Timothy is a true servant shaped by the example of Christ.

The timing of the incarnation: insight from Thomas Aquinas

For some Protestants the very mention of Thomas Aquinas creates anxiety. However, this medieval theologian beloved by so many Roman Catholic thinkers is one of the pre-eminent minds of the Christian tradition along with Augustine, Calvin and Barth. To say this is not to say that our critical faculties are to be suspended at the mere mention of the name. Rather it is to be open to learn as well as to critique. As the saying goes, 'Have many teachers [Aquinas would be one, Calvin another] but only one master [Christ].'

Aquinas turned his considerable intelligence to the matter of the timing of the incarnation. Paul A. Glenn accurately captures Aquinas's reasoning in this paraphrase:

> The time of the Incarnation was most suitable. Had God become man to redeem us immediately after the first sin was committed, human pride would not have been humbled in consequence of that sin; man would not have realized, through an impressive stretch of time, the greatness of the treasure he had lost. And it was good for

---

[45] Some scholars argue that Paul has an Adam–Christ contrast in mind and that the incarnation per se is not in view in the passage. For example, see Hooker (2002: 504–505) who contends that 'The use of Adamic imagery elsewhere encourages us to suppose that it underlies Philippians 2–3, where we have similar ideas of Christ's becoming human, with the result that men and women become what he is.' For a fine discussion of the scholarly possibilities and also his defence of the more traditional incarnational view see R. Murray 2001: 1184–1186; see also G. D. Fee in C. S. Evans 2006: 30–35 for a convincing exegesis of the text and an able counter to the Adam–Christ thesis.

man to prepare, by prayerful longing, for the redemption; thus he would gain a keen awareness of the value of redemption; and of his need for it, so that, when it came, he would ardently take advantage of it. On the other hand, it would not do to have the Incarnation delayed, lest human longing turn to hopelessness and despairing disappointment. Therefore at exactly the right time, in the 'fullness of time,' as St. Paul says (Gal. 4:4), God became man.[46]

Aquinas's three reasons are clearly in view in this part of the *Summa Theologica*. If the incarnation had taken place too soon, then human pride would not have been challenged sufficiently. We would not have appreciated what was lost by the Fall. Additionally, to use Augustine's famous words, 'You have formed us for Yourself, and our hearts are restless till they find rest in You'.[47] Without the elapse of time would our hearts have grown sufficiently restless? Would we have appreciated redemption's cost and therefore its worth? On the other hand, however, if the incarnation were too long in coming, then despair would have triumphed. The divine timing then was exquisite.

Another question needed addressing in Aquinas's time: Why not delay the incarnation until the end of human history? Aquinas had an answer to that question too:

The perfection of glory to which human nature will finally be raised by the Word Incarnate will appear when souls and bodies are united again at the end of the world in the time of the general judgment. Yet it could not be fitting to have the Incarnation deferred to that moment. For man needed a remedy for sin, knowledge of God, reverence, good morals. And the Incarnation gave man these needed things: first, by hope and anticipation in those who lovingly awaited it, and then, by faith and devotion in those who actually experienced it in fact and in its fruits. None of these things would have come to man had the Incarnation been delayed to the end of the world. Hope and longing would have disappeared; the hearts of men would have grown cold.[48]

---

[46] Glenn 1963: 312. For the original see the *Summa Theologica* III.a, Q. 5. For the online version see Aquinas 2007.

[47] Augustine 2007b: 1.1.

[48] Glenn 1963: 312, Q. 6. Aquinas (2007) wrote, '**I answer that**, As it was not fitting that God should become incarnate at the beginning of the world, so also it was not fitting that the Incarnation should be put off till the end of the world' (original emphasis).

Once more the divine timing of the incarnation was just right, or, to use a term favoured by Aquinas, 'fitting'.[49] Belief in a sovereign God would expect no less.

Conclusion

As I write this conclusion the USA is in the grip of the presidential race. All over the country there are surrogates for the incumbent president and for the rival speaking on behalf of their respective leaders. Surrogates abound as do television ads. Some of the surrogates are former or presently serving politicians, some are business successes, some are entertainers. None by definition is the leader. The wonderful news of the gospel is that God did not send a mere revelatory spirit nor a mere prophetic surrogate but the Son himself (Mark 12:1–12). No other could reveal the Father as the Son could. No other could redeem alienated humanity as the Son could. No other could both represent and substitute for us as the Son could. No other could defeat the evil one as the Son could. No other could model all that Adam and Israel should have been as the sinless, ever obedient, ever trusting Son could. And he did!

Excursus: Did the divine Son assume fallen or unfallen human nature?

In classic Chalcedonian terms Jesus Christ is one Person who is truly God and truly human. With reference to Christ's humanity, Chalcedon affirms that he is 'of one substance with us as regards his manhood; like us in all respects, apart from sin'.[50] But what sort of humanity did he assume in this post-Fall world? Did he assume a fallen human nature as Karl Barth maintained or did he assume an unfallen human nature as Oliver Crisp argues?[51] And what is the dogmatic rank of the answer?

Crisp usefully distinguishes two kinds of temptation and two possible subjects of temptation when it comes to men and women.

---

[49] The concept of the fittingness of divine action to circumstance has solid New Testament grounding (see *prepon*, 'fitting'; see Matt. 3:15; Heb. 2:10 and esp. 7:26).

[50] For the Chalcedonian definition see Bettenson and Maunder 1999: 56. Macleod (1998: 221) suggests that to ascribe sinlessness to Christ means asserting that Christ 'was free of actual sin' and 'free from inherent sin'. For a useful discussion of Christ's sinlessness see B. Ware 2010: 9–17.

[51] For Barth's position see *CD* I/2: 155–159 and IV/1: 159, 234, 252. For Crisp's see Crisp 2009: 122–136.

One kind of temptation is external. The serpent comes from outside Eden. The other kind is internal. This temptation comes from the appetites of fallen flesh. One kind of subject of temptation is an innocent human being (e.g. Adam in Gen. 2). Another kind of subject is a sinful human being (e.g. the wretched person of Rom. 7).[52]

What then of Christ? Certainly Jesus experienced external temptation.[53] In Matthew 4:1 we read, 'Then Jesus was led by the Spirit into the wilderness to be tempted by the devil.' The tempter clearly comes from the outside in an attempt to tempt Jesus into deviating from the Father's will. However, there is no evidence in the Gospels that Jesus faced internal temptation. Internal turmoil, yes! The agony in Gethsemane makes that plain. In Luke 22:44 we find, 'And being in anguish [*agōnia*, lit. 'agony'], he prayed more earnestly, and his sweat was like drops of blood falling to the ground.' Even so, internal turmoil is not necessarily the product of temptation, as the Gethsemane account shows. Paul does ascribe to Christ 'the likeness of sinful flesh' (Rom. 8:3). Does this Pauline phrase suggest that Christ possessed a fallen human nature? N. T. Wright argues that such a question is beside the point:

> To debate whether Jesus' humanity was therefore 'sinful humanity' or 'sinless humanity,' whether 'fallen' or 'unfallen,' seems to me beside the point. What matters is that it was genuine humanity, not a sham (cf. Phil 2:7), where . . . [*en homoiōmati anthrōpōn*, 'in the likeness of humans'] does not mean 'like a human being, but not actually one,' but rather 'a true human being, bearing the true likeness.' Jesus could and did suffer and die, truly and really; he was in principle capable of sinning, but unlike all other humans did not. It was God's design that, in his truly human death, sentence would be meted out on sin once for all.[54]

J. D. G. Dunn adds, 'Hence whatever the precise force of the *homoiōmati* [likeness] it must include the thought of Jesus' complete

[52] For the substance of this paragraph I am drawing on Crisp 2009: 122–136.

[53] The question might be raised as to whether Jesus' experience of hunger and tiredness point towards his assuming a fallen human nature. However, there is no reason to think that hunger is a post-Fall phenomenon only. In the Garden why would the first couple eat unless hungry? Hunger is not necessarily starvation. As for tiredness, there is a tiredness that is pathological, but there is also a tiredness that simply indicates the need for rest. Indeed even outside Eden there is a tiredness that is pleasant when it comes with the satisfaction of a job achieved.

[54] N. T. Wright 2002b: 578.

identification with "sinful flesh" (cf. NJB: "the same human nature as any sinner").'[55] Calvin understands the phrase differently: 'But he says, that he came in the likeness of the flesh of sin; for though the flesh of Christ was polluted by no stains, yet it seemed apparently to be sinful, inasmuch as it sustained the punishment due to our sins, and doubtless death exercised all its power over it as though it was subject to itself.'[56] Calvin seems in no doubt that Christ's human flesh was unfallen. In no doubt also is W. J. Dumbrell who comments, 'Greek *homoiōma* (likeness) is chosen to further understand that, though Jesus shared fully with humanity, he did not share sinful humanity.'[57] Dumbrell makes the important point that '"Flesh" here is not a physical term but the this-worldly orientation shared by all as a result of the Fall, hence its character as a force.'[58] If so, then Wright is correct to maintain that to argue from this verse (Rom. 8:3) whether Christ's human nature was fallen or unfallen is beside the point. A different approach is needed that takes into account wider considerations.

Given the way Paul in his letter to the Romans appeals to Adam as a type of the one to come and Christ as the antitype that corresponds to Adam, it is important to reflect theologically on the features of the correspondence between them.[59] Regarding human nature, both came to be in this world without a human father. In T. V. Morris's categories Adam and Christ are essentially human but not commonly human.[60] Commonly human beings are the result of a union of a male and female. Both Adam and Christ are in their own ways the first of a race of creatures. Adam comes before us as the head of the old creation of humankind. Christ in contrast is the head of the new creation of humankind. Furthermore, both Adam and Christ were innocent when facing the tempter. (Adam fell. Christ did not.) Christ was therefore tempted not internally but externally like Adam. Given these correspondences it seems more likely that Christ assumed unfallen human nature. In other words, as Crisp rightly contends Christ was impeccable (not liable to sin) and not merely

---

[55] Dunn 2004, comment on Rom. 8:3.

[56] Calvin 2002c, comment on Rom. 8:3.

[57] Dumbrell 2005: 85.

[58] Ibid.

[59] Rom. 5:14 is the key text: 'Nevertheless, death reigned from the time of Adam to the time of Moses, even over those who did not sin by breaking a command, as did Adam, who is a pattern of the one to come [*typos tou mellontos*, 'a type of the one coming'].'

[60] T. V. Morris 2001.

sinless.[61] Even so, Barth is right to maintain, 'True, the Word assumes our human existence, assumes flesh, i.e., He exists in the state and position, amid the conditions, under the curse and punishment of sinful man.'[62] Christ did not become incarnate in some unreal unfallen creation, but in this actual fallen one. Even so, it does not follow that the human nature he assumed was a fallen one.[63]

What I argued in an earlier excursus, on the question whether Christ would have come if there had been no Fall, applies here as well. In terms of dogmatic rank both the question and my answer are speculative. However, Gunton is worth quoting once more, 'Hypothetical questions are dangerous in theology, because it [theology] is concerned with what God has done, not what he might have done instead. But in this case the question enables us to bring out the point of what has happened.'[64]

---

[61] Crisp 2009: 136.

[62] Barth, *CD* I/2: 155.

[63] For a useful discussion of the theological entailments of embracing either the unfallen or the fallen human nature view see Macleod 1998: 221–230. He sees real strengths in Edward Irving's, Karl Barth's, Thomas Torrance's and James Torrance's arguments for the assumption of fallen human nature by the Son of God. However, in my view he rightly points out the even greater weaknesses in them and so advocates the classical unfallen human nature position. In particular he points out the difficulties in distinguishing the idea of Christ's assuming fallen human nature and that of Christ's assuming sinful human nature. He also addresses the legitimacy of the use of the principle enunciated by Gregory Nazianzen, by pointing to the original context in which the principle was proposed in contradistinction to the contemporary debate about unfallen versus fallen human nature, that the unassumed cannot be healed. For a contrary view see Torrance 2008: 61–65 and Gunton 2002: 67–68, 101.

[64] Gunton 2002: 67.

Chapter Six

The significance of
the incarnation

This study thus far has yielded conclusions that are classically patristic. In terms of the Nicene Creed of AD 325, the Son of God came down from heaven to save us. In terms of the ancient hymn the *Te Deum* (fourth century AD), in so doing the Son of God overcame the sting of death and opened the kingdom of heaven to all believers. In terms of the famous Chalcedonian definition of AD 451, Jesus Christ the incarnate Son of God is one Person in two natures, truly God and truly human. The task now is to consider the question 'So what?' Or, put another way, what is the significance of the incarnation? Theologically considered, just how important is the incarnation? As we shall see, that significance is manifold but for the purposes of this discussion I shall divide significance into two kinds: theological and existential. I make no pretence to being exhaustive in so doing.

Theological significance

The theological significance of the incarnation will be explored in terms of its methodological implications for the doing of theology, its import for the question of God and change, for its affirmation of the value of creation, for the valuing of human life, for our understanding of mission, for its importance in the Christian's encounter with other religions in the world, for theodicy and defence in the face of evil, and for matters of the dogmatic ranking of doctrines.

For theological method

Paul G. Hiebert maintains that there are three types of theology. Systematic theology examines 'the fundamental categories of and structures implicit in Scripture' in a synchronic way.[1] Biblical theology reads Scripture diachronically with sensitivity to its storyline as it unfolds in space and time. Narrative is to the fore. He then suggests a

---

[1] Hiebert 2000: 242.

third kind of theology, which he calls 'missiological theology'. This form of theology asks, 'What does God's Word say to humans in this particular situation?'[2] Others might call this 'applied theology'. Whether the theology in view is systematic theology or biblical theology or missiological theology so called, theology cannot be done as though we do not live on a visited planet.[3] In other words we ought not to do Christian theology as though Christ had never come.

Karl Barth draws out the methodological implications of Christ's coming for theological thought in the following terms:

> We must realize that the Christian message does not at its heart express a concept or an idea, nor does it recount an anonymous history to be taken as truth and reality only in concepts and ideas. Certainly the history is inclusive, i.e. it is the one which includes in itself the whole event of 'God with us' and to that extent the history of all those to whom 'God with us' applies. But it recounts this history and speaks of its inclusive power and significance in such a way that it declares a name, binding the history indissolubly to this name and presenting it as the story of this name. *This means that all the concepts and ideas used in this report (God, man, world, eternity, time, even salvation, grace, transgression, atonement and any others) can derive their significance only from the bearer of this name and from His history, and not the reverse.* They cannot have any independent importance or role based on a quite different prior interpretation. They cannot say what has to be said with some meaning of their own or in some context of their own abstracted from this name. They can only serve to describe this name – the name of Jesus Christ.[4]

Barth is stating an important principle in the theological methodological realm that St Peter expressed in the soteriological one. Peter preached, 'And there is salvation in no one else, for there is no other

---

[2] Ibid. 244.

[3] The term 'visited planet' I have taken from the short story written by J. B. Phillips (n.d.). The idea of visitation has solid biblical roots. In Luke 19:42–44 Jesus laments over Jerusalem, 'Would that you, even you, had known on this day the things that make for peace! But now they are hidden from your eyes. For the days will come upon you, when your enemies will set up a barricade round you and surround you and hem you in on every side and tear you down to the ground, you and your children within you. And they will not leave one stone upon another in you, because you did not know the time of your visitation [*episkopē*]' (ESV).

[4] Barth, CD IV/1: 16–17, my emphasis. If Barth had included Scripture in his list, then he might have developed a more robust doctrine of inspiration than he actually did.

name under heaven given among men [*anthrōpoi* includes both males and females] by which we must [*dei*, 'of necessity'] be saved' (Acts 4:12 ESV). In both cases there is in a pluralistic culture an unavoidable scandal in attaching so much methodologically, soteriologically and, I would add, epistemologically to that Name with its sufficiency, supremacy and finality. The scandal of particularity remains.

In a nutshell, as Barth realized, we cannot do theology as though Christ has not come in the flesh.

For the doctrine of God and change

If we indeed live on a visited planet, then did that event change God, and if so in what ways? After all, John 1:14 claims that the Word (*logos*) became (*egeneto*) something other than the Word, namely flesh (*sarx*).

There are several logical possibilities here. One is that the incarnation changed the very being of God. This seems to be an implication of kenoticist Christologies that argue that either the Son of God divested himself of his omnipotence, omniscience and omnipresence in becoming incarnate (e.g. Gottfried Thomasius) or put them into abeyance.[5] For the most radical kenoticist of them all, Thomas J. J. Altizer, in becoming incarnate God ceased to be God and thus the death on the cross was the death of God. He writes, 'The radical Christian proclaims that God has actually died in Christ, that this death is both a historical and a cosmic event, and, as such, it is a final and irrevocable event, which cannot be reversed by a subsequent religious or cosmic movement.'[6] If that were so, it is utterly mystifying why a New Testament was ever written predicated as it is on the assumption of a living God. Taking another tack, perhaps God's being per se was not changed by the incarnation. Rather God's character has been changed by a matter of degree. God is now more loving and more compassionate because of the experience of incarnation. However, the fact that the divine love and compassion are more in view in the incarnate Son of God may be better understood as an epistemological claim, not an ontological one. Is there a better answer?

The better answer is the classical one. As in the Athanasian Creed (sixth century) the incarnation is claiming 'not the conversion of Godhead into flesh, but the assumption of manhood into God' (Lat. *non conversione divinitatis in carnem, sed assumptione humanitatis in*

---

[5] Thomasius (1802–75) was the most eminent of the nineteenth-century kenoticists. See the useful discussion of his view in Thompson 2006: 78–85.

[6] Altizer n.d.

THE GOD WHO BECAME HUMAN

Deum). That is to say, the Trinity now relates to itself qua Trinity in a new way through the humanity of Christ. As Bruce Milne rightly argues, we are not talking about the triune Godhead and minus regarding the incarnation. As he states it, 'At a theological level kenosis appears to move in the wrong direction. Its basic equation is: incarnation = God minus. The biblical equation is rather: incarnation = God plus.'[7] The plus is the new way the Father, Son and Holy Spirit relate through the assumed humanity of the Son. Rather we are speaking of the Trinity and plus. The change is relational and permanent.[8]

For the affirmation of the created order

Archbishop of Canterbury William Temple famously said that Christianity is the most materialistic of all religions.[9] Clearly he wasn't suggesting that here is a faith interested only in materialistic pursuits. Rather his point was that Christianity affirms the material order. The Creator created matter. Indeed the world to come of Scripture and the classic creeds does not leave matter behind.

As Jason Byassee argues, 'Grace does not destroy nature, nor does it leave it alone, but transfigures it.'[10] Romans 8:19–22 is eloquent testimony to this prospect. Creation has a future:

> For the creation waits in eager expectation for the children of God to be revealed. For the creation was subjected to frustration, not by its own choice, but by the will of the one who subjected it, in hope that the creation itself will be liberated from its bondage to decay and brought into the freedom and glory of the children of God.
>
> We know that the whole creation has been groaning as in the pains of childbirth right up to the present time.

---

[7] Milne 2009: 200.

[8] Contra Marcellus of Ancyra (c. AD 280–374) who thought that in salvation history we see an extrapolation from the Godhead in the coming of the Son and further extrapolation from the Godhead in the coming of the Holy Spirit. However, at the denouement of all things these extrapolations were returned to the Godhead and thus God returns to oneness. This is how he understood 1 Cor. 15:28: 'When he [Jesus] has done this [put down all opposition to the divine rule], then the Son himself will be made subject to him who put everything under him, so that God may be all in all.' See Pelikan 1971: 207–209. The Niceno-Constantinopolitan Creed of AD 381 includes the phrase 'and his kingdom will have no end' to exclude Marcellianism.

[9] Quoted in Harkness 1961. She writes that Temple concludes, 'Christianity is the most "materialistic" of all religions because, though it subordinates matter to spirit, it finds sacredness in everything God has made.'

[10] Byassee 2007: 127.

Paul personifies creation under the figure of a pregnant woman about to give birth. Creation's destiny is intertwined with that of God's children. The Christian hope is not for the individual alone but has cosmic implications. As for the individual, our material bodies likewise have a future, according to Paul in verses 23–24: 'Not only so, but we ourselves, who have the firstfruits of the Spirit, groan inwardly as we wait eagerly for our adoption to sonship, the redemption of our bodies. For in this hope we were saved.' Paul adds to the picture in his Philippians letter. He sees the incarnate Son of God's own glorified body as the paradigmatic prospect for the believer: 'But our citizenship is in heaven. And we eagerly await a Saviour from there, the Lord Jesus Christ, who, by the power that enables him to bring everything under his control, will transform our lowly bodies so that they will be like his glorious body' (Phil. 3:20–21).

However, some in the early church period had difficulty embracing the affirmation of flesh, as 1 John 4:1–3 shows:

> Dear friends, do not believe every spirit, but test the spirits to see whether they are from God, because many false prophets have gone out into the world. This is how you can recognize the Spirit of God: every spirit that acknowledges that Jesus Christ has come in the flesh is from God, but every spirit that does not acknowledge Jesus is not from God. This is the spirit of the antichrist, which you have heard is coming and even now is already in the world.[11]

John is opposing a Christology that finds a real incarnation difficult to entertain. Jesus Christ may not have been rejected but the idea of his enfleshment, as in John 1:14, is rejected.

The erroneous view that John is contesting seems to be a precursor to the full-blown Docetist ones of the next century that are associated with Gnosticism.[12] John Macquarrie writes of the challenge that a robust doctrine of creation and incarnation posed to some of the

---

[11] This Johannine text contains many important ideas. Theological claims need to be tested (*dokimazein*). The nature of one's Christology constitutes a key test. The incarnation is a facet of Christology that serves as a theological criterion.

[12] There is debate as to whether 1 John 4 addresses full-blown Docetism; hence I have used the language of 'precursor'. For a judicious discussion of the debate see Carson and Moo 2005: 677–682. Carson and Moo conclude that John is dealing with some form of 'proto-Gnosticism'. Carson and Moo (678) in discussing Gnosticism describe it as 'theosophical potpourri . . . anchored in neoplatonic dualism'. Neoplatonism came to the fore in the third century AD with Plotinus, who died in 270. Middle Platonism, which came earlier than Plotinus, is a better candidate in my view.

religious thinkers in the early church period. He states the threat in these terms:

> Thus very early in Christian history the Church was threatened by the rise of various Gnostic and docetic sects. Sometimes these denied that the creation is the work of God and assigned it to demons; or in the case of Marcion, it was even claimed that the god of the Hebrew Scriptures is himself a demonic power. Likewise, the doctrine of the incarnation was explained away as mere appearance.[13]

What provoked such responses to Christian claims? Mark A. Noll captures the conceptual challenge of incarnation to the Docetist in particular in these arresting words:

> [I]t is obvious that early Christian writers were making unusually bold claims about the person and work of Jesus Christ. He appears on earth and appears to be human, but he is also said to possess – and to bestow – the glory of the one true God. Mysteries, conundrums, paradoxes and apparent contradictions abound . . . How could an apparently ordinary human born to an apparently ordinary Galilean woman be said to partake of what the one true God enjoyed as his sole prerogative? If Jesus somehow did embody the divine glory, why was it recorded that he seemed to lack the prerogatives of deity – that he needed to eat and drink, that he became weary, that he professed not to know everything, and (most counterintuitively) that he could die? But maybe, if testimonies about the glory of God in Christ were true, then the reports of human limitations were deceptive and Jesus never *really* experienced human weaknesses he only *seemed* to experience.[14]

Noll's last sentence captures the essence of ancient Docetism. Jesus only seemed (*dokein*, 'to appear') human.

How does the incarnation then affirm the material order? The Word really did become flesh. As Michael Williams states:

> John 1:14 does not say that the Word became *nous* [mind]. It says that the Word became *sarx* [flesh] – the bodily stuff of God's good

---

[13] Macquarrie 1996: 30.
[14] Noll 2011: 7, original emphases. Noll does not state that he is addressing Docetism per se in these words, but they are eminently applicable to that view.

creation. The Word became flesh not in some abstract realm of truth where only minds exist, but in history. . . . Dwelling among us, he was seen by flesh and blood, a particular human being. Pretty material stuff. Pretty historical. Glorious.[15]

John in his letter adds his own testimony (1 John 1:1): 'That which was from the beginning, which we have heard, which we have seen with our eyes, which we have looked at and our hands have touched – this we proclaim concerning the Word of life.' And the Word made flesh, Jesus Christ, remains flesh albeit now glorified post-resurrection. Matter and spirit are not antithetical.[16] A biblically informed Christianity is not Platonism in religious guise. The body is not a body-tomb (sōma-sēma) from which the soul must escape to some ethereal realm.[17]

For the valuing of human life

In 1969 Quaker philosopher Elton Trueblood summarized years of his own thinking about human life and its value in these ominous words:

A quarter of a century ago a few of us began to say that faith in the possibility of a cut-flower civilization is a faith which is bound to fail. What we meant was that it is impossible to sustain certain elements of human dignity, once these have been severed from their cultural roots. The sorrowful fact is that, while the cut flowers seem to go on living and may even exhibit some brightness for a while, they cannot do so permanently, for they will wither and be discarded. The historical truth is that the chief sources of the concepts of the dignity of the individual and equality before the law are found in the biblical heritage. Apart from the fundamental convictions of that heritage, symbolized by the idea that every man

[15] Quoted in Noll 2011: 34. Noll himself (35) concludes, 'In sum, to confess the material reality of the incarnation is to perceive an unusual dignity in the material world itself.'

[16] Scripture knows of a number of antitheses: light versus darkness (e.g. 1 John 1:5), Spirit versus the flesh in the Pauline sense of flesh (e.g. Gal. 5:17), and faith versus sight (e.g. 2 Cor. 5:7), to name a few. Spirit versus matter is not one of them.

[17] Plato n.d. Plato's *Gorgias* reads, 'Socrates compliments Callicles on his frankness in saying what other men only think. According to his view, those who want nothing are not happy. "Why," says Callicles, "if they were, stones and the dead would be happy." Socrates in reply is led into a half-serious, half-comic vein of reflection. "Who knows," as Euripides says, "whether life may not be death, and death life?" Nay, there are philosophers who maintain that even in life we are dead, and that the body (soma) is the tomb (sema) of the soul.'

is made in the image of God, there is no adequate reason for accepting the concepts mentioned.[18]

In his startling statement Trueblood did not exhaust the range of relevant 'fundamental convictions' made available through the biblical heritage.

The very fact that God became truly human underlines the value of human life. The Creator did not become a lion (apologies to C. S. Lewis) or a dolphin or a parrot. He became one of us.[19] True, medieval divine and of nominalist fame William of Ockham, with his idea of the absolute sovereignty of God (*potestas absoluta*, 'absolute authority' or 'absolute power'), did argue that God could have become incarnate as a stone or an ass or a wooden object. But his view has been judged rightly as absurd (e.g. John Macquarrie).[20] As another philosopher, this time the eminent twentieth-century Roman Catholic Jacques Maritain, argued often, 'the sanctity of human life ultimately rests in the fact that Christ became incarnate as a human creature, not some other sort of creature'.[21] Protestant theologian Karl Barth adds to the chorus: 'The respect for human life which becomes a command in the recognition of the union of God with humanity has an incomparable power and width.'[22] It is no surprise then to find in the Gospels that Jesus operated with a scale of creaturely value. Human life is more valuable (*diapherō*, lit. 'carry through', tr. 'are of more value than' in the context) than that of a sparrow, even a flock of them (Matt. 10:29–31). Human life is more valuable (*diapherō*) than that of a sheep (Matt. 12:11–12).[23] This valuing of human life over that of other creatures is criticized by some as 'speciesism' but is fundamental to a sound theological anthropology that factors in the reality of an incarnation.[24]

The fact of the incarnation has profound implications for Christian ethical thinking and moral practice whether in view are the issues

[18] Trueblood 1969: 14–15.

[19] Interestingly, although the notion of *imago Dei* is integral to any biblically informed theological anthropology, I am unaware of any biblical text that connects it with the incarnation of Christ. John's Prologue tells us that the *logos* (the Word) became *sarx* (flesh), not *eikōn* (image).

[20] See the discussion in Macquarrie 1996: 33.

[21] Post 2011: 702.

[22] Quoted in ibid.

[23] These are comparative claims. Jesus is not arguing that sparrows and sheep are valueless.

[24] Secular ethicist Peter Singer is highly critical of Christianity for its 'speciesism'. 'Speciesism' is the privileging of one species over another in respect to moral status. For a critique of Singer from a Christian perspective see Preece 2002.

surrounding the beginnings of life (e.g. abortion) or the endings of human life (e.g. euthanasia). Regarding the beginnings of human life, Jürgen Moltmann points out:

> If the Son of God became wholly and entirely human, and if he assumed full humanity, then this does not merely take in human personhood; it includes human nature as well. It does not embrace adult humanity alone; it comprehends humanity diachronically, in all its phases of development – that is, it includes the being of the child, the being of the foetus [sic] and the embryo. The whole of humanity in all its natural forms is assumed by God in order that it may be healed. So it is 'human' and 'holy' in all its natural forms, and is prenatally by no means merely 'human material', or just the preliminary stage of humanity.[25]

Indeed if Christ were not incarnate at conception, then Christology becomes adoptionist, with an already fertilized human ovum becoming divinely endorsed, or even Nestorian, with an already fertilized human ovum becoming a vehicle for divine presence, resulting in both a human presence and a divine one.

For our understanding of mission

It is popular these days to make much of the incarnation as the model for Christian mission in the world – a balanced mission of word and deed. The second Lausanne Conference held in Manila in 1989 states in its manifesto, 'True mission is incarnational. It necessitates entering humbly into other people's worlds, identifying with their social reality, their sorrow and suffering, and their struggles for justice against oppressive powers.'[26] At the earlier Lausanne Conference held in 1974 the eminent John Stott in his addresses argued that the Johannine text below (John 20:19–23) is the 'crucial form' of the Great Commission:

> On the evening of that first day of the week, when the disciples were together, with the doors locked for fear of the Jewish leaders, Jesus came and stood among them and said, 'Peace be with you!' After he said this, he showed them his hands and side. The disciples were overjoyed when they saw the Lord.

---

[25] Moltmann 1990: 85.
[26] Quoted in Green 2003: 129.

Again Jesus said, 'Peace be with you! As the Father has sent me, I am sending you.' And with that he breathed on them and said, 'Receive the Holy Spirit. If you forgive anyone's sins, their sins are forgiven; if you do not forgive them, they are not forgiven.'[27]

This passage is widely appealed to in order to justify an incarnational model of mission to embrace, and not just by John Stott. The argument runs in general along the following lines. Just as Christ identified with us in becoming human, we too need to identify with those whom we are trying to reach with the love of God. James Davison Hunter expresses the point in this way as he teases out the implications of the incarnation: 'For the Christian, if there is a possibility for human flourishing in a world such as ours, it begins when God's word of love becomes flesh in us, is embodied in us, is enacted through us.'[28] We are to be a faithful presence in a broken world as a kind of *incarnatus prolongus* (the incarnation prolonged) in concert with the quintessential faithful presence of the Word who became flesh.[29] However, the accent in Jesus' words is not on identification but on the reception of the Holy Spirit and the promise of forgiveness. As Andreas Köstenberger rightly comments, 'The fact that Jesus shows to his disciples his pierced hands and his side (cf. 20:19), as well as his commission to forgive or retain sins, ties the disciples' mission to Jesus' death (cf. chaps 18–20; cf. also 17:4 and 19:30).'[30] J. Todd Billings adds to the point by drawing attention to the reference to the Holy Spirit in the Johannine passage. He explores the implication of Jesus' saying 'Receive the Holy Spirit' as follows: 'It is not our own "incarnation," then, but the Holy Spirit who makes Christ present in us and beyond us.'[31] In his view the New Testament model for mission is not an incarnational one but 'the much richer theology of servant-witness and cross-cultural ministry . . . in union with Christ by the

---

[27] Ibid.
[28] Hunter 2010: 241, a most stimulating work.
[29] The idea that the church is an extension of the incarnation has contemporary advocates. Brown and Loades (1996: 7, 75) maintain that our bodies are taken into Christ's when we partake of the sacrament. Thus his incarnation is extended. They write (7), 'Eating Christ's body means becoming part of him. If we likewise allow the images of the Fourth Gospel mutually to enrich one another, then to drink his blood *must* mean becoming part of the vine that is Christ, and by implication eating his flesh *must* mean becoming part of the flesh in which the Word tabernacles' (my emphases). This sacramental mysticism with its accent on 'must' takes us well beyond anything that the exegesis of the Fourth Gospel allows.
[30] Köstenberger 1998: 195.
[31] Billings 2012: 60.

Spirit'.[32] Furthermore he contends that the popular slogan in some circles of 'live the Good News rather than preach the Good News' fails in the light of the biblical witness.[33] He is right.[34]

That Christ in the incarnation identified with humankind is a truth to affirm and prize.[35] Who can deny that identifying with those one hopes to reach has no better exemplar than Christ? He came to the lost sheep of Israel as a Jew of the house of David. However, the question is where the emphasis falls in the New Testament literature in so far as mission is concerned. It is instructive that neither the Matthean version of the Great Commission nor the Lucan one thematize the incarnation. The accent in Matthew falls on disciple-making, baptizing, teaching and obedience (Matt. 28:18–20). In Luke's account we read, 'The Messiah will suffer and rise from the dead on the third day, and repentance for the forgiveness of sins will be preached in his name to all nations, beginning at Jerusalem. You are witnesses of these things' (Luke 24:46–48). These disciples were not witnesses of the Bethlehem manger but of Christ's death and resurrection. And, as in John 20:19–22, the forgiveness of sins is to the fore.

Better then to speak of the Christological model for mission where the incarnation is an important facet yet not the centre of gravity but the presupposition for that centre's cruciform shape.

For the encounter with other religions

I have lived in three countries. Most of my life I lived in Australia. Twice I lived in England and now for a number of years in the USA. The religious scene in the three countries is plural. Judaism, Christianity of various sorts, Islam, Buddhism and a host of others look for their place in the sun. Theology of religions is increasingly popular as a subject for publication. Yet for those Christians with a high view of scriptural authority encountering other religions cannot be done with integrity as though Christ had never come in the flesh. But the

---

[32] Ibid.

[33] Ibid.

[34] The Marcan account is instructive here. When people needed to be taught the kingdom, out of compassion Jesus taught them, as in Mark 6:32–34; but when contextually the presenting need was sustenance, out of compassion he fed them, as in Mark 8:1–8. However, his exercise of compassion was expressed within the fundamental priority of preaching the kingdom, which is thematized right from the start of the Gospel of Mark (1:38): 'Jesus replied, "Let us go somewhere else – to the nearby villages – so that I can preach there also. *That is why I have come*"' (my emphasis).

[35] As Hiebert (1985: 91–110) does in his ch. 4, entitled 'The Incarnational Missionary'.

nature of that claim and its particularity is becoming increasingly problematical for many in a multifaith world. Our discussion at this point needs to be selective, so for our purposes only one other religion will be our focus: Islam.[36]

To a Muslim the *very idea of a God who could become incarnate and weep human tears* is nonsensical. How can the transcendent Allah weep, let alone weep human tears? I made this point a few years ago in a conference and the question was raised about one of the names of Allah in the Qur'ān, namely *al-Rahim* (The Merciful). Indeed the Qur'ān opens with 'In the name of Allah, the Beneficent, the Merciful [*al-rahim*]'.[37] However, Abu Hamid Al-Ghazali (1058–1111) argues in discussing this name:

> Mercy is not without a painful empathy which affects the merciful, and moves him to satisfy the needs of the one receiving mercy. *Yet the Lord – praise be to him most high – transcends that,* so you may think that this diminishes the meaning of mercy. But you should know that this is a perfection and does not diminish the perfection of mercy inasmuch as the mercy depends on the perfection of its fruits. So long as the needs of those in need are perfectly fulfilled, the one who receives mercy has no need of suffering or distress in the merciful one; rather the suffering of the merciful only stems from a weakness and effect in himself.[38]

Divine perfection and transcendence exclude suffering in this view.[39] Furthermore the Christian claim that Jesus the Christ is God incarnate presupposes that God is Trinity and that God can become a human being. In fact to describe Jesus as the Son of God to a Muslim's ear implies sexual intercourse between God and Mary.[40] All these claims are problematical in the extreme for Muslims. In Islam, Allah is the only God there is and Allah's transcendence is such that having a son is unthinkable: 'Verily, God is only one God; too exalted (*subhanahu*)

[36] For a broader discussion of the problematic of the deity of Christ as the flashpoint see Jennings 2011.
[37] *Al-Fātihah* (The Opening), in Ali 2002: 3 (Ali's tr.).
[38] Quoted from *The Ninety-Nine Beautiful Names of God*, in Markham 1996: 292, my emphasis. A *hadith* (lit. 'story') is a saying about Muhammad and his behaviour, and part of the *Sunna* literature.
[39] In the appendix the questions of divine suffering, incarnation and evil are further addressed.
[40] Hence the translation controversy over whether to use the title 'Son of God' in any translation of the New Testament destined for a Muslim readership. For a discussion of the issues at a popular level see Hansen 2011.

is He that He should have a son (*walad*).'[41] Islam has a Christology but it is a low one that sees Jesus as a human creature only – albeit the second greatest prophet. Only Muhammad is greater.[42] In fact ascribing deity to Christ is to commit the sin of *shirk* (regarding someone as the partner of another).[43] That is to say, another, namely Jesus, is being associated with Allah. This is idolatry and for Muslim thinker Shabbir Akhtar 'blasphemous mythology' and 'only fantasy'.[44]

By way of contrast, the classic Christian view of Jesus as expressed in the Chalcedonian definition of AD 451 is a high Christology. This definition affirms that Christ is one Person in two natures. He is truly human and truly God. Richard Bauckham makes this illuminating point about the early Christian creeds and definitions: 'The Trinitarian definitions of the faith at Nicea and Constantinople and the Christological definition at Chalcedon are not, of course, in any sense substitutes for the apostolic witness to Christ in the New Testament. They are formulated essentially as guides to reading the Gospel story of Jesus.'[45] Of these definitions the Chalcedonian one that Bauckham cites is of particular importance for what it both said and left unsaid. It affirms that Jesus Christ is one Person in two natures, truly God and truly human. It did so in categories not found in any Bible concordance (e.g. *homoousios*, 'of the same being'). However, as B. B. Warfield argued in relation to the Trinity – and it applies to

---

[41] Nisa' (Women) 4:171, quoted in Mattson 2008: 39. For a sensitive discussion of this key difference between Islam and Christianity see Migliore 2008: 126–127.

[42] Not all agree that Islam has a Christology. Renard (1998: 108) argues, 'Strictly speaking, there is and can be no Islamic "Christology," since Jesus is not the "Christ" in Muslim thought.' But for a contrary view see Cotterell 1982: 282–298. Contra Renard, Muslim scholar Kateregga (Kateregga and Shenk 1981: 131) has no difficulty in regarding Jesus/Isa as the Messiah.

[43] According to Ali (2002: 1257), in the last chapter of the Qur'ān (*Al-Iḫlās* [The Unity]) four kinds of *shirk* are excluded: (1) believing in a plurality of gods (e.g. the Trinity [*sic*]), (2) belief that another who is not Allah can possess the attributes of deity, (3) belief that God is either a father or a son, and (4) a belief that others can do what only Allah can do.

[44] Akhtar 2011: 37. Akhtar is an Oxford-trained analytical philosopher whose critique of the Trinity and incarnation is very disappointing. He argues (163–164) that both notions are incoherent and unintelligible but shows little understanding of the Christian claim, and the authorities he draws on to state the doctrines are non-Christian Western critics of Christianity (Michael Martin and Michael Durrant). He faults Aquinas, to whom he barely refers, but does not expound, appealing to mystery, which is the very category Akhtar himself applies (1990: 181) to the knowledge of Allah's attributes.

[45] Bauckham 2002. Bauckham very helpfully addresses the question whether Chalcedon distorted the biblical witness by the use of non-biblical Greek philosophical speak, and argues convincingly that it did not.

Christology as well – sometimes other than Bible words are needed to preserve the sense of Scripture. He argues:

A doctrine [of the Trinity] so defined can be spoken of as a Biblical doctrine only on the principle that the sense of Scripture is Scripture. And the definition of a Biblical doctrine in such un-Biblical [better, 'non-biblical'] language can be justified only on the principle that it is better to preserve the truth of Scripture than the words of Scripture.[46]

The use of non-biblical terminology becomes all the more non-biblical when deviant versions of Christology come quoting Scripture (e.g. the ancient Arians). What Chalcedon left unsaid was any theory of how metaphysically speaking Jesus Christ can be one Person in two natures, truly God and truly human. This is one of its strengths in my view. Its great affirmations make it clear that to deny that Jesus Christ is one Person, as popular Nestorianism did, it seems, is to fall off a doctrinal cliff.[47] To deny that he is truly God is likewise to go over the edge. This is the problem with Islam's low Christology and many a liberal theology. To deny that Jesus Christ is truly human is to go into free fall likewise. One thinks here of Gnostics like the second-century Basileides.[48] The mystery of Jesus Christ as the *theoanthrōpos* (the God-man) is not to be dissolved by a reductionism of his divine aspect: he was only human as in Islam. Nor is it to be dissolved by a reductionism of his human aspect: he was divine only. The Chalcedonian fathers read their Scriptures aright. Crucially this classic answer withstands biblical scrutiny.

Incidentally the story of the incarnation shows us why all religious stories cannot be equally true. Islam affirms that Jesus was miraculously born of a virgin but is not the incarnate Son of God. Classic Christianity affirms both claims. Someone has clearly got the story wrong. If I may update an observation of the philosopher E. S. Brightman: a universe in which both Christianity and Islam were true would be a

---

[46] Warfield 1958: 79.

[47] Rightly or wrongly Nestorius, Bishop of Constantinople, was accused of teaching that God has two sons at work in the one body: a divine one and a human one and thus Mary bore a human son as the *Christotokos* (Christ bearer), but not God the Son. Consequently she was not *theotokos* (God bearer). For a competent discussion of Nestorianism see González 1987: I, 353–364.

[48] Basileides fancifully argued that the Christ spirit miraculously exchanged places with Simon of Cyrene on the way to the cross, and it was Simon looking like Jesus who was crucified while the Christ spirit now appearing as Simon stood by laughing at human folly. For him a spirit could not be human. See Stevenson 1970: 81–82.

madhouse.[49] The principle of non-contradiction needs to be observed. 'A' cannot be non-'A' at both the same time and in the same respect. A typewriter cannot be blue all over and red all over at the same time and in the same respect. For, make no mistake, both Christianity and Islam claim that their foundational stories are not merely useful fictions, or, to use Plato's expression, 'a noble lie'.[50] Rather both religions assert that they are making truth claims.

For theodicy and defence

As I write, the war in Afghanistan continues and there is further violence in Iraq. Syria is in a particularly bloody period, and a friend has just been diagnosed with stage 3 breast cancer. A few years ago one of my close friends died on Christmas Day. We went through theological college together. Every Christmas now reminds of that fact. Death, disease, destructive behaviour stalk humankind. In a world of so much manifest suffering what can the historic Christian faith say? John 11:35 tells us that 'Jesus wept'. In other words, God incarnate wept. But what more might be said?

Following a helpful distinction found in the work of Alvin Plantinga, let me suggest that in the face of evil all that may be offered is a defence rather than a theodicy.[51] A theodicy gives *the* reason God allows or does X, whereas a defence offers a more moderate proposal. A theodicy might argue that *the* reason is that God so prizes human free will that it was worth a creation that might have evils in it. The Creator desired a creature that could love its maker freely. In contrast, a strong defence would give reasons for trusting in God's moral integrity (e.g. the love of God expressed through the cross) and also offer a theory of how that integrity is not compromised by the presence of evils in creation. A moderate defence would likewise give reasons for trusting in God's moral integrity, but unlike the strong defence offer no account of how the existence of evil comports with that integrity.[52] I would contend that

---

[49] Brightman (1925: 56) actually said, 'Christian Science and Roman Catholicism . . . both cannot be true at the same time unless the universe is a madhouse.'

[50] I am basing the substance of this paragraph on Cole 2009a.

[51] A. Plantinga 1980: 10–11, 26–29. A good example of such a defence is found in Dulles 2006: 324–335.

[52] Although he does not use the category of moderate defence, C. S. Evans (2006: 7) illustrates the notion: 'Despite the assurances of theologians and philosophers, when we humans look honestly at the suffering present in the natural order it is not always easy to believe that the God of heaven and earth is a God who is both all-powerful and all-loving. When theodicies fail to satisfy, most Christians are steadied by faith: a trust and confidence that God is good and had good reasons for creating and governing the

because of the limitations in scope of special revelation – not all has been revealed (Deut. 29:29) – only some kind of defence is possible. Integral to any such defence would be the fact that God incarnate wept human tears. Outside Eden God in Christ knows human pain and grief from the inside of the human condition. More than that, God in Christ has acted to defeat evil through Christ's coming and cross, as Hebrews 2:14–15 makes plain: 'Since the children have flesh and blood, he too shared in their humanity so that by his death he might break the power of him who holds the power of death – that is, the devil – and free those who all their lives were held in slavery by their fear of death.'

On the one hand Dietrich Bonhoeffer was right to argue that 'Only the suffering God can help.'[53] Historic Christianity of the Bible and the creeds says he has indeed helped. On the other hand Baron von Hügel was right to argue we need help, and not just a fellow sufferer. God in Christ instantiated both desiderata.[54] As Kevin J. Vanhoozer argues, 'God is not Whitehead's "fellow sufferer who understands" but the "sovereign sufferer who withstands."'[55]

For dogmatic rank

The sixteenth-century reformer Martin Luther was many things: a transformative leader, an engaging preacher, a pioneering Bible translator into the vernacular, a hymn writer and a still influential theological writer, among other contributions. He was also astute in judging his times. He argued:

If I profess, with the loudest voice and clearest exposition, every portion of the truth of God except precisely that little point which

world as he has, even if we do not always know those reasons. It is far more credible to believe that God does care about human suffering when he has himself demonstrated his love by sharing in our suffering [through the incarnation and the cross].'

[53] Quoted in McWilliams 1985: 44. To a Muslim intellectual such as Shabbir Akhtar (2011: 37) such a notion is unthinkable given the following statement: 'The Quran rejects the Judeo-Christian notion of sympathetic divine kingship: a God concerned for his people or for his faithful believer like a loving father for his children.' His Qur'ānic evidence comes from Sura 5:18, which reads in part, 'And the Jews and the Christians say: We are the sons of Allah and His beloved ones. Say: Why does He then chastise you for your sins? Nay, you are mortals from among those whom He has created.' His use of this evidence is obscure.

[54] I have developed these ideas at length in Cole 2011.

[55] Vanhoozer 2010: 466. In this work Vanhoozer writes with his usual theological adroitness but his discussion in my view would have been strengthened even further if he had drawn a distinction between biblical anthropmorphisms and biblical anthropopathisms (e.g. see his 483, n. 36).

the world and the devil are at that moment attacking, I am not confessing Christ, however boldly I may be professing Christ. Where the battle rages there the loyalty of the soldier is proved, and to be steady on all the battle field beside is mere flight and disgrace if he flinches at that point.[56]

Church history illustrates Luther's contention. Some examples are in order. In the first century the emphasis was on grace, not works of the law, contra the Judaizers. In the second century it was the reality of Christ's humanity contra Gnosticism. In the third century it was the reality of the three eternal persons of the one God contra Sabellianism. In the fourth century it was the essential Trinity contra the Arians. In the fifth century it was the two natures of Christ, truly God and truly human, contra the Eutychians. And so forth. These days, as we have seen above, it is both Trinity and Christology contra Islam.

A good way to ascertain the dogmatic rank of a theological proposition is to ask what would be lost if the claim were untrue. In the case of the incarnate Son of God's humanity a whole host of other key claims fall to the ground. If the Son of God had not become truly human, then he could not have served as the prophet like Moses of Deuteronomy 18:15–18, nor as the messianic Davidic king of Psalm 2, nor as the servant of the Lord of Isaiah 53, nor as the cursed substitute of Galatians 3:13, nor as our representative great high priest of Hebrews 4:14–16, nor as the role model of 1 Peter 2:18–25. In other words he could not have been the mediator of whom Paul wrote in 1 Timothy 2:5–6, where Paul accents Christ's humanity: 'For there is one God and one mediator [*mesitēs*] between God and mankind [*anthrōpōn*, pl.; includes males and females], the man [*anthrōpos*, sg.] Christ Jesus, who gave himself as a ransom for all people.' Clearly the incarnation is no minor doctrinal claim. Both its relevance and importance remain acute. Even so, it is significant that the two ordinances Jesus left with his disciples – baptism and the Lord's Supper – focus on his death, resurrection and return, not his coming into the world in the first place. The latter is important, yes! All important, no![57]

[56] Luther quoted in Piper 1999: 41.

[57] Some in the early church period wrote at times as though the incarnation were sufficient in itself to save. For example, Athanasius in the fourth century in his *Letter to Epictetus* 7, maintained, 'Because the Word of God, the eternal Son of the Father, clothed himself with flesh and became man, we are delivered' (quoted in Hendry 1959: 48, n. 48). Athanasius seems to have worked within a Platonic metaphysic in which by assuming the universal of manhood the Son informed all human particulars.

Existential significance

By 'existential significance' I mean the significance of the incarnation for the individual living in the broken creation that longs itself to be remade. Two aspects of the significance will be explored: appreciating the depths of the divine love as seen in the incarnation, and cultivating a sense of wonder. Again this discussion is not exhaustive.

Appreciating the depths of divine love

This is not an easy world in which to believe in a God of love. Death stalks us all. Disease is humanity's constant companion. And we destroy one another in war and crime. So to claim that God is not only there but is also good raises the questions 'How do you know this? Where is the evidence?' The New Testament tells us where to look.

The evidence provided by 1 John 4:9–10 is crucial for answering the questions posed above. John writes, 'This is how God showed his love among us: he sent his one and only Son into the world that we might live through him. This is love: not that we loved God, but that he loved us and sent his Son as an atoning sacrifice for our sins.' The Christian is to look to the coming and cross of Christ to know that God is indeed love. The genius of Scripture is to offer narratival definitions of key terms. If we want to know what biblical forgiveness looks like, we go back to the story of how Joseph forgave his brothers who sold him into slavery (Gen. 50:15–21). If we want to know what repentance is, we think of the story Jesus told of the return of the prodigal son to his father (Luke 15:11–32). And if we want to know what divine love is in our sort of world and the evidence for it, we tell the story of the incarnation and the atonement: Christmas and Easter. Philosopher Roger Scruton captures in some measure the divine goodness in his Gifford Lectures when he writes:

> God revealed himself on that occasion as we do – by coming to the threshold of himself. He came before Moses as a point of view, a first person perspective, the transcendental 'I am' that cannot be known as an object but only as a subject. This perspective can become a real presence among us only if it can be revealed in the world of objects, as the human subject in the human face. But how can this be? . . . Christianity's answer to that question and that answer is the incarnation. God, in the person of Christ, is present

among us. It is from the life of Christ that we can understand the true nature of God's goodness.[58]

Similarly Hans Urs von Balthasar argues, 'But this love is no mere diffused, all-pervading medium, dissolving everything in vague sentiment; on the contrary, it becomes present in the exact features of one particular, historical Person. . . . It attains visibility in his very precise words, actions, sufferings and miracles.'[59] Without the incarnation the human story becomes a very dark one indeed. In Shakespearean terms, as Macbeth states it, humanity's story becomes

> a tale
> Told by an idiot, full of sound and fury,
> Signifying nothing.[60]

However, in Johannine terms the good news is that light – the light of life – has come into the world (John 1:4–9).

Cultivating a sense of wonder

Famously Aristotle maintained that philosophy begins in wonder. If that is true of philosophy, how much more so the Christian life? Wonder at what Paul described in Ephesians 1:7–8 as 'the riches of God's grace that he lavished on us'. Lavished on us in Christ is Paul's argument.

In this section we look at the wonder that quite properly stems from looking back to what God in Christ has done and then the wonder that flows from looking forward to what God in Christ will do.

Wonder in retrospect

To state the obvious, Christianity, unlike say Scientology, is not a new religion on the human scene. Generally speaking, for us as moderns the new has an attraction the old has not. C. S. Lewis even coined a phrase for it: 'chronological snobbery'.[61] For the chronological snob the new is always to be preferred over the old. As a consequence, for many in the West the Christian story is a very old hat and worthy only

[58] Scruton 2012: 172.

[59] Balthasar 1986: 57.

[60] *Macbeth*, Act 5, Scene 5, Lines 26–28. These lines are among those spoken by Macbeth upon hearing of his wife's death and realizing how badly wrong the murder of the king and the seizing of his throne had turned out.

[61] Duriez 1990: 41. Duriez points out that Lewis used the phrase in his inaugural lecture (*De descriptione temporum*) at the University of Cambridge in 1955.

of satire, as in the Monty Python film *The Life of Brian*. In the film Jesus' words 'Blessed are the peacemakers' gets misheard as 'Blessed are the cheese makers.' Brian and a host of others ultimately are crucified and happily sing on their crosses, 'Look on the bright side of life.' A hideously cruel form of punishment becomes a vehicle for comedy.

Someone who was aware of the loss of wonder at the stupendous nature of the Christian story was Christian essayist, playwright and lay theologian Dorothy Sayers. She had a deep appreciation of the nature of drama. Sayers expresses her wonder with a great deal of verve as she looks back to the coming of Christ into the world and to his cross:

> So that is the outline of the official story – the tale of the time when God was the underdog and got beaten, when he submitted to the conditions he had laid down and became a man like the men he had made, and the men he had made broke him and killed him. This is the dogma we find so dull – this terrifying drama of which God is the victim and hero . . . If this is dull, what, in Heaven's name, is worthy to be called exciting?[62]

In her conclusion she reinforces her point:

> Now, we may call that doctrine exhilarating, or we may call it devastating; we may call it revelation, or we may call it rubbish; but if we call it dull, then words have no meaning at all. That God should play the tyrant over man is the usual dreary record of human futility; but that man should play the tyrant over God and find him a better man than himself is an astonishing drama indeed. Any journalist, hearing of it for the first time, would recognize it as news; those who did it for the first time actually called it news, and good news at that; though we are likely to forget that the word *Gospel* ever meant anything so sensational.[63]

Sayers felt the wonder of it. And she rightly sees the drama is not reducible to the Christmas story. Easter is crucial as well. Significantly the drama has not ended. There is the world to come.

---

[62] Sayers 1979: 24–25.
[63] Ibid. 28–29, original emphasis.

Wonder at the prospect

One of the great milestones in Christian history was the call and conversion of Saul of Tarsus on the Damascus road as narrated in the book of Acts. He encountered the risen Christ and it transformed his life. However, in what form did he meet Jesus on that day? Was Jesus embodied in some post-resurrection sense or was he a disembodied spirit? Paul's letters make it clear that Jesus was embodied in some way. He informed the Corinthians in his magnificent cumulative argument for the resurrection that he had seen the Lord, as had other apostles (1 Cor. 15:7–8): 'Then he appeared to James, then to all the apostles, and last of all he appeared to me also, as to one abnormally born.' 'As one abnormally born' clearly has the Damascus road in view. In fact the very term 'resurrection' entails 'embodiment'.[64] Moreover he encourages the Philippians by reminding them of their citizenship in heaven and of the great prospect ahead of them (Phil. 3:20–21): 'But our citizenship is in heaven. And we eagerly await a Saviour from there, the Lord Jesus Christ, who, by the power that enables him to bring everything under his control, will transform our lowly bodies so that they will be like his glorious body.' The prospect of seeing the glorified incarnate Christ ought to fill the believer with longing, according to the apostle in 2 Timothy 4:8, 'Now there is in store for me the crown of righteousness, which the Lord, the righteous Judge, will award to me on that day – and not only to me, but also to all who have longed for [ēgapēkosi, 'have loved'] his appearing.'[65]

Paul was not the only apostle who lived *sub specie aeternitatis* (under the aspect of eternity). John in his first letter (1 John 3:1–3) spells out the prospect in an intimate way:

> See what great love the Father has lavished on us, that we should be called children of God! And that is what we are! The reason the world does not know us is that it did not know him. Dear friends,

---

[64] N. T. Wright 2003: 31.

[65] The ESV is to be preferred here: 'Henceforth there is laid up for me the crown of righteousness, which the Lord, the righteous judge, will award to me on that Day, and not only to me but also to all who have loved his appearing.' The aspect is important: 'have loved' is in the perfect. As G. H. Guthrie (1990: 188) rightly comments, 'As the perfect tense suggests, they have loved his appearing in the past and will continue to do so to the moment of receiving the reward.' Interestingly this Pauline statement also shows that *agapē* love cannot be reduced in every instance simply to seeking the good of the other. Also see 2 Tim. 4:10 and Demas's *agapē* love for the present age. The use of the word in context is the key to its meaning.

now we are children of God, and what we will be has not yet been made known. But we know that when Christ appears, we shall be like him, for we shall see him as he is. All who have this hope in him purify themselves, just as he is pure.

For John the end-time prospect is the transformation of the children of God. The *visio Dei* in this text is actually the *visio Christi*. There is an ancient epistemic principle that only like can know like. In the end, to see Christ there needs to be ontological transformation. Paul in his letters calls it 'glorification' (e.g. Rom. 8:30).

God-with-us (concomitance) will find its apogee in the consummation represented by the new heavens and the new earth of Revelation 21 – 22. In Revelation 21:1–4 (ESV) the seer reports:

> Then I saw a new heaven and a new earth, for the first heaven and the first earth had passed away, and the sea was no more. And I saw the holy city, new Jerusalem, coming down out of heaven from God, prepared as a bride adorned for her husband. And I heard a loud voice from the throne saying, 'Behold, the dwelling place of God is with man. He will dwell with them, and they will be his people, and God himself will be with them as their God. He will wipe away every tear from their eyes, and death shall be no more, neither shall there be mourning, nor crying, nor pain anymore, for the former things have passed away.'

The great covenant goal of God-with-us is now met. In the words of my biblical theology teacher Graeme Goldsworthy, which I heard in class so many times, 'God's people are in God's place under God's rule.'

All is now sacred space. Jürgen Moltmann sums up the end-time picture in these colourful terms: 'With this the whole creation becomes the *house of God*, the *temple* in which God can dwell, the *home country* in which God can rest.'[66] Spatially speaking, the New Jerusalem like the Holy of Holies of Old Testament times is a cube (Rev. 21:16). Again, as Moltmann observes, 'In this respect the city resembles no earthly city, and no earthly temple either. But it does correspond to the Holy of Holies in Israel's temple, the inner sanctuary (1 Kgs 6:17–20).'[67] Any distinction between the sacred and the profane no

---

[66] Moltmann 1996: 307, original emphases.
[67] Ibid. 315.

longer applies. For this city is filled with priest-kings. As priests they
worship God and the Lamb (Rev. 22:3), and as kings they reign with
the Lamb on the throne (Rev. 22:5). As Augustine wrote in his classic
work *The City of God* with reference to the world to come, 'There we
shall rest and see, see and love, love and praise.'[68]

Conclusion

Bernard Ramm reminds us that 'The great theologian differs from
the ordinary in the former's ability to draw out these larger implications of the text. It was in men like Augustine, Luther, Calvin, and
Barth that the genius of theological exegesis came into its own.'[69]
In this chapter I have endeavoured to draw out some of the larger
implications of the texts dealing with the incarnation – texts we have
explored in previous chapters. The incarnation has theological implications for theological method, the question of whether God can
change in some way, for the value of the created order, for the valuing
of human life, for our understanding of mission, for the Christian
encounter with other religions, especially Islam with its low Christology, for theodicy and defence, and for the weighting of doctrines
in some kind of dogmatic rank. Christian theology cannot be
properly done as though Christ had never come. The incarnation
also has implications for the individual. The love of God as displayed
in the entry of the Son of God into the world is, in the words of
James Davison Hunter, 'the most breathtaking demonstration in
history of God's love for his creation and his intention to make all
things new'.[70] What God has done is astonishing. John Murray states
it well:

> The infinite became finite, the eternal and supratemporal entered
> time and became subject to its conditions, the immutable became
> mutable, the invisible became visible, the Creator became the
> created, the sustainer of all became dependent, the Almighty
> infirm. All is summed up in the proposition, God became
> man.[71]

[68] Augustine, quoted in Aquinas 1939: 53, n. 6, *Ibi vacabimus, et videbimus: videbimus,
et amabimus: amabimus, et laudabimus* (There we shall rest, and we shall see; we shall
see, and we shall love; we shall love, and we shall praise). This is the climax of Augustine's
City of God.
[69] Ramm et al. 1974: 28–29.
[70] Hunter 2010: 240.
[71] J. Murray 1977: 132.

Doxology is the appropriate response and also the cultivation of a sense of wonder at what God has done in the past and will do in the world to come.

Chapter Seven

Conclusion

Scripture presents a living God who is transcendent and immanent. The transcendent God is not confined by creation. He is not limited by time or space. As immanent, this same God is at work within the created order, sustaining its existence. As Thomas Chalmers suggested, 'the uniformity of nature is but another name for the faithfulness of God'.[1] Yet these two broad categories do not exhaust the reality of the living God's relation to us. God is also concomitant – he comes alongside, dwells with and travels with his people. Divine concomitance finds its quintessential expression in the incarnation of the Son who pitched his tent among us in real space and real time. As John Murray says, 'The thought of incarnation is stupendous, for it means the conjunction in one person of all that belongs to godhead and all that belongs to manhood.'[2] This is a staggering claim. No surrogate came. Concerning God the Son, Irenaeus the second-century church father writes of 'the only true and steadfast Teacher, the Word of God, our Lord Jesus Christ, who did, through His transcendent love, become what we are, that He might bring us to be even what He is Himself'.[3] If this is not a reason for doxology, what can be?

Chapter 1 explored the purpose of creation in terms of God's creating and fashioning a palace-temple as his habitation for dwelling with the creature made in the divine image. In addition how God prepared the way for his ultimate incarnate concomitance from the very beginning by revealing himself in anthropomorphic, anthropopathic and anthropopraxic ways was canvassed. In this chapter these latter three terms were defined. From the start, in the first book of the Bible, Genesis, we found that the God of the Bible is often spoken of as though embodied. Herman Bavinck is even more bold: 'It follows that Scripture does not merely contain a few anthropomorphisms; on the contrary, *all* Scripture is anthropomorphic.'[4] Moreover the chapter argued that a third category needs to be added

---

[1] Quoted in Trueblood 1969: 125.
[2] J. Murray 1977: 133.
[3] Irenaeus 2007: V, preface.
[4] Bavinck 1977: 86, original emphasis.

to the two traditional ones of transcendence and immanence to discuss God's relation to creation. The third category is concomitance. An excursus examined a venerable question: Would the incarnation have taken place irrespective of the Fall? Speculatively I argued yes.

In the second chapter the portrait of God was amplified as we considered the divine deeds in Israel's history with its fountainhead in the call of Abram. God was at work to redeem a people of his own among whom he could dwell. Once more God's anthropomorphic, anthropopathic and anthropopraxic ways were reviewed as we followed the biblical plotline. In this chapter the mysterious figure of the angel of the Lord was also considered, as was the phenomenon of anthropomorphic theophany.

The third chapter explored Israel's hope and the promise of the divine presence with his people in the midst of the created order. Key texts were examined, including Psalms 45:6, 110:1, Isaiah 9:6 and Daniel 7:13. Some argue that the Old Testament expected a divine Messiah and that the deity of Christ was taught in the Old Testament. Others disagree. I argued that the idea that the Christ is God is consistent with the Old Testament testimony but not demanded by it. We also considered how the Old Testament held out the promise of Yahweh himself coming to rescue his people. These ideas are left unsynthesized by Old Testament writers. We also saw that recent approaches to the typological reading of Scripture help us to understand how the incarnation was prepared for in a subtle way in the descriptors and promises relating to David and his house.

In chapter 4, as we continued to follow the biblical plotline, we saw how the preparatory gave way to the actual as the testimony of the New Testament came into full view. The Word became flesh and dwelt among us (John 1:14). God stooped. Concomitance was now enfleshed as Immanuel ('God with us', Matt. 1:23). In the Old Testament in Genesis 6:6 God grieved over wayward humankind. In the New Testament we saw how Christ wept human tears at the tomb of Lazarus (John 11:35). He is the window into the heart of God. To hear Jesus is to hear the Word of God; to see Jesus is to see the character of God; to watch Jesus in action is to see God in action. R. T. France makes the point strikingly: 'God no longer simply *told* His people about Himself, or even showed them by His actions. He came Himself, and walked among them, and men *saw* the invisible, God in a human body, the ultimate anthropomorphism.'[5] John's

---

[5] France 1970: 99–101, original emphasis.

testimony was joined to that of Matthew, for whom Jesus was the Immanuel of Isaianic hope, and to that of Mark, for whom God in Jesus comes to Zion, and to that of Hebrews, which affirmed both the deity and humanity of the incarnate Son. In retrospect these New Testament writers could ground their belief in the deity and humanity of Christ in the Old Testament Scriptures. This chapter also argued that the incarnation was of the one to whom the Old Testament anthropomorphisms, anthropopathisms and anthropopraxisms pointed. Nicholas Wolterstorff's theory of theories gave conceptual tools for understanding how the Old Testament prepared the way for an incarnation, although the incarnation in prospect was never explicitly in view in the Old Testament. The Pauline notion of mystery underlined the latter point and reinforced the argument that the Old Testament believers were not expecting an actual incarnation of the God of Israel. An excursus dealt with the debate over whether Old Testament saints knowingly encountered the pre-incarnate Christ. I remained unconvinced by those who argued that they did.

Chapter 5 addressed the question raised by Anselm of Canterbury in the Middle Ages: Why did God become human? Unlike Anselm, however, New Testament answers rather than speculative ones were sought to the question. The appeal was to Scripture, not to reason with the Bible intentionally shut. A plethora of New Testament testimonies were canvassed that address the question of the rationale of the incarnation. I argued that Christ's revelatory, representative, substitutionary, devil-defeating and moral-modelling roles are predicated on his assuming a truly human nature. An excursus was attached that tackled the question of whether the divine Son assumed fallen or unfallen human nature in the incarnation. I sided with the traditional view that Christ assumed an unfallen human nature.

In chapter 6 we considered the value of the incarnation in two aspects: theological and existential. We saw the value of the incarnation for theological method, for epistemology, for the doctrine of God and change, for affirming the created order, for valuing human life, for our understanding of mission, for the encounter between Christianity and other religions, with special reference to Islam, for the question of theodicy and defence, given evils, and for matters of dogmatic rank. We also explored the value of the incarnation at the personal or existential level. The incarnation matters with regard to our appreciation of the depths of the divine love and our sense of wonder at what the Lord has done on the plane of human history in this age and what he will do in the age to come.

The canonical story ends on a note of hope, a hope in which con-comitance (God-with-us) is consummated in the world to come. In the end all is sacred space. The divine habitation is definitively built. The New Jerusalem has no need of a temple. God dwells in the midst of his people. The palace-temple has both rulers and priests. Creation has been reclaimed and transfigured. Order has been restored. Signifi-cantly the Lamb on the throne remains the incarnate one. The end point is no ethereal Platonic-style heavenly existence but a robust new heavens and a new earth. Christianity is not Gnosticism. The biblical testimony calls for discipleship, doxology and great expectation as we live as God's people in between the comings of the great king. We are to set our minds on things above, as Paul expressed to the Colossians (Col. 3:1). In this life we walk by faith, in the world to come, by sight. Thus there is a day coming when the veiling will no longer pertain. All will be revealed. Hence the longing that ends the canonical presentation (Rev. 22:20): 'Come, Lord Jesus.'

Above all, the incarnation of the Son of God ought to fill us with humble wonder. A loving Father did not send a mere prophetic or priestly or royal surrogate, but the Son who both instantiates the perfection of all three and yet transcends them. This is what divine love looks like, as John makes plain: 'This is how God showed his love among us: he sent his one and only Son into the world that we might live through him' (1 John 4:9).

Appendix

The theological interpretation of Scripture[1]

My wife is a fashion designer and college teacher of fashion. To be a good designer, she tells me, you need to listen to the fabric. You need to engage the fabric on its terms. You can't stitch leather the way you stitch knits. A different needle is needed. An ordinary needle would break. Biblical theology likewise is a discipline that seeks to listen to its fabric. The fabric is the Word of God written. In practice this means placing a biblical text or passage in its context in its literary unit or argument in its book in the canon within the flow of revealed redemptive history.[2] Presuppositions are always at work, of course, as I endeavoured to make clear in the introductory chapter of this study. By way of reminder, evangelical biblical theology presupposes the living God who speaks and acts, the unity of Scripture, inspiration and the canon. Scripture then is not reducible to an anthology of ancient Near Eastern and early church texts but is the inspired – in the strong Pauline *theopneustos* sense – Word of God, albeit in human words (*concursus*). Put another way, we try to be good phenomenologists of the text. I like the way the Jewish thinker Abraham Joshua Heschel summed up phenomenology: knowing what you see rather than seeing what you know.[3] I once worked with a Bible teacher who found the same meaning in every text, whether in Genesis, Isaiah or Mark: read your Bible, say your prayers, share your faith, have fellowship with other Christians, and give to the work. He saw what he knew rather knew what he saw. Happily what he knew had good biblical warrant, but not in the texts he was expounding, I would argue. So,

---

[1] A version of this material appears in Cole 2010. Used with permission.
[2] I see similarities between my view and that of Kevin J. Vanhoozer (2009: 180–181), who writes of 'canon sense'. Vanhoozer describes 'canon sense' as having been trained 'to see things not simply from the perspective of eternity (*sub specie aeternitatis*) but from the perspective of the theodrama (*sub specie theodramatis*)'.
[3] Heschel 1969: I, xi.

as much as lies within us, we seek to see what is actually there in the text before us.

Evangelical systematic theology also appeals to what is there but goes further than the descriptive. It is a normative or prescriptive discipline. Systematic theology wants to find out what we ought to believe (our head), what we ought to value (our heart) and how we ought to live (our hands and feet) as the sacred text is brought to bear on the broken world in which we live and are to serve. However, to do so responsibly systematic theology needs to know how to listen to the fabric. This is where the discipline of biblical theology is vital to the discipline of systematic theology. The traditional way to do systematic theology is to make a claim and supply proof texts (*dicta probantia*) to back it up. For example, take the claim that Christ is God incarnate. The classic proof text is John 1:14, 'The Word became flesh and made his dwelling among us.' It might appear like this: 'Christ is God incarnate' (John 1:14). I am sure many a reader has had the experience of looking up the string of proof texts in a standard systematic theology text and being mystified as to the relevance of some of them to the claim. Now proof texts are needed. You can't say everything at once. I remember a student in England who had been warned off systematic theology by his pastor, who valued only biblical theology. The student was having problems of a practical kind. If he was asked after church about an issue, people simply didn't have the time to take the tour with him from Genesis to Revelation to find out what all the relevant texts had to say. Some kind of synthesis, some kind of theological shorthand, was needed. Systematic theology supplies that shorthand.

Systematic theology's proof texts, however, need to be derived from the application of a sound biblical theology method. Let us return to John 1:14. If I am challenged on appealing to that text as a systematic theologian I would seek to show that it is part of an argument beginning at John 1:1, in eternity as it were, and ending in time, with John 1:14–18. In other words our text is integral to the Prologue of John and is the climax of the story of how God seeks to dwell in the midst of his people. This story started in the garden (Eden), continued with Israel (esp. tabernacle and temple) and climaxed in Jesus Christ. Incarnation is the zenith of divine presence. To use Brian Rosner's way of expressing it – I am appealing to John 1:14 in the light of the Bible's 'overarching narrative and Christocentric focus'.[4]

---

[4] Rosner 2001.

In other words a text needs not only to be seen in its context but also seen in its literary unit, in its book in the canon and with the flow of redemptive history firmly in mind.[5]

Biblical theology serves systematic theology in another way. Here my example is that great gospel benefit of the forgiveness of our sins. Read your standard systematic theology texts and you would not know how important as a biblical motif the forgiveness of our sins is, but Luke-Acts, which constitutes about a third of the New Testament, is clear. The risen Christ thematizes the forgiveness of sins as the great gospel benefit in Luke 24:47 (the Great Commission Lucan style), and in Acts we see it held out both to Jews (Acts 2:38 – Pentecost) and Gentiles (Acts 10:43 – Cornelius).[6] In the light of the overarching narrative of Scripture, which identifies the God to whom we pray, we can see why this benefit is so important. God is not only love (1 John 4:8), but is also light (1 John 1:5). How can a holy God dwell with an unholy people? Sin needs to be addressed. The Word become flesh is the linchpin to that address: his coming, his cross and his coming to life again. In other words biblical theology helps systematic theology get the proportions right in its accents. This is an exceedingly important contribution. In my opinion there is a crying need for a systematic theology text to be written that does just that.

A final question to consider – what has all the above to do with the increasingly influential notion of the theological interpretation of Scripture? Are biblical theology and the theological interpretation of Scripture synonymous? I like to distinguish the two tasks. Other theologians appear to treat them more as synonymous (e.g. Brian S. Rosner).[7] I am aware that I am being stipulative in arguing this. Biblical theology on the one hand helps me to know what I see, whereas the theological interpretation of Scripture helps me to know how to serve the church with what I see as I endeavour to bring the text and the present together in a meaningful fashion. For example, John 1:14 viewed through the theological interpretation of Scripture's

[5] Literary unit is important. I once had a bizarre argument with a church deacon who contended that if a real historical incident did not lie behind the story of the Good Samaritan in Luke 10:25–37 he would give up Christianity. 'Why?' was my question. His answer was that the real Son of God could not tell a truth through a lie. I tried to point out, but to no avail, that the story was a parable.

[6] Early Christianity appears to have recognized the importance of the forgiveness of sins as a gospel benefit. It is a line item in both the Apostles' Creed and the Nicene Creed.

[7] Rosner (2001) writes, 'What is biblical theology? To sum up: *biblical theology may be defined as theological interpretation of Scripture in and for the church*' (original emphasis).

lens cannot be merely described as the climax of a biblical theology of presence, true though that is. The theological interpretation of Scripture also wants to say that John 1:14 tells of a God who so loved the world that he came himself and tabernacled among us. We do not live in a divinely abandoned landscape, adrift in space as cosmic flotsam and jetsam. Put another way the theological interpretation of Scripture draws out the larger implication of the text of Scripture, or of several texts of Scripture that have been placed in a conversation with each other with an eye on the flow of redemptive history. Bernard Ramm's wise words on the subject are worth quoting once more: 'The great theologian differs from the ordinary in the former's ability to draw out these larger implications of the text. It was in men like Augustine, Luther, Calvin, and Barth that the genius of theological exegesis [or what I prefer to call the theological interpretation of Scripture] came into its own.'[8] The disciplines of biblical theology and the theological interpretation of Scripture are thus in my view complementary. Both disciplines are indispensible. Put yet another way, when systematic theology uses biblical theology to connect text and present in a normative fashion, we are engaged in the theological interpretation of Scripture.

---

[8] Ramm et al. 1974: 28–29.

Bibliography

Akhtar, S. (1990), *A Faith for All Seasons: Islam and the Challenge of the Modern World*, Chicago: Dee.

—— (2011), *Islam as Political Religion: The Future of an Imperial Faith*, London: Routledge.

Ali, M. M. (2002), *The Holy Qur'an: Arabic Text with English Translation and Commentary*, Dublin: Ahmadiyya Anjuman Isha'at Islam Lahoire.

Allison, Jr., D. C. (2001), *Matthew*, OBC.

Altizer, T. J. J. (n.d.), 'The Gospel of Christian Atheism' <http://www.religion-online.org/showchapter.asp?title=523&C=531>, accessed 22 Aug. 2012.

Anderson, W. T. (ed.) (1995), *The Truth About the Truth: De-confusing and Re-constructing the Postmodern World*, New York: Tarcher/Putnam.

Aquinas (1939), *The Catechetical Instructions of St. Thomas Aquinas*, tr. J. B. Collins <http://www.documentacatholicaomnia.eu/03d/1225-1274,_Thomas_Aquinas,_Catechismus,_EN.pdf>, accessed 22 Nov. 2012.

—— (2007), *Summa Theologica*, tr. Kevin Knight <http://www.newadvent.org/summa/4001.htm>, accessed 26 Oct. 2012.

Archer, Jr., G. L. (1997), *Daniel*, EBC.

Attridge, G. H. W. (2001), *Hebrews*, OBC.

Augustine (2007a), *The City of God*, NA.

—— (2007b), *The Confessions*, NA.

—— (2007c), *The Trinity*, NA.

Balthasar, H. U. von (1986), *Prayer*, tr. G. Harrison, San Francisco: Ignatius.

Banks, R. (2011), *And Man Created God: Is God a Human Invention?*, Oxford: Lion Hudson.

Barr, J. (1960), 'Theophany and Anthropomorphism in the Old Testament', VTSup, Leiden: Brill.

Barrett, C. K. (1963), *The Pastoral Epistles*, Oxford: Clarendon.

Bauckham, R. (1990), 'In Defence of *The Crucified God*', in N. M. de S. Cameron (ed.), *The Power and Weakness of God: Impassibility and Orthodoxy*, Edinburgh: Rutherford House, 93–118.

———— (1998), *God Crucified: Monotheism and Christology in the New Testament*, Grand Rapids: Eerdmans.

———— (2002), *Orthodoxy in Christology* <http://richardbauckham. co.uk/uploads/Accessible/Orthodoxy%20in%20Christology.pdf>, accessed 9 July 2012.

Bavinck, H. (1977), *The Doctrine of God*, tr. W. Hendriksen, Edinburgh: Banner of Truth.

Beale, G. K. (1994), 'Positive Answer to the Question Did Jesus and His Followers Preach the Right Doctrine from the Wrong Texts?', in G. K. Beale (ed.), *The Right Doctrine from the Wrong Texts? Essays on the Use of the Old Testament in the New*, Grand Rapids: Baker, 387–404.

———— (2004), *The Temple and the Church's Mission: A Biblical Theology of the Dwelling Place of God*, Downers Grove: InterVarsity Press; Leicester: Apollos.

———— (2011), *A New Testament Biblical Theology: The Unfolding of the Old Testament in the New*, Grand Rapids: Baker Academic.

Beale, G. K., and D. A. Carson (2007), 'Introduction', CNTUOT.

Benin, S. D. (1993), *The Footprints of God: Divine Accommodation in Jewish and Christian Thought*, Albany: State University of New York Press.

Bennett, G. (1860), *Gatherings of a Naturalist in Australasia: Being Observations Principally on the Animal and Vegetable Productions of New South Wales, New Zealand and Some of the Austral Islands*, London: John Van Voorst.

Bercot, D. W. (ed.) (2002), *A Dictionary of Early Christian Beliefs*, Peabody: Hendrickson.

Berding, K., and J. Lunde (eds.) (2008), *Three Views on the New Testament Use of the Old Testament*, Grand Rapids: Zondervan.

Berkhof, H. (1979), *Christian Faith: An Introduction to the Study of Faith*, tr. S. Woudstra, Grand Rapids: Eerdmans.

Berlin, A., and M. Z. Brettler (2004), 'Psalms', in *JSB*.

Bettenson, H. (ed.) (1967), *Documents of the Christian Church*, Oxford: Oxford University Press.

———— (ed. and tr.) (1977), *The Later Christian Fathers*, Oxford: Oxford University Press.

———— (ed. and tr.) (1978), *The Early Christian Fathers*, Oxford: Oxford University Press.

Bettenson, H., and C. Maunder (1999), *Documents of the Christian Church*, 3rd ed., Oxford: Oxford University Press.

Billings, J. T. (2012), 'The Problem with "Incarnational Ministry"', in *Christianity Today*, July–Aug., 59–63.

Blackham, P. (2001a), 'Faith in Christ in the Old Testament' <http://www.theologian.org.uk/bible/blackham.html>, accessed 22 Nov. 2011.

—— (2001b), 'Gen 16–17' <http://old.efac.org.au/Gen%2016-17.htm>, accessed 22 Nov. 2012.

—— (2005), 'The Trinity in the Hebrew Scriptures', in P. L. Metzger (ed.), *Trinitarian Soundings in Systematic Theology*, London: T. & T. Clark, 35–48.

Blomberg, C. L. (2007), 'Matthew', CNTUOT.

Bock, D. L. (2005), 'Messiah/Messianism', in *DFTIB*.

Bray, G. (2002), 'The Church Fathers and Their Use of Scripture', in P. Helm and C. R. Trueman (eds.), *The Trustworthiness of God: Perspectives on the Nature of Scripture*, Grand Rapids: Eerdmans, 157–174.

Brightman, E. S. (1925), *An Introduction to Philosophy*, New York: Holt.

Broderick, R. C. (ed.) (1987), *The Catholic Encyclopedia: Revised and Updated Edition*, Nashville: Nelson.

Brown, D., and A. Loades (1996), *Christ: The Sacramental Word: Incarnation, Sacrament and Poetry*, London: SPCK.

Brueggemann, W. (2002), 'Biblical Authority: A Personal Reflection', in W. Brueggemann, C. W. Placher and B. K. Blount, *Struggling with Scripture*, Louisville: Westminster John Knox, 5–31.

—— (2009), *An Unsettling God: The Heart of the Hebrew Bible*, Minneapolis: Fortress.

Burns, L. (2009), The *Nearness of God: His Presence with His People*, Phillipsburg: P. & R.

Byassee, J. (2007), *Praise Seeking Understanding: Reading the Psalms with Augustine*, Grand Rapids: Eerdmans.

Caird, G. B. (1980), *The Language and Imagery of the Bible*, London: Duckworth.

Calvin, J. (2002a), *Genesis*, CJCC.

—— (2002b), *Institutes of the Christian Religion*, ed. J. T. McNeill, tr. F. L. Battles, Philadelphia: *CJCC*.

—— (2002c), *Romans*, *CJCC*.

Carson, D. A. (2000), *The Difficult Doctrine of the Love of God*, Wheaton: Crossway; Leicester: Inter-Varsity Press.

———— (2004), 'Mystery and Fulfillment: Toward a More Comprehensive Paradigm of Paul's Understanding of the Old and the New', in D. A. Carson, P. T. O'Brien and M. A. Seifrid (eds.), *Justification and Variegated Nomism*, vol. 2: *The Paradoxes of Paul*, Tübingen: Mohr Siebeck; Grand Rapids: Baker Academic, 393–436.

———— (2010), *The God Who Is There: Finding Your Place in God's Story*, Grand Rapids: Baker.

———— (2012), *Jesus the Son of God: A Christological Title Often Overlooked, Sometimes Misunderstood, and Currently Disputed*, Wheaton: Crossway; Nottingham: Inter-Varsity Press.

Carson, D. A., and D. J. Moo (2005), *An Introduction to the New Testament*, 2nd ed., Grand Rapids: Zondervan; Leicester: Apollos.

Chilton, B. (2001), *The Temple of Jesus: His Sacrificial Program Within a Cultural History of Sacrifice*, Annandale-On-Hudson: Comparisons Institute of Advanced Theology, Bard College.

Christensen, D. L. (2004), *Deuteronomy 1:1–21:9*, WBC 6a.

Clark, K. J., R. Lints and J. K. A. Smith (2004), *101 Key Terms in Philosophy and Their Importance for Theology*, Louisville: Westminster John Knox.

Coggins, R. (2001), *Isaiah*, OBC.

Cole, G. A. (1990), 'Sola Scriptura: Some Historical and Contemporary Perspectives', *Chm* 104.1: 20–34.

———— (2000), 'The Living God: Anthropomorphic or Anthropopathic?', *RTR* 59.1: 16–27.

———— (2008), 'Exodus 34, the Middoth and the Doctrine of God: The Importance of Biblical Theology to Evangelical Systematic Theology', *SBJT* 12.3: 4–23.

———— (2009a), 'Do Christians Have a Worldview?' <http://thegospelcoalition.org/cci/article/do_christians_have_a_worldview>, accessed 28 Aug. 2012.

———— (2009b), *God the Peacemaker: How Atonement Brings Shalom*, Downers Grove: InterVarsity Press; Nottingham: Apollos.

———— (2010), 'SBJT Forum – Theological Interpretation of Scripture', *SBJT* 14.2.

———— (2011), 'The God Who Wept a Human Tear: Some Theological Reflections' <http://ojs.globalmissiology.org/index.php/english/article/view/612>, accessed 26 Oct. 2012.

———— (forthcoming), 'Why a Book? Why This Book? Why the Particular Order Within This Book? Some Theological Reflections on the Canon', Grand Rapids: Eerdmans.

Colle, R. D. (1994), *Christ and the Spirit: Spirit-Christology in Trinitarian Perspective*, Oxford: Oxford University Press.

Collins, C. John (2006), *Genesis 1–4: A Linguistic, Literary and Theological Commentary*, Phillipsburg: P. & R.

Cotterell, F. P. (1982), 'The Christology of Islam', in H. H. Rowdon (ed.), *Christ The Lord: Studies in Christology Presented to Donald Guthrie*, Leicester: Inter-Varsity Press, 282–298.

Craigie, P. C. (2002), *Psalms 1–50*, WBC 19.

Crisp, O. D. (2008), 'The Logic of Penal Substitution Revisited', in D. Tidball, D. Hilborn and J. Thacker (eds.), *The Atonement Debate: Papers from the London Symposium on the Theology of Atonement*, Grand Rapids: Zondervan, 208–227.

———— (2009), *God Incarnate: Explorations in Christology*, London: T. & T. Clark.

Davis, E. F., and R. B. Hays (eds.) (2003), *The Art of Reading Scripture*, Grand Rapids: Eerdmans.

Day, J. (2001), *Hosea*, OBC.

Dearman, J. A. (2002), 'Theophany, Anthropomorphism, and the Imago Dei: Some Observations About the Incarnation in the Light of the Old Testament', in S. T. Davis, D. Kendall and G. O'Collins (eds.), *The Incarnation: An Interdisciplinary Symposium on the Incarnation of the Son of God*, Oxford: Oxford University Press, 31–46.

Deedat, A. (n.d.), *Crucifixion or Cruci-fiction?*, Woodside: Islamic Propagation Center International.

Dempster, S. G. (2007), 'The Servant of the Lord', in S. J. Hafemann and P. R. House (eds.), *Central Themes in Biblical Theology: Mapping Unity in Diversity*, Grand Rapids: Baker Academic; Nottingham: Apollos, 128–178.

d'Holbach, Baron (2007), *The System of Nature*, vol. 2, Sioux Falls: NuVision.

Dines, J. M. (2001), *Amos*, OBC.

Drury, C. (2001), *The Pastoral Epistles: 1 & 2 Timothy and Titus*, OBC.

Dulles, A. (2009), 'Divine Providence and the Mystery of Human Suffering', in J. F. Keating and T. J. White (eds.), *Divine Impassibility and the Mystery of Human Suffering*, Grand Rapids: Eerdmans, 324–335.

Dumbrell, W. J. (1988), *The Faith of Israel: Its Expression in the Books of the Old Testament*, Grand Rapids: Baker; Leicester: Apollos.

———— (2001a), *The End of the Beginning: Revelation 21–22 and the Old Testament*, Eugene: Wipf & Stock.

—————— (2001b), *The Search for Order: Biblical Eschatology in Focus*, Eugene: Wipf & Stock.

—————— (2005), *Romans: A New Covenant Commentary*, Eugene: Wipf & Stock.

Dunn, J. D. G. (2004), *Romans 1–8*, WBC 38a.

—————— (2009a), 'Incarnation', in *NIBD* 3.

—————— (2009b), 'Mystery', in *NIBD* 4.

Duriez, C. (1990), *The C. S. Lewis Handbook: A Comprehensive Guide to His Life, Thought and Writings*, Eastbourne: Monarch.

Dyrness, W. (1998), *Themes in the Old Testament Theology*, Carlisle: Paternoster.

Eisenbaum, P. (2011), *The Letter to the Hebrews*, JANT.

Elbert IV, D. J. (2011), *Wisdom Christology: How Jesus Becomes God's Wisdom for Us*, Phillipsburg: P. & R.

Evans, C. S. (ed.) (2006), *Exploring Kenotic Christology: The Self-Emptying of God*, Vancouver: Regent College Publishing.

Evans, E. (ed. and tr.) (1972), *Tertullian Adversus Marcionem*, London: Oxford University Press.

Fox, N. S. (2003), 'Numbers', in *JSB*.

France, R. T. (1970), *The Living God: A Personal Look at what the Bible Says About God*, London: Inter-Varsity Press.

—————— (1985), *Matthew: An Introduction and Commentary*, TNTC 1.

Fretheim, T. E. (1984), *The Suffering of God: An Old Testament Perspective*, Philadelphia: Fortress.

Friedman, R. E. (1995), *The Disappearance of God: A Divine Mystery*, Boston: Little, Brown.

Gignilliat, M. S. (2011), 'The Gospel Promised by the Prophets: The Trinity and the Old Testament', in T. George (ed.), *Evangelicals and Nicene Faith: Reclaiming the Apostolic Witness*, Grand Rapids: Baker Academic, 20–33.

Glenn, P. J. (1963), *A Tour of the Summa*, St. Louis: Herder.

Goldsworthy, G. (1981), *Gospel and Kingdom: A Christian Interpretation of the Old Testament*, Exeter: Paternoster.

—————— (2000), *Preaching the Whole Bible as Christian Scripture: An Application of Biblical Theology to Expository Preaching*, Grand Rapids: Eerdmans; Leicester: Inter-Varsity Press.

—————— (2001), 'The Blackham–Goldsworthy Debate' <http://www.theologian.org.uk/bible/blackham.html>, accessed 29 Mar. 2011.

González, G. L. (1987), *A History of Christian Thought: From the Beginnings to the Council of Chalcedon*, rev. ed., Nashville: Abingdon.

——— (ed.) (2006), *The Westminster Dictionary of Theology*, Louisville: Westminster John Knox.

Goppelt, L. (1982), *Typos: The Typological Interpretation of the Old Testament in the New*, tr. D. H. Madvig, Grand Rapids: Eerdmans.

Gowan, D. E. (2006), *Eschatology in the Old Testament*, 2nd ed., London: T. & T. Clark.

Green, C. (2003), 'The Incarnation and Mission', in D. G. Peterson (ed.), *The Word Became Flesh: Evangelicals and the Incarnation*, Carlisle: Paternoster, 110–151.

Greidanus, S. (1999), *Preaching Christ from the Old Testament: A Contemporary Hermeneutical Method*, Grand Rapids: Eerdmans.

Grenz, S. J., D. Giretzki and C. F. Nordling (1999), *Pocket Dictionary of Theological Terms*, Downers Grove: InterVarsity Press.

Grogan, G. W. (1997), *Isaiah*, EBC.

Guinan, M. D. (2008), 'Adam, Eve and Original Sin' <http://www.americancatholic.org/Newsletter/CU/ac0507.asp>, accessed 10 June 2008.

Gunton, C. E. (2002), *The Christian Faith: An Introduction to Christian Doctrine*, Malden: Blackwell.

Guthrie, D. (1983), *Hebrews: An Introduction and Commentary*, TNTC 15.

——— (1990), *Pastoral Epistles: An Introduction and Commentary*, TNTC 14.

Guthrie, G. H. (1998), 'The Reasons for the Incarnation (2:14–16)', in NIVACNT, *Hebrews*.

——— (2007), 'Hebrews', CNTUOT.

Hafemann, S. J. (ed.) (2002), *Biblical Theology: Retrospect and Prospect*, Downers Grove: InterVarsity Press; Leicester: Apollos.

Hafemann, S. J., and P. R. House (eds.) (2007), *Central Themes in Biblical Theology: Mapping Unity in Diversity*, Grand Rapids: Baker Academic; Nottingham: Apollos.

Hahn, S. W. (2009), *Covenant and Communion: The Biblical Theology of Pope Benedict XVI*, Grand Rapids: Brazos.

Halverson, W. H. (1981), *A Concise Introduction to Philosophy*, 4th ed., Boston: McGraw Hill.

Hamilton, J. A., Jr. (2006), 'The Skull Crushing Seed of the Woman: Inner-Biblical Interpretation of Genesis 3:15', *SBJT* 11: 30–55.

——— (2010), *God's Glory in Salvation Through Judgment: A Biblical Theology*, Wheaton: Crossway.

Hamori, E. J. (2008), *'When Gods Were Men': The Embodied God in Biblical and Near East Literature*, Berlin: de Gruyter.

Hansen, C. (2011), 'The Cross and the Crescent' <http://www. christianitytoday.com/ct/2011/february/soncrescent.html?start=2>, accessed 28 Aug. 2012.

Hanson, A. T. (1963), 'Typology', in *OGB*.

—— (1965), *Jesus Christ in the Old Testament*, London: SPCK.

Harkness, G. (1961), 'Beliefs That Count' <http://www.religion-online. org/showchapter.asp?title=582&C=774>, accessed 25 Aug. 2012.

Harris, M. J. (1992), *Jesus as God: The New Testament Use of Theos in Reference to Jesus*, Grand Rapids: Baker.

Harvey, V. A. (1997), *A Handbook of Theological Terms*, New York: Simon & Shuster.

Hendry, G. S. (1959), *The Gospel of the Incarnation*, London: SCM.

Heschel, A. J. (1962), *The Prophets*, vol. 2, New York: Harper & Row.

Hiebert, P. G. (1985), *Anthropological Insights for Missionaries*, Grand Rapids: Baker Academic.

—— (1994), *Anthropological Reflections on Missiological Issues*, Grand Rapids: Baker.

—— (2000), 'Spiritual Warfare and Worldview', *ERT* 24.3: 240–256.

Hill, D. (1993), 'Mystery', in *OGB*.

Hooker, M. D. (2002), *The Letter to the Philippians: Introduction, Commentary, and Reflections*, *NIB* 11.

House, P. R. (1998), *Old Testament Theology*, Downers Grove: Inter-Varsity Press.

Hugenberger, G. P. (1994), 'Introductory Notes on Typology', in G. K. Beale (ed.), *The Right Doctrine from the Wrong Texts? Essays on the Use of the Old Testament in the New*, Grand Rapids: Baker, 331–341.

Hunter, J. D. (2010), *To Change the World: The Irony, Tragedy, and Possibility of Christianity in the Late Modern World*, Oxford: Oxford University Press.

Irenaeus (2007), *Against Heresies*, *NA*.

Jacob, E. (1958), *Theology of the Old Testament*, tr. A. W. Heathcote and P. J. Allcock, London: Hodder & Stoughton.

Jennings, J. N. (2011), 'The Deity of Christ, for Missions, World Religions, and Pluralism', in C. W. Morgan and R. A. Peterson (eds.), *The Deity of Christ*, Wheaton: Crossway, 253–281.

Kaiser, Jr., W. C. (1979), *Toward an Old Testament Theology*, Grand Rapids: Zondervan.

Kaiser, Jr., W. C., P. H. Davids, F. F. Bruce and M. T. Brauch (2001), 'Genesis 32:23–32 with Whom Did Jacob Wrestle?', *HSOB* (EIRC).

Kasper, W. (1984), *God of Jesus Christ*, tr. Matthew J. O'Connell, London: SCM.

Kateregga, B. D., and D. W. Shenk (1981), *Islam and Christianity: A Muslim and a Christian in Dialogue*, rev. ed., Grand Rapids: Eerdmans.

Keating, J. F., and T. J. White (eds.) (2009), *Divine Impassibility and the Mystery of Human Suffering*, Grand Rapids: Eerdmans.

Kee, H. C. (1980), *The Origins of Christianity: Sources and Documents*, London: SPCK.

Keener, C. S. (1993), *Mark*, BBCNT (EIRC).

Kelly, J. N. D. (1977), *Early Christian Doctrines*, 5th ed., London: A. & C. Black.

Kidner, D. (1973), *Psalms 1–72*, TOTC 15.

———— (1995), *Psalms 73–150: An Introduction and Commentary*, TOTC 16.

Kieffer, R. (2001), *John*, OBC.

Kierkegaard, S. (1936) *Philosophical Fragments* <http://www.religion-online.org/showchapter.asp?title=2512&C=2384>, accessed 2 Dec. 2011.

———— (1941a), *Concluding Unscientific Postscript*, tr. D. F. Swenson, Princeton: Princeton University Press.

———— (1941b) Quotation <http://www.utas.edu.au/docs/humsoc/kierkegaard/resources/Kierkquotes.html>, accessed 17 Sept. 2012.

Klein, R. W. (2004), *1 Samuel*, WBC 10.

Kline, M. G. (1977–8), 'Primal Parousia', *WTJ* 40: 245–280.

The Koran, tr. N. J. Dawood, 4th rev. ed., Harmondsworth: Penguin, 1980.

Köstenberger, A. J. (1998), *The Missions of Jesus and the Disciples According to the Fourth Gospel*, Grand Rapids: Eerdmans.

———— (2007), 'John', CNTUOT.

———— (2011), 'The Deity of Christ in John's Gospel', in C. W. Morgan and R. A. Peterson (eds.), *The Deity of Christ*, Wheaton: Crossway, 91–114.

Kruse, C. G. (1987), *2 Corinthians: An Introduction and Commentary*, TNTC 8.

———— (2003), *The Gospel According to John: An Introduction and Commentary*, TNTC 4.

Kugel, J. L. (2003), *The God of Old: Inside the Lost World of the Bible*, New York: Free.

———— (2007), *How to Read the Bible: A Guide to Scripture Then and Now*, New York: Free.

Kuntz, J. K. (1967), *The Self-Revelation of God*, Philadelphia: Westminster.

Lane, W. L. (2002), *Hebrews 1–8*, WBC 47a.

Law, D. R. (2000), 'Kierkegaard, Søren', in T. A. Hart (ed.), *The Dictionary of Historical Theology*, Grand Rapids: Eerdmans, 301–303.

Letham, R. (1993), *The Work of Christ*, Leicester: Inter-Varsity Press.

Levenson, J. D. (2004), 'Genesis', in *JSB*.

Lewis, C. S. (1958), *Mere Christianity*, London: Collins.

Lewis, D. L. (2008), *God's Crucible, Islam and the Making of Europe, 570–1215*, New York: Norton.

Liddon, H. P. (1908), *The Divinity of Our Lord and Saviour Jesus Christ: Eight Lectures Preached Before the University of Oxford in the Year 1866*, London: Longmans, Green.

Longenecker, R. N. (1994), 'Negative Answer to the Question "Who Is the Prophet Talking About? Some Reflections on the New Testament Use of the Old', in G. K. Beale (ed.), *The Right Doctrine from the Wrong Texts? Essays on the Use of the Old Testament in the New*, Grand Rapids: Baker, 375–386.

——— (2002), *Galatians*, WBC 41.

Lossky, V. (1976), *The Mystical Tradition of the Eastern Church*, Crestwood: St. Vladimir's Seminary Press.

Louth, A. (2001), *Genesis 1–11*, ACC.

McCormack, B. L. (ed.) (2006), *Justification in Perspective: Historical Developments and Contemporary Challenges*, Grand Rapids: Baker Academic.

MacDonald, M. (2001), *2 Corinthians*, OBC.

McGrath, A. E. (2007), *Christian Theology: An Introduction*, 4th ed., Oxford: Blackwell.

——— (ed.) (2007), *The Christian Theology Reader*, 3rd ed., Oxford: Blackwell.

——— (2011), *Christian Theology: An Introduction*, 5th ed., Malden: Wiley-Blackwell.

McGuckin, J. A. (2004), *The Westminster Handbook to Patristic Theology*, Louisville: Westminster John Knox.

McKelvey, R. J. (2001), 'Temple', in *NDBT* (EIRC).

Macleod, D. (1998), *The Person of Christ*, Downers Grove: Inter-Varsity Press; Leicester: Inter-Varsity Press.

Macquarrie, J. (1996), 'Incarnation as Root of the Sacramental Principle', in D. Brown and A. Loades (eds.), *Christ: The Sacramental Word: Incarnation, Sacrament and Poetry*, London: SPCK, 29–39.

McWilliams, W. (1985), *The Passion of God: Divine Suffering in Contemporary Protestant Theology*, Macon: Mercer University Press.

Maimonides (1995), *Maimonides, the Guide of the Perplexed*, tr. Chaim Rabin, Indianapolis: Hackett.

Malone, A. S. (2005), 'John Owen and Old Testament Christophanies' <http://www.theologian.org.uk/doctrine/johnowen.html>, accessed 29 Mar. 2011.

Markham, I. S. (ed.) (1996), *A World Religions Reader*, Cambridge: Blackwell.

Marshall, I. H. (1982), 'Incarnational Christology in the New Testament', in H. H. Rowdon (ed.), *Christ the Lord: Studies in Christology Presented to Donald Guthrie*, Leicester: Inter-Varsity Press, 1–16.

Martin, D. B. (2008), *Pedagogy of the Bible: An Analysis and Proposal*, Louisville: Westminster John Knox.

Martin, R. P. (2001), 'Hymns, Hymn Fragments, Songs, and Spiritual Songs', in *DPHL* (EIRC).

———— (2002), *2 Corinthians*, WBC 40.

Matthews, V. H., M. W. Chavalas and J. H. Walton (2000), *The IVP Bible Background Commentary: Old Testament*, Downers Grove: InterVarsity Press.

Mattson, I. (2008), *The Story of the Qur'an: Its History and Place in Muslim Life*, Oxford: Blackwell.

Metzger, P. L. (ed.) (2005), *Trinitarian Soundings in Systematic Theology*, London: T. & T. Clark.

Meyendorff, J. (1975), *Byzantine Theology: Historical Trends and Doctrinal Themes*, London: Mowbray.

Migliore, D. L. (2008), *The Power of God and the Gods of Power*, Louisville: Westminster John Knox.

Milne, B. (2009), *Know the Truth: A Handbook of Christian Belief*, Nottingham: Inter-Varsity Press; Downers Grove: IVP Academic.

Moltmann, J. (1990), *The Way of Jesus Christ*, tr. Margaret Kohl, New York: HarperCollins.

———— (1996), *The Coming of God: Christian Eschatology*, tr. Margaret Kohl, Minneapolis: Fortress.

Moritz, T. (2001), 'Mark, Book of', in *DFTIB*.

Morris, L. (1997), *Hebrews*, EBC.

Morris, T. V. (2001), *The Logic of God Incarnate*, Eugene: Wipf & Stock.

Motyer, J. A. (1999), *Isaiah: An Introduction and Commentary*, TOTC 20.

Mounce, W. D. (2002), *Pastoral Epistles*, WBC 46.

Muller, R. A. (1986), *Dictionary of Latin and Greek Theological Terms: Drawn Principally from Protestant Scholastic Theology*, Grand Rapids: Baker.

Murray, J. (1977), *Collected Writings of John Murray 2: Systematic Theology*, Edinburgh: Banner of Truth.

Murray, R. (2001), *Philippians*, OBC.

Neusner, J. (1992), *The Incarnation of God: The Character of Divinity in Formative Judaism*, Atlanta: Scholars Press.

Niditch, S. (2001), *Judges*, OBC.

Niehaus, J. J. (1997), 'Theophany', in *NIDOTTE* 4.

Noll, M. A. (1993), 'B. B. Warfield', in W. E. Elwell (ed.), *Handbook of Evangelical Theologians*, Grand Rapids: Baker, 26–39.

———— (2011), *Jesus Christ and the Life of the Mind*, Grand Rapids: Eerdmans.

O'Brien, P. T. (1993), 'Mystery', in *DPHL* (EIRC).

Oden, T. C. (1992), *Classic Christianity: A Systematic Theology*, New York: HarperCollins.

Ortlund, Jr., R. C. (2011), 'The Deity of Christ and the Old Testament', in C. W. Morgan and R. A. Peterson (eds.), *The Deity of Christ*, Wheaton: Crossway, 39–60.

Packer, J. I. (1986), 'What Do You Mean When You Say God?', *Christianity Today*, 19 Sept., 27–31.

Pao, D. W., and E. J. Schnabel (2007), 'Luke', CNTUOT.

Pelikan, J. (1971), *The Christian Tradition: A History of the Development of Doctrine*, vol. 1: *The Emergence of the Catholic Tradition (100–600)*, Chicago: University of Chicago Press.

Peterson, D. (1994), *Hebrews*, NBC (EIRC).

———— (ed.) (2003), *The Word Became Flesh: Evangelicals and the Incarnation*, Carlisle: Paternoster.

Phillips, J. B. (n.d.), 'The Visited Planet' <http://home.earthlink.net/~paulrack/id81.html>, accessed 22 Aug. 2012.

Piper, J. (1999), 'Why the Glory of God Is at Stake in the "Foreknowledge" Debate', Modern Reformation (Sept.–Oct.): 41–42.

Pittenger, N. (n.d.), 'Preaching the Gospel' <http://www.religion-online.org/showchapter.asp?title=3038&C=2576>, accessed 26 Oct. 2012.

Plantinga, A. (1980), *God, Freedom and Evil*, Grand Rapids: Eerdmans.

Plantinga, C. (1995), *Not the Way It Is Supposed to Be: A Breviary of Sin*, Grand Rapids: Eerdmans.

Plato (n.d.), 'Gorgias' <http://www.ancienttexts.org/library/greek/ plato/gorgias.html>, tr. Benjamin Jowett, accessed 25 Aug. 2012.

Post, S. (2011), 'Sanctity of Human Life', in J. B. Green (ed.), *Dictionary of Scripture and Ethics*, Grand Rapids: Baker Academic, 702–703.

Poythress, V. S. (1994), 'Divine Meaning of Scripture', in G. K. Beale (ed.), *The Right Doctrine from the Wrong Texts? Essays on the Use of the Old Testament in the New*, Grand Rapids: Baker, 82–113.

Preece, G. (ed.) (2002), *Rethinking Peter Singer*, Downers Grove: InterVarsity Press.

Ramm, B., et al. (1974), *Hermeneutics*, Grand Rapids: Baker.

Ramsey, A. M. (1969), *God, Christ and the World: A Study in Contemporary Theology*, London: SCM.

Renard, R. (1998), *Responses to 101 Questions on Islam*, New York: Paulist.

Reymond, R. L. (2006), 'Christology's Future in Systematic Theology', in A. T. B. McGowan (ed.), *Always Reforming: Explorations in Systematic Theology*, Nottingham: Apollos; Downers Grove: IVP Academic, 67–124.

Richardson, A. (1972), *Creeds in the Making: A Short Introduction to the History of Christian Doctrine*, London: SCM.

Rodd, C. S. (2001), *Psalms*, OBC.

Rosner, B. S. (2001), 'Biblical Theology', in *NDBT* (EIRC).

Ross, A. P. (2006), *Recalling the Hope of Glory: Biblical Worship from the Garden to the New Creation*, Grand Rapids: Kregel.

Ryken, L. L. (1980), *The Literature of the Bible*, 6th ed., Grand Rapids: Zondervan.

——— (1998), 'Comedy as Plot Motif', in *DBI*.

Sailhamer, J. H. (1997), *Genesis*, EBC.

Sanders, J. (ed.) (2006), *Atonement and Violence: A Theological Conversation*, Nashville: Abingdon.

Sargant, W. (1957), *Battle for the Mind: Physiology of Conversion and Brainwashing*, Melbourne: Heinemann.

Saville, A. (n.d.), 'Paul Blackham: A Trinitarian Reading of the Old Testament' <http://www.churchsociety.org/churchman/documents/ Cman_123_4_Saville.pdf>, accessed 29 Mar. 2012.

Sayers, D. (1979), 'The Greatest Drama Ever Staged', in *The Whimsical Christian: 18 Essays by Dorothy Sayers*, Boston: Hall, 20–29.

Schnabel, E. J. (2012), 'Paul, Timothy, and Titus: The Assumption of a Pseudonymous Author and of Pseudonymous Recipients in the Light of Literary, Theological and Historical Evidence', in J. K. Hoffmeier and D. R. Magary (eds.), *Do Historical Matters Matter to Faith? A Critical Appraisal of Modern and Postmodern Approaches to Scripture*, Wheaton: Crossway, 383–404.

Scobie, C. H. H. (2003), *The Ways of Our God: An Approach to Biblical Theology*, Grand Rapids: Eerdmans.

Scruton, R. (2012), *The Face of God: The Gifford Lectures for 2010*, London: Continuum.

Scrutton, A. P. (2005), 'Emotion in Augustine of Hippo and Thomas Aquinas: A Way Forward for the Im/passibility Debate?', *International Journal of Systematic Theology* 7 (Apr.): 169–177.

———— (2011), *Thinking Through Feeling: God, Emotion and Passibility*, New York: Continuum.

Segal, A. F. (2002), 'The Incarnation: The Jewish Milieu', in S. T. Davis, D. Kendall and G. O'Collins (eds.), *The Incarnation: An Interdisciplinary Symposium on the Incarnation of the Son of God*, Oxford: Oxford University Press, 116–139.

Sheppard, J. A. (2005), *Christendom at the Crossroads: The Medieval Era*, Louisville: Westminster John Knox.

Smalley, S. S. (2002), *1, 2, 3 John*, WBC 51.

Snodgrass, K. (1994), 'The Use of the Old Testament in the New', in G. K. Beale (ed.), *The Right Doctrine from the Wrong Texts? Essays on the Use of the Old Testament in the New*, Grand Rapids: Baker, 29–54.

Soloveichik, M. Y. (2010), 'Torah and Incarnation', *First Things* 206 (Oct.): 44–48.

Sommer, B. D. (2004), 'Isaiah', in *JSB*.

Staniforth, M. (ed. and tr.) (1972), *Early Christian Writings: The Apostolic Fathers*, Harmondsworth: Penguin.

Stevenson, J. (ed.) (1970), *A New Eusebius: Documents Illustrative of the History of the Church to A.D. 337*, London: SPCK.

———— (1976), *Creeds, Councils, and Controversies: Documents Illustrative of the History of the Church A.D. 337–461*, London: SPCK.

Stott, J. R. W. (1986), *The Message of Galatians: Only One Way*, Leicester: Inter-Varsity Press.

Stuart, D. (2004), *Hosea–Jonah*, WBC 31.

Sunshine, G. (1985), 'Accommodation in Calvin and Socinus: A Study in Contrasts', Trinity International University, Deerfield, Masters thesis.

Sweet, L. M. (1949), 'The Christological Approach to the Christian Doctrine of God', *Int* 3.1: 19–29.

Tennent, T. C. (2007), *Theology in the Context of World Christianity: How the Global Church Is Influencing the Way We Think About and Discuss Theology*, Grand Rapids: Zondervan.

Terrien, S. T. (1978), *The Elusive Presence: Towards a New Biblical Theology*, Eugene: Wipf & Stock.

Thierry, P. H. (2007), *The System of Nature*, vol. 2, Sioux Falls: Nuvision.

Thomas, G. J. (1997), 'A Holy God Among a Holy People in a Holy Place: The Enduring Eschatological Hope', in K. E. Brower and M. W. Elliot (eds.), *'The Reader Must Understand': Eschatology in Bible and Theology*, Leicester: Apollos, 53–69.

Thompson, T. R. (2006), 'Nineteenth-Century Kenotic Christology: The Waxing, Waning, and Weighing of a Quest for a Coherent Orthodoxy', in C. S. Evans (ed.), *Exploring Kenotic Christology: The Self-Emptying of God*, Vancouver: Regent College Publishing, 74–111.

Tigay, J. H. (2003), 'Exodus', in *JSB*.

Torrance, T. F. (1992), *The Mediation of Christ*, new ed., Colorado Springs: Helmer & Howard.

——— (2008), *Incarnation: The Person and Life of Christ*, Carlisle: Paternoster; Downers Grove: InterVarsity Press.

Towner, P. H. (1994), *1–2 Timothy and Titus*, Downers Grove: Inter-Varsity Press; Leicester: Inter-Varsity Press.

Treier, D. (2005), 'Wisdom', in *DFTIB*.

Trueblood, E. (1969), *A Place to Stand*, New York: Harper & Row.

Tuckett, C. M. (2001), *Mark*, OBC.

Turner, J. M. (1974), 'God's Three Ways of Being God', *ExpTim* 85: 43.

Vanhoozer, K. J. (2002), *God, Scripture and Hermeneutics: First Theology*, Downers Grove: InterVarsity Press; Leicester: Apollos.

——— (2005), *The Drama of Doctrine: A Canonical Linguistic Approach to Christian Theology*, Louisville: Westminster John Knox.

——— (2009), 'A Drama-of-Redemption Model', in S. N. Gundry and G. T. Meadows (eds.), *Four Views on Moving Beyond the Bible to Theology*, Grand Rapids: Zondervan, 151–199.

——— (2010), *Remythologizing Theology: Divine Action, Passion, and Authorship*, Cambridge: Cambridge University Press.

Vischer, W. (1949), 'The Anthropomorphisms of the Biblical Revelation', *Int* 3.1: 3–18.

Walton, J. H. (2009), *The Lost World of Genesis One: Ancient Cosmology and the Origins Debate*, Downers Grove: IVP Academic.

Ware, B. (2010), 'The Man Christ Jesus', *JETS* 53.1: 5–18.

Ware, K. (1995), *The Orthodox Way*, rev. ed., Crestwood: St. Vladimir's Seminary Press.

——— (2000), *The Inner Kingdom: Volume I of the Collected Words*, Crestwood: St. Vladimir's Seminary Press.

Warfield, B. B. (1958), *Biblical Foundations*, London: Tyndale.

——— (1968), *Biblical and Theological Studies*, Philadelphia: P. & R.

——— (1970), *The Person and Work of Christ*, Philadelphia: P. & R.

Watts, J. D. W. (2002a), *Isaiah 1–33*, WBC 24.

——— (2002b), *Isaiah 34–66*, WBC 25.

Watts, R. E. (2002), 'Making Sense of Genesis 1' <http://www.asa3.org/ASA/topics/bible-science/6-02watts.html>, accessed 21 Apr. 2010.

——— (2007), 'Mark', CNTUOT.

Webber, R. E. (2008), *Who Gets to Narrate the World? Contending for the Christian Story in an Age of Rivals*, Downers Grove: InterVarsity Press.

Weber, J. (2012), 'Quotation Marks', *Christianity Today*, July–Aug., 13.

Weinandy, T. (2001), 'Does God Suffer?', *First Things* 117: 35–41.

Wenham, G. J. (2004), *Genesis 1–15*, WBC 1.

Wilkens, R. L. (2003), *The Spirit of Early Christian Thought: Seeking the Face of God*, New Haven: Yale University Press.

Williams III, H. H. D. (2001), 'Mystery', in *NDBT* (EIRC).

Wills, L. M. (2004), 'Daniel', in *JSB*.

Wolterstorff, N. (1984), *Reason Within the Bounds of Religion*, 2nd ed., Grand Rapids: Eerdmans.

Wood, L. J. (1997), *Hosea*, EBC.

Wright, C. J. H. (1992), *Knowing Jesus Through the Old Testament*, Downers Grove: InterVarsity Press.

——— (2006), *The Mission of God: Unlocking the Bible's Grand Narrative*, Downers Grove: InterVarsity Press; Leicester: InterVarsity Press.

Wright, N. T. (1986), *Colossians*, TNTC 12.

——— (2002a), 'Jesus' Self-Understanding', in S. T. Davis, D. Kendall and G. O'Collins (eds.), *The Incarnation: An Interdisciplinary Symposium on the Incarnation of the Son of God*, Oxford: Oxford University Press, 47–61.

———— (2002b), 'The Letter to the Romans: Introduction, Commentary, and Reflection', NIB 10.

———— (2003), *The Resurrection of the Son of God*, Minneapolis: Fortress.

———— (2008), *Surprised by Hope: Rethinking Heaven, the Resurrection, and the Mission of the Church*, New York: HarperCollins.

Wyschogrod, Michael (1996), *The Body of Faith: God in the People of Israel*, Lanham: Rowman & Littlefield.

Zahniser, M. A. H. (2008), *The Mission and Death of Jesus in Islam and Christianity*, Maryknoll: Orbis.

Zaspel, F. G. (2010), *The Theology of B. B. Warfield: A Systematic Summary*, Wheaton: Crossway; Nottingham: Apollos.

Index of authors

Index of Scripture references

Index of ancient sources